A REORDERED WORLD

Other Potomac Associates Books

HOPES AND FEARS OF THE AMERICAN PEOPLE

THE LIMITS TO GROWTH*

A NEW ISOLATIONISM: THREAT OR PROMISE?

U.S. HEALTH CARE: WHAT'S WRONG AND WHAT'S RIGHT

STATE OF THE NATION

BEYOND CONTAINMENT: U.S. FOREIGN POLICY IN TRANSITION

POTOMAC ASSOCIATES is a nonpartisan research and analysis organization which seeks to encourage lively inquiry into critical issues of public policy. Its purpose is to heighten public understanding and improve public discourse on significant contemporary problems, national and international.

POTOMAC ASSOCIATES provides a forum for distinctive points of view through publication of timely studies and occasional papers by outstanding authorities in the United States and abroad. Although publication implies belief by Potomac Associates in the basic importance and validity of each study, views expressed are those of the author.

POTOMAC ASSOCIATES is a non-tax-exempt firm located at 1707 L Street, NW, Washington, D.C. 20036.

POTOMAC ASSOCIATES books are distributed by Basic Books, 10 East 53 Street, New York, New York 10022.

*THE LIMITS TO GROWTH is published by Universe Books, 381 Park Avenue South, New York, New York 10016.

A REORDERED WORLD
EMERGING INTERNATIONAL
ECONOMIC PROBLEMS

EDITED BY RICHARD N. COOPER

POTOMAC ASSOCIATES
WASHINGTON, D.C.

Published in the United States of America in 1973 by Potomac Associates, 1707 L Street NW, Washington, D.C. 20036

First Printing: November 1973

Library of Congress Catalog Card Number: 73-82986
Cloth edition: ISBN 0-913998-02-8
Paperback edition: ISBN 0-913998-03-6

Typographical design by Ronald Clyne

Foreign Policy is published by National Affairs, Inc., in association with the Carnegie Endowment for International Peace, which bears no responsibility for the editorial content. Editorial Office: 345 East 46 Street, New York, New York 10017. Business Office: P.O. Box 379, Old Chelsea Station, New York, New York 10011.

This book is distributed by Basic Books, 10 East 53 Street, New York, New York 10022

Printed in the United States of America

CONTENTS

ALLOCATION OF THE WORLD'S RESOURCES ⸺

FOREWORD

Potomac Associates was formed just over three years ago as a nonpartisan organization dedicated to encouraging independent and lively inquiry into critical issues of public policy. Our goal has been to heighten public understanding and improve public discourse on significant contemporary problems. With each of our publications we have tried to contribute to the positive interaction between citizens and policymakers that is at the heart of a representative democratic system.

The present volume, *A Reordered World: Emerging International Economic Problems*, and its companion, *Beyond Containment: U.S. Foreign Policy in Transition*, are the products of Potomac Associates' cooperation with another relative newcomer to the forums of policy analysis, *Foreign Policy*. In bringing together some of the best articles from their first three years of publication with an original commentary and interpretation, we are guided by our belief that constructive change in our policies—both foreign and domestic—can only come from wider understanding and debate of the issues.

We hope that these books will serve that end.

William Watts
President
Potomac Associates

FOREIGN POLICY

We founded *Foreign Policy* in late 1970. It seemed to us then that the time was right for such a venture. As we wrote in the first issue,

the two editors of this magazine are old friends who have, during the past six years, disagreed sharply over Vietnam. Now, however, that there is broad agreement that the United States must withdraw militarily from Vietnam—although the how and the when may remain in dispute—we have decided to join together in an effort to stimulate rational discussion of the new directions required in American foreign policy. . . . The basic purposes of American foreign policy demand re-examination and redefinition. . . . A new magazine, having no institutional memory, can commence this task with a keener awareness that an era in American foreign policy which began in the late 1940s has ended.

Today, three years later, we think we can truthfully say that *Foreign Policy* has made a start on this task. Our pages have been open to contributors expressing the most divergent viewpoints, and their exchanges have demonstrated that rational foreign policy debate is again possible after the schisms over Vietnam. Our Editorial Board, whose advice and contributions have been invaluable to the magazine reflects our broad political spectrum: Thomas L. Hughes (Chairman), W. Michael Blumenthal, Zbigniew Brzezinski, Richard N. Cooper, Richard A. Falk, David Halberstam, Morton H. Halperin, Stanley Hoffmann, Joseph S. Nye, Jr., John E. Rielly, James C. Thomson, Jr., and Richard H. Ullman. We have focused on the new issues confronting American foreign policy in the 1970s, such as international finance and trade, energy and resources, the shifts in the balance of power, the defects in our policy-making processes. And we have tried to deal with these issues in a fresh, constructive, and at times iconoclastic manner, reflecting our initial editorial commitment that *Foreign Policy* should be *"serious but not scholarly, lively but not glib, and critical without being negative."*

Foreign Policy owes much of its character and style to the late John Franklin Campbell, who did such a brilliant job as Managing Editor for the first five issues, and whose work has been carried on so successfully by the current Managing Editor, Richard Holbrooke, and the Associate Managing Editor, Pamela Gilfond. Beginning with Issue No. 7 the Carnegie Endowment for International Peace has shared in our operating costs, while bearing no responsibility for editorial content, and we are grateful for their help.

We are pleased that many of the articles on international economic policy we have published in the past three years have now been collected in this volume. Many of them received wide attention when they appeared, but all of them deserve this second reading. A companion volume of articles on foreign policy is being published simultaneously, and other volumes in this series will be issued from time to time.

Samuel P. Huntington
Warren Demian Manshel

A REORDERED WORLD

INTRODUCTION
by Richard N. Cooper

It is now commonplace to say that the world is becoming much more interdependent. But what exactly does this proposition imply? Certainly international relations, and U.S. foreign policy in particular, will take on a character quite different from that of the period following 1945. Greater interdependence means, among other things, that international relations will become more like domestic relations, which are much concerned with the allocation of resources and the distribution of income. Domestic policy has a very heavy economic content, and the same may be expected of future foreign policy.

The essays in this book, a selection from the first three years of the journal *Foreign Policy*, all illustrate the effect of economic issues on international relations. Many of them address events that occurred not long before publication, though they are grouped here by theme rather than in the order in which they were published. To the extent that they are topical, they must be read in context. All, however, have an interest that ranges well beyond the immediate circumstances in which they were written. No attempt will be made here to summarize the essays comprehensively, but a word or two will be said about the context in which each was written and about its major thrust.

The lead essay, "Don't Take Japan for Granted" (pp. 3-21) by Yasuo Takeyama, editor of the prestigious *Nihon Keizai Shimbun* (Japanese Economic Journal), describes the impact of U.S. economic policies on Japanese attitudes and the willingness of the Japanese to regard their relations with the United States cooperatively rather than competitively. It was written in the immediate aftermath of President Richard M. Nixon's announcement of his New Economic Policy (August 1971), in which, *inter alia*, he imposed unilaterally and without any advance consultation a 10 percent tariff surcharge on all dutiable imports. The White House was known to have been especially irritated because Japan failed to carry out the president's campaign commitment to limit U.S. imports of wool and synthetic textiles, some of which come from Japan. Takeyama draws attention to the lag in American perceptions of what was actually happening in Japan's economy and to Japan's economic policies, and he points out the dangers of the oversimplified and implicitly hostile "Japan, Inc." view that has been fostered in the United States. The final five points of Takeyama's essay—his strong plea against protectionism, his concern about the U.S. balance of payments and its contribution to world inflation, his argument for promoting internal adjustment (rather than resistance) to the changing economic structure of the world, his preference for negotiations among private parties rather than among governments, and his case for laying down rules of conduct for multinational corporations—set the stage for the essays that follow.

The second article, "Coming Trade Wars?" (pp. 22-45), written by Harald B. Malmgren before he was appointed deputy special trade representative to President Nixon, draws attention to the strong and virulent strain of neo-mercantilism now observable in the world, to its roots in domestic politics, and to the dangers it poses for a cooperative world order. Malmgren reveals a strong irritation, increasingly found in the United States, with the evolving economic policies of the European Community, the establishment of which America vigorously encouraged in the mid-fifties, largely for noneconomic reasons.

The economic aspects of foreign policy were not, to be sure, given much consideration in the fifties. Because of the General Agreement on Tariffs and Trade (GATT), which in 1947 laid down a well-defined but flexible framework for handling trade relationships among those countries adhering to it, it was possible during the two decades following World War II to regard trade as "low level" foreign policy. The framework of the GATT has eroded badly during the past decade, however, owing to worsening U.S. balance-of-payments deficits (or, more generally, to a faulty balance-of-payments adjustment mechanism), to the failure of the European Community, now the world's largest single trading unit, to live up to the spirit and even to the letter of the Agreement, and to demands of less developed countries, generally granted, to be exempt from the GATT rules. "Trade Policy Is Foreign Policy" (pp. 46-61) suggests several possible routes back to some sort of world order in international trade and points to the advantages of a long-term commitment to free trade.

The next three essays turn from trade to finance. They focus on the key difficulties in the international monetary system and interpret some of the recent changes in it. Like Takeyama's essay, Harold van Buren Cleveland's "How the Dollar Standard Died" (pp. 65-74) was written soon after the announcement of President Nixon's New Economic Policy, which in addition to imposing a 10 percent surcharge on dutiable imports also declared that the United States would no longer convert dollars presented by other governments into gold. Cleveland sees the end of a dollar standard, by which he means (in contrast to other authors who have used the same term) a dollar-based monetary system supporting an open, expansive, and basically harmonious international economy. He argues that what was misleadingly called the gold-dollar system was really a dollar standard. Gold convertibility was an important fig leaf symbolizing the fact that the United States would pursue domestic economic policies that, while inwardly oriented, were nonetheless considered "responsible" by foreign observers; they would thus be suitable for the world economy as well as for the United States. Cleveland wrote his essay before the Smithsonian Agreement of December 1971, which resulted in elimination of the irritating tariff surcharge, in an 8 percent devaluation of the dollar relative to gold (less or more relative to other currencies), and in the reestablishment of "central" exchange rates to be supported by purchases and sales of dollars by other countries. The Agreement did *not* reestablish the gold convertibility of the dollar, and it thereby put the world formally on a "dollar standard" in a sense different from that used by Cleveland. Cleveland foresaw, however, the evolution of the world economy toward a series of currency blocs, with exchange rates between them determined largely by market factors. This is precisely what happened in March 1973, after a second devaluation of the dollar, when a number of European countries agreed on a "joint float" of their currencies against the dollar. The Japanese yen was also allowed to float; the Canadian dollar had already been floating since 1970.

As this book goes to press, the fate of this system of floating exchange rates is still unclear. Some observers hope it will prove to be durable. But the sharp depreciation of the dollar in the spring and early summer of 1973 caused grave anxiety in several European countries, which feared strong economic dislocation from overcompetitive American goods. All indications suggest that international financial unsettlement will continue to be a major irritant between the United States and Europe.

"The Future of the Dollar" (pp. 75-91) suggests that the international position of the dollar, in both official and private uses, will in the future come under severe strain, but that the dollar will retain its primacy because of the lack of a clear rival and because its functions are at least essential enough so that no contrived substitute is likely to be established by the end of the decade. This essay was written after the Smithsonian Agreement but before the developments of March 1973, and, like Cleveland's, it attempts to explain why the monetary system broke down.

The more technical question of the structure of the U.S. balance of payments is explored in "Why Exports Are Becoming Irrelevant" (pp. 92-99) by Lawrence Krause of the Brookings Institution. Krause suggests, controversially, that it is a mistake for the United States to think of reestablishing its large trade surplus, which by 1971 had ebbed to a deficit for the first time in this century. He emphasizes the marked shift toward production of services in the domestic economy and sees similar forces extending to U.S. transactions with the rest of the world. Its heavy investments overseas will enable the United States to receive increasing earnings from abroad, which may then finance a trade deficit, as similar investment earnings did for Britain before World War I. From his analysis Krause draws several implications for the politics of trade policy: first, the United States will lose interest in taking the initiative on further trade liberalization; second, American labor will become increasingly protectionist in its orientation as employment in the export industries diminishes relative to other forms of employment; and, third, there will be greater integration of the world economy, going well beyond the exchange of merchandise. This essay, written before the August 1971 measures, represents an implicit criticism of the U.S. government's concentrating its effort to improve the balance of payments or enlarging the trade balance.

C. Fred Bergsten introduces quite a different topic in "The Threat from the Third World" (pp. 103-22). He argues that U.S. policy has neglected the less developed part of the world (other than Southeast Asia) and that this neglect will in time be repaid in damaging actions by frustrated governments or other groups within the less developed countries. The costs of neglect will, in Bergsten's view, fall largely in the economic arena. The United States increasingly depends on developing countries for raw materials and for markets; those that have raw materials and manufacturing capacity can disrupt the U.S. economy by denying it needed materials and by flooding it with cheap manufactures; large reserve holders, such as the oil nations, can play havoc with the world financial system. To avoid these possible costs, Bergsten argues, the United States should make more generous concessions to the less developed countries—trade preferences, concessional aid, and the like—which will alter the climate favorably and reduce the risks that the damaging actions will come to pass.

But should the United States extend tariff preferences to less developed countries, as Bergsten proposes? "Third World Tariff Tangle" (pp. 123-35) argues that it is important that the United States provide assured access to its market for the products of less developed countries, even at existing tariffs (Bergsten would certainly agree), but that the extension of preferences will provide little economic stimulation for these countries. (The actual system adopted by the European Community tends to confirm this pessimistic view.) On the contrary, it might do much harm by introducing a wide variety of "safeguard" clauses and in that way, paradoxically, reduce assured market access. Any political gains from the grant of trade preferences would thus be short lived, for disillusionment would soon set in. It is argued, in addition, that with appropriate economic policies the developing countries can do very well at exporting manufactured goods, even without tariff preferences.

One of the vehicles through which developing countries can improve export performance is the multinational corporation. John Diebold ("Multinational Corporations," pp. 136-50) argues that these corporations will become major agents of economic transformation by shifting a substantial portion of the world's manufacturing activity to developing countries (a thesis that is consistent with Krause's view of the evolving structure of U.S. balance of payments). Much friction will result, however, if relations between the host country, the multinational firm, and the firm's home country are not well handled. Diebold suggests a number of behavioral guidelines to reduce these frictions.

Bergsten laid heavy weight on growing American dependence on raw materials imported from less developed countries. The last five articles return to the raw material problem. It is now known that abundant resources lie both on and below the bottom of the sea. Evan Luard of Oxford University discusses the allocation of seabed resources now that advancing technology is making them increasingly accessible ("Who Gets What on the Seabed?" pp. 153-67). So long as the costs of extracting these resources are high relative to their market value, the question of property rights will remain moot—as it has in the past. But once the appropriate technology becomes operative, the rewards of extraction may be high, and a whole new set of problems will develop. Will the oceans be carved up into national properties as European nations carved up the world's "backward" areas before World War I? Already, to protect their fishing interests, Peru and Iceland have asserted that their jurisdiction extends far out into open waters. Luard describes the current debate on the seabed and the oceans above it and identifies the issues that will have to be faced in the forthcoming UN Conference on the Law of the Sea.

To the extent that extracting resources from the seabed is practical—heavy investments have already been made for mining manganese nodules (they also contain copper, cobalt, and nickel), and there has long been offshore drilling for oil and natural gas—then some of Bergsten's anxieties about heavy dependence on developing countries may be exaggerated. In the long run, after allowance for the development of new technologies and new exploration, the supply of raw materials may be ample. Broadly speaking, this is the view of Theodore Moran, who in "New Deal or Raw Deal in Raw Materials" (pp.168-81) discusses the tough stance that developing countries might take in policies governing the production of raw materials for export and the difficulties they are likely to encounter if they do. It is also the view of Morris Adelman, who discusses the world oil situation in the next article, "Is the Oil Shortage Real?" (pp. 182-213). Moran argues that nationalization of raw material production, as Chile has done with its copper mines, while politically attractive, may well be damaging to the nationalizing country because of the high variability in demand for raw materials. The nationalizing country becomes the residual supplier and is treated as such. Moran might have added that the country could also end up with lower earnings because with national-ization the *average* output is likely to be less than it would be with integrated ownership, and the country also loses the benefits of generous tax-crediting provisions in the laws of the home countries of multinational firms.

Morris Adelman, in a celebrated and controversial article, argues that the energy shortage is a contrived one. Its causes are the near monopoly position of the Organization of Petroleum Exporting Countries (OPEC) in the world oil market and the marked cost advantage of oil over competing fuels. So long as this situation exists, oil prices may be expected to rise much higher than they have already. But such a rise would reflect the OPEC's monopoly position, not real scarcity, for world reserves are ample and extraction costs are low. Adelman faults U.S. policy with encouraging rather than resisting the exercise of market power by OPEC.

A second article on oil, "An Atlantic-Japanese Energy Policy" (pp. 214-40), by the highly respected petroleum consultant Walter J. Levy, complements Adelman's essay by pointing to some of the unpleasant implications of the industrial countries' heavy dependence on Middle East oil. Levy urges the consumer countries to confront OPEC with a unified position, which he outlines in general terms, in order to es-tablish a countervailing power on the international oil scene.

In "Seabeds Make Strange Politics" (pp. 241-60) Ann Hollick returns to the question of the sea and the seabed with a fascinating account of the shifting U.S. policy position and the diverse and conflicting domestic interests—the oil and mineral firms, the fishing industry, the scientific community, the U.S. Navy—behind the shifts. The essay represents a nice case study of the point that domestic and foreign policy interests are increasingly intertwined and that the declining prominence of security concerns will both shift the focus and greatly complicate the formulation of future foreign policy.

2

Throughout all these essays there is a common thread of thought: that economic issues are important in our relations with other countries, that they are likely to grow more important in the future, and that they will call for new policies. The writers reflect a view that economic issues have received insufficient high-level attention in the formulation of recent U.S. foreign policy and that U.S. relations with friendly developed and less developed countries have been allowed to deteriorate largely over economic issues, even while considerable strides were being made to improve relations with the Soviet Union and China.

The unraveling of international economic relations has been intimately related to the growing fusion of domestic and international concerns. Apart from matters of war and peace, no foreign policy issues arouse the public so thoroughly as economic issues do—though, in this case, the public is usually limited to particular groups, vested interests, who bring pressure through political channels for favorable government action on myriad economic fronts. The dairy farmers, the citrus growers, the beef herders, the textile manufacturers, the oil refiners, the international bankers, the arms producers, and dozens of other groups all take a strong and highly focused interest in particular aspects of foreign trade, investment, and finance.

The heavy involvement of these special interests is entirely appropriate in a democracy based on constituency politics, but it greatly complicates the formulation and pursuit of foreign policy, and it greatly increases both the responsibility and the burden on the president to balance particularistic interests against the national interest. The latter is often concrete enough, but highly diffuse in impact, as in decisions affecting the price of heating oil for consumers. At other times the national interest is quite intangible, though nonetheless important, as in preserving "good" relations with other countries, the special interests of which can play for private advantage on any general ill-will toward the United States, thereby causing damage to American interests in areas quite remote from the area where the ill-will was generated.

None of this is, of course, qualitatively new. Vested interests have been around for a long time, and government actions have long had international repercussions. What, then, is new in the present situation? A variety of factors, both real and psychological, can be identified. At a general level, however, two considerations are of particular importance. First, in the world at large, and in the United States in particular, there has been a lessening of anxiety about national security and the threat posed by international communism. Second, within the last fifteen years a very great thickening of economic relations has taken place among noncommunist countries.

So long as peoples feel militarily insecure, they are willing to subordinate narrower economic considerations to security interests. Concretely, this ultimate concern with security meant that for the two decades or so following World War II, the industrial countries of the West were willing to follow the lead of the United States in economic matters because they depended heavily upon the United States for their security. And unless they thought vital national interests were at stake, they were reluctant to adopt policies that deeply offended the United States. For its part, America was willing to adopt a position of leadership—with all the responsibility that entails—and it often subordinated narrow economic interests to the broader, collective interests of the Western nations. Thus, for the sake of European economic and political recovery in the late forties and early fifties the United States tolerated and even encouraged systematic discrimination against American goods in other markets. It also bore a heavy share of expenditure for the common defense, giving other countries to that extent a "free ride."

The advent in the late fifties of intercontinental ballistic missiles—which meant that the United States could be directly threatened—cast some doubt on the credibility of the U.S. atomic deterrent in Western Europe. The pursuit of alternative arrangements resulted in the French *force de frappe*, the German *Ostpolitik*, and the NATO countries' development of an increased capacity for nonnuclear response (with larger requirements for conventional forces, more difficult to justify to the American public than a "trip wire" force). In addition, there was also a series of steps to reduce tension between the Soviet Union and the noncommunist industrial countries: agreements on nuclear testing and nonproliferation, the Strategic Arms Limitation Talks, the normalization of the status of Berlin, discussions concerning mutual force reduction in Central Europe—in sum, a general atmosphere of détente was gradually established after the dangerous confrontations over Berlin and Cuba in the early sixties. Tensions, of course, have remained, especially in Southeast Asia and the Middle East, but they have been remarkably muted as far as relations between the superpowers are concerned. In this kind of emerging climate, the issue of national security has receded into the background and has been replaced by the more mundane and apparently more divisive pursuit of economic interests. To take only one example: when its virulent anti-communism abated as the cold war thawed, organized labor in America became far less willing to subordinate protection-ist inclinations to overriding security considerations.

The second new and important development in foreign rela-tions is the growth of economic interdependence. Actions in one country are transmitted ever more quickly and some-times irritatingly to other countries. Economic relationships are no longer confined to the traditional exchange of manu-factures for food and raw materials, although much of that remains. Rather, economic transactions have increasingly become exchanges of manufactures for manufactures (an enterprise in which the mutual benefits of an international di-vision of labor are far less intuitively evident), financial capital movements between countries, transfers of tech-nology, and, not least, direct investment abroad, with owner-ship of an establishment lying outside the country in which it is located. These developments reflect a growing mobility in factors of production, and this greater mobility in turn im-plies less natural insulation between national economies. The monopoly of a new idea or production technique is not as long lasting as it used to be; the influence of differential pat-terns of corporate taxation on the choice of a location for manufacturing activity is greater than it used to be; the pull or push of divergent national monetary policies on interna-tional movements of funds is stronger than it used to be; and so on.

Two important implications can be drawn from these devel-opments. First, any change in national economic policy (us-ing this term in its broadest sense, which would include the regulation of business) can have substantial "spillover" into other countries, affecting production, employment, the de-gree of competition, and the like. Second, increased mobility and the greater willingness of firms and funds to escape onerous taxation or regulation undercut and hence constrain national economic policy. Any country that deviates in its policies too sharply from its neighbors simply drives firms and funds abroad—or attracts them in droves. These two implications create a profound tension between the kind of open international economy that has been successfully fostered for the past three decades, and the parallel growth in national governmental responsibility to manage national economies effectively. As governments have taken on greater responsibility for managing economies, they have also seen their traditional instruments of economic policy diminish in effectiveness.

A correlative development is the steady improvement of production techniques, which increasingly give economic value to the earth's resources where none existed before. Just as petroleum was once transformed from an offensive and worthless black fluid that polluted streams to a decisively important source of energy, many of the earth's formerly "worthless" resources are now becoming valuable. Radio frequencies, the stratosphere (for civil overflights), the oceans, and more recently the seabed and space, all raise questions about efficient exploitation and about distribution of gains. In short, the problem of property rights is brought into ever new areas, where established conventions usually offer little guidance for proper handling. Once again, the effect on international relations can be profound. Historically, disputes over property rights have frequently been at the heart of international—or intercommunity—relations.

The articles in this book taken as a group suggest the importance of economic questions for general foreign policy, not so much because of a more intensified economic *dependence* of one country on another—the opposite is probably true, given our increasing technological capacity to substitute one limited resource for another—but because as bread and butter matters economic issues greatly influence the context in which all international relations, at least among the noncommunist countries, will evolve. If economic relations among countries go well, other relations are likely to go well. If economic relations go sour, they are likely to poison other areas as well. In democratic societies, favorable or unfavorable public attitudes toward other countries can enlarge or constrain the freedom of chief executives to act in all areas of foreign policy, once security matters cease to be of preoccupying concern. To ply their trade effectively and comprehensively, students of international relations must therefore concern themselves more with economic issues than they have in the past. As U. Alexis Johnson, former under secretary of state for political affairs, recently acknowledged: "I expect that economic considerations may dominate foreign policy over the next two decades, as security concerns dominated the last two." The traditional separation between economics and diplomacy, and between domestic politics and international relations, is becoming untenable.

THE SETTING:
ECONOMICS AND FOREIGN POLICY

DON'T TAKE JAPAN FOR GRANTED
by Yasuo Takeyama

The two major economic powers, the United States and Japan, are now facing the crucial test to prove whether they are wise and mature enough to redefine their mutual relations. . . . The Nixon-Sato summit conference of November 1969 ended an old friction with the historic decision to return Okinawa to Japan in 1972, but it created a new strain because of the "unhappy misunderstanding" between the two leaders concerning the textile issue. Secretary of Commerce Stans' high posture on textile import limitations only aggravated the tension. The dollar crisis of the past year [1971] and President Nixon's dramatic announcements July 15 of a China trip and August 15 of a wage-price freeze and import surcharge have raised further serious strains in U.S.-Japanese relations.

In his February 1971 foreign policy report to Congress, President Nixon cautioned, "My Administration shares with the government of Japan the conviction that our relationship is vital to the kind of world we both want. We are determined to act accordingly. But the future will require adjustments in the U.S.-Japanese relationship, and the issues involved are too important and their solutions too complicated to be viewed with any complacency on either side." The great problem for both sides is to view their economic conflicts in a broader context of political realism, free from unsettling emotionalism.

Viscount Shibuzawa's Tragic Struggle

To this end, it may be especially timely to review the history of earlier U.S.-Japanese economic relations. A biography recently published in Tokyo describes the career of Viscount Eiichi Shibuzawa (1840-1931), one of the founding fathers of the modern Japanese business economy. An advocate of close transpacific ties, Shibuzawa organized the U.S.-Japan Relations Council in 1916 and traveled frequently to America to promote better understanding between the two countries. Some tragic parallels exist between the ultimate failure of

"Don't Take Japan for Granted" was published originally in *Foreign Policy*, Number 5, Winter 1971-72.

men like Shibuzawa to promote transpacific cooperation half a century ago and the clouded atmosphere of our relations today.

In 1909 Shibuzawa crossed the Pacific to visit President Taft as chairman of the Honorary Commercial Commission of Japan to the United States. He declared at the same time that the "U.S. people overestimated the strength of Japan. It may be an honor for us to be thus overestimated, but also it is not good." When in 1922 the United States enacted its notorious immigration law, discriminating against Asians, men like Shibuzawa were deeply frustrated. Shibuzawa's biographer has written:

The United States is a big country and its affection is extremely capricious. As long as another country behaves in a manner acceptable to American thoughts, tastes, and standards, Americans love that country like a pet. However, if and when the "pet" grows up or starts to show independence, America spurns that country without the slightest hesitation. American caprice created the dangerous triangular relations between the United States, mainland China, and Japan in the Pacific area, which eventually led to the tragic Second World War. . . . This "love-hate" cycle occurred twice in U.S.-Japanese relations in the last 100 years.

It is an unhappy historical fact that both sides have failed to establish solid "competitive, but cooperative relations," like those the United States has with many Western European countries. Perhaps, as Shibuzawa's biographer maintains, it is because "no other countries exist which are so different from each other as the United States and Japan. These two countries seem to have been destined to misunderstand one another."

Times have changed since the days of Viscount Shibuzawa. Yet there are three lessons we have to keep in mind if we are to improve our relations. The first of these is that there must be sympathetic insight by both Japanese and Americans into each other's socio-politico-psychological character, or misunderstandings will make it impossible for us to tackle the pressing problems before us. The second valuable and bitter lesson is that realistic, healthy relations with the United States are a vital requirement for Japan's survival, and also that Sino-Japanese relations are of paramount importance for U.S.-Japanese relations. The final lesson is that Japan, when faced by pressing necessity, must be prepared to make flexible changes in her policy toward the United States in order to reverse a rise in anti-Japanese sentiment among the American public.

Japan Under Heavy Attack

In May 1971, when the Bonn Government, overriding the strong opposition of France, unexpectedly floated the mark, U.S. criticism against Japan was intensified. Public hearings of the Senate Finance Committee were accompanied by hostile news stories such as a broadside in *Time* magazine (May 10) entitled "Japan, Inc." and a *Wall Street Journal* headline (May 26): "Oriental Invasion: Japanese Cars Score Success in U.S. Market." These attacks made many Japanese suspect that a well-organized anti-Japanese campaign was in full swing to arouse U.S. public opinion.

With a relatively high rate of unemployment, a sluggish economy, a deteriorating balance of payments, and then a "dollar crisis," the United States had to find a scapegoat to put the blame somewhere. Well, there was Japan, which has been enjoying comfortable trade surpluses: a most convenient scapegoat for all the economic evils Americans were suffering. This, at any rate, is how many Japanese see it. The basic problem for both sides is to analyze with cool heads why this scapegoat theory and "Japanese invasion" myth are now being spread on such a wide scale in the United States. From the American viewpoint the central issue has been Japan's alleged slowness to lift import restrictions and bars to foreign direct investment in the Japanese economy. The fact is that Japan has been steadily, step by step, liberalizing. Today only seven industries—as defined by OECD (Organization for Economic Cooperation and Development) rules—remain with restrictions on foreign capital. In import liberalization, the number of items subjected by Japan to residual import restriction was reduced to forty as of autumn 1971 (down from ninety at the beginning of the year), which compares with seventy such items restricted by France and thirty-eight by West Germany. Japan is keeping its promise to liberalize and has no intention of reverting to a closed internal market.

I would also emphasize the fact, which many Americans may not know, that the United States is the lucky beneficiary of a number of waivers (rights not to liberalize) from GATT (General Agreement on Tariffs and Trade) rules, a privilege denied to many products of Japan. The United States has been benefiting from the right of waiver for such important items as dairy products, cotton, wheat and wheat products, and peanuts, in which the United States has a strong competitive edge in the world market.

U.S. man-made textile imports from Japan amounted to barely 1.1 percent of total U.S. domestic consumption in 1968, when suddenly the U.S. textile industry sought to make these imports a hot political issue. Under heavy political pressure from the U.S. administration and Congress the Japanese textile industry was forced to declare "unilateral voluntary export restraint" toward the United States. This left Japanese taxpayers to shoulder the expenditure of $200 million as adjustment relief to their suddenly depressed textile enterprises.

This is a portrait of the recent economic tension between the United States and Japan viewed through the eyes of Japanese. Many Japanese seriously wonder whether the United States really knows about our recent endeavors to liberalize trade and increase defense spending. The direct defense expenditures of Japan for fiscal year 1970 were 534 billion yen, a fivefold increase since 1958. With American industry seemingly inefficient and American monetary policy increasingly one of undisciplined "benign neglect" for the rest of the world, many Japanese feel it is not fair for their own strong currency and economy to be singled out as the villain of the piece.

A look at the balance-of-payments position of the two countries should help show what is behind the so-called "Japanese invasion" myth. In 1964 Japan's exports to the United States amounted to $1,842 million compared to imports from the United States of $2,366 million, leaving Japan with a trade deficit of $494 million. The year 1965 marked a watershed change in this adverse balance. Japan achieved a $113 million surplus in bilateral trade with the United States in that year, rising to $311 million in 1966, $559 million in 1968, $868 million in 1969 and $380 million in 1970 (though suffering a deficit of $200 million in 1967). In 1970 Japan's exports to the United States reached $5,940 million and U.S. exports to Japan were $5,560 million.

An Oriental Invasion?

In 1970 10.7 percent of all U.S. exports went to Japan, 5.8 percent went to the United Kingdom, 3.4 percent to France, 6.3 percent to West Germany, and 3.3 percent to Italy. U.S. exports to Japan had increased by 33.3 percent in the single year 1969-70, the largest such increase for the United States in any market. International Monetary Fund (IMF) statistics show that the United States incurred heavy payments deficits in 1970 of $478 million to the United Kingdom, $103 million to Western Europe outside the European Economic Community (EEC), $625 million to Canada, and $1,610 million to Japan. To some extent, profit remittances generated by U.S. direct investment in these countries compensated for these deficits. Such remittances were $365 million from the United Kingdom, $1,034 million from Western Europe, $939 million from Canada, and $92 million from Japan.

The balance-of-payments problem of one country should be viewed and dealt with not on a bilateral basis but on a multilateral or global basis. This principle, strongly emphasized over the years by U.S. cabinet officials to their Japanese counterparts, seems to be forgotten by American officials today.

Many of my American friends complain that Japan treats the United States, the most advanced industrial nation, like a developing country, because Japan imports from the United States raw materials such as coking coal, cotton, and wood and in return exports to the United States such sophisticated industrial goods as televisions and radios, motorbicycles, steel products, and automobiles. Americans claim also that they are anxious to export to Japan advanced technological products, but Japan won't let them. These complaints seem to me exaggerated and hence a distortion of the true picture of the trade between the two countries. For example, Japan in 1970 imported $401 million worth of chemical products from the United States. Of Japan's total machinery imports, 61.4 percent valued at $1,412 million and 98.4 percent of aircraft imports (the most typical U.S. high-technology product) came from America. In the case of computers, IBM Japan, a wholly owned subsidiary of IBM International, is said to have more than a 40 percent sales share in the burgeoning Japanese market.

The high-technology industries are, needless to say, sensitive areas in many advanced industrial countries, for future opportunities for employment and export earnings of individual countries heavily depend on them. The United States has exerted strong politico-economic pressure on Japan to secure complete liberalization in her import of these high-technology products. At the same time, paradoxically, the United States is forcing Japan to restrict *its* export to the United States of products of *its* matured industries, such as textiles and shoes.

The import of Japanese automobiles has also aroused a clamor in the United States. In 1970 America imported 1,230,000 autos, or 14.67 percent of its total registered cars for the year. Volkswagen ranked first among the imports with 569,182 cars. Japanese Toyota was second with 184,898, and Nissan was in third place with 100,541. Total Japanese cars imported for the year amounted to 285,439, about half of the Volkswagen total. But Volkswagen's record sales prompted no charges of a "German invasion" like the *Wall Street Journal*'s allegation of an "Oriental invasion" in the automobile market. It is true that Japan imposes a 10 percent import tariff on foreign-made cars, which is far higher than America's normal 3.5 percent tariff (13.5 percent with the Nixon import surcharge) but is lower than the EEC's 13.2 percent and the United Kingdom's 13 percent. Another reproach is that Japan has been slower than Europe to permit the Big Three Detroit automakers to operate subsidiaries. Chrysler, however, has finally received approval from the Japanese government to acquire a 35 percent share in the Mitsubishi Motor Corporation, and General Motors has acquired 34.2 percent of the Isuzu Motor Corporation. Ford is expected to follow suit with similar investments.

The American auto industry really should be asking itself why American consumers prefer imported foreign cars and why U.S. cars do not have higher sales in Japan. A part of the answer is that Detroit has not been satisfying the needs of the American consumer, who increasingly prefers to buy cars that are less expensive and better built. With respect to Detroit's exports to Japan, Japanese consumers usually have to pay $500 to $600 just to have a U.S. imported car adjusted to conform to the safety standards of Japan. If Detroit is export minded, it should make cars that conform to these safety regulations. Then it could sell more cars in Japan.

The Nixon Assault of August 15

Along with the invasion myth, United States resentment has also charged that Japanese firms "play by different rules" than U.S. firms—that government-industry cooperation in Japan cushions competition. This charge is, I believe, wholly unfounded when one takes a close look at the two econo-mies. Japan has been following the rule of free competition, which the United States preached to it, since the end of World War II. We have been firm adherents to the GATT prin-ciples. With the strenuous efforts of its people and enormous fixed-capital investment during the last ten years, Japan has finally built up its industrial strength so as to enable itself to compete freely and fairly in the world market. We want to contribute to a healthier world economy, and to achieve this end we believe it is necessary to work toward the develop-ment of freer competition.

Last March, Henry Scott Stokes, in a perceptive article,* has noted the pervasive misunderstanding of Japan's economic performance and the pressures this created for U.S. retali-ation, which has now sadly occurred. "The Japanese," wrote Stokes,

have made enormous progress in trade liberalization at least in the last half dozen years. Japan's reputation on this score is poor, largely because it delayed liberalization until very late in the game. But this reputation reflects the state of affairs of four or five years ago rather than the condition today. The situation is, after all, that Japan will shortly have only forty items under quota restriction—and its tariffs are, by international standards, not all that high. . . . The argument that Japan is "invading," "conspir-ing," or "plotting to take over" becomes hard to sustain, when Japan *is simply using the free trade and free enterprise system set up under GATT and the OECD* to its own advantage, because it is stronger than its competitors.

Mr. Stokes concluded, "Japan it seems is going to go on winning *under the present rules,* and the temptation to change the rules is therefore a real one—and will get stronger in times of serious economic difficulty in the United States and United Kingdom." This astute prophecy came true when President Nixon delivered his tremendous blows to the GATT and IMF principles by his New Economic Policy of August 15, 1971.

*In *Far Eastern Economic Review*, March 27, 1971.

Time, Inc. on Japan, Inc.

On May 10, three months prior to the Nixon speech, *Time* magazine in its cover story on "Japan, Inc." portrayed the Japanese commercial system as a corporate monolith. The story implied that Japan was an unfair competitor because it did not adhere to Western principles on anything. "Industry is cartelized," said *Time*. "The Japanese economy is directed toward a national goal and almost everybody feels a sense of participation in achieving it. Bureaucrats, bankers, business executives, workers—all labor hard to make Japan a world power through economics." We were said to practice an "inscrutable economics." "Nowhere in the non-Communist world do business and government coexist so closely," with "most of the government's influence . . . exercised by the all-important Ministry of International Trade and Industry (MITI)." We were accused of maintaining a "closed-door policy" and of "refusal to observe the rules of the game of world trade."

It is more than an irony that just at the time this mythical conception of "Japan, Inc." was gaining ground in the United States, a challenging book entitled *America, Inc.* appeared. Its coauthors, Morton Mintz, a prizewinning investigative reporter of *The Washington Post*, and Jerry Cohen, former chief counsel and staff director of the Senate Anti-Trust and Monopoly Subcommittee, described barriers to competition and concentrations of government-business power in America.

Apart from obvious American frustrations—over Vietnam, a sluggish economy, a high rate of unemployment, social conflict and malaise—it seems to me that the sources of difficulty and "scapegoating" in U.S.-Japanese relations are based on an American misperception of Japan. You oscillate between underestimating and overestimating us.

Like Viscount Shibuzawa sixty years ago, a recent Japanese visitor to America, Mr. Yoshizane Iwasa, chairman of the Fuji Bank, has come to this conclusion in trying to sort out the myths that separate our thinking. While visiting New York in 1964 at the head of an economic mission, Iwasa identified three of these myths. The first myth, he declared, was the impression, held by many Americans, that behind its facade of democracy and modern industry Japan is fundamentally a backward, inscrutable, feudal society that has little or nothing in common with the industrialized West. The second myth was that the Japanese economy consists of a thin veneer of modern industries and teeming cottage workshops based on low wages and thriving on low-priced competition in world markets. The third myth was that Japan had an unfair edge in trade and payments balances with America. Finally, Iwasa said, there was the myth that Japan is an "automatic ally" that can safely be taken for granted.

Only four years later, in another address to an American audience, Iwasa found it necessary to warn against overestimating Japan's economic potential. For in the short span of those four years, 1964-68, the U.S. stereotype of the Japanese economy and character had radically shifted. The new myths of 1968 were: (1) that Japan, having developed her international competitive power quite rapidly, was now a formidable threat to the economies of even the strongest industrial nations; (2) that despite this great economic potential Japan was obsessed with a desire to amass foreign currency through exports and was concerned only with her own economic growth, disregarding the welfare of her trading partners and of the world economy; and (3) that Japan selfishly restricts imports while imposing tighter controls than any other advanced country on the inflow of foreign capital.

The way to cut through these misconceptions is to face them squarely. I confess that it may not be easy for Americans to understand at a glance the relationship and *modus operandi* between government and business in Japan. Nor is it easy for us Japanese to comprehend the realities of the relationship between state and federal governments and business in the United States.

Beyond Inscrutability

The crucial problem of what kind of business-government "partnership" one country has depends on that country's socio-historical environment, stage of economic development, and the relationship between its political elites and business elites. As professors Clark Kerr, John Dunlop, Frederick Harbison, and Charles Meyers conclude in their book *Industrialism and Industrial Man*, each country has its own pattern of industrialization and structure of leadership. Different patterns of relationship between government and industry exist in every country, and the U.S. pattern is by no means the only one. The Japanese pattern, not unlike the

French pattern, can be described as one of "creative tension" between government and business, or, as World Bank official Sol Sanders puts it, "a complicated set of checks and controls, compromises and orders, between the Japanese business complex and the Japanese government [which] gives Japan 'a planned unplanned economy.'"

Japan is neither a totalitarian state nor a rigidly planned economy. The government has no unilateral directive power over the business management of individual enterprise. As a policy advisory member of MITI, my opinion is that MITI's proper role is to select broad economic policy targets and then try to persuade and guide private industries to meet those targets.

To Americans who allege that there is an "inscrutable" relationship between government and business in Japan, we Japanese reply by wondering whether the U.S. economic system is really a free enterprise system or free market economy in the true sense of those terms. An ample literature (of which *America, Inc.* is only the most recent example) exists to show that it is not. While it is often alleged that the relationship of government to business in the United States is one of cold war, it is difficult for us foreigners to take that allegation at face value. No other country has such an elaborate system of dollar-a-year-men from business in the highest posts of government, smoothly coordinating public and private policies. And no other country has such a well-developed military-industrial complex of government-business collaboration.

Yet U.S. trade policy often seems to follow a haphazard course, influenced, as one observer has stated, "by the extremes of little lobbyists or great events."* Certainly with respect to the textile dispute Americans "have neither the kind of leaders nor the overwhelming concern with foreign trade to easily and clearly define a trade policy like Japan or any other nation. Hence, foreign trade policy is formed by the flow of events."

It may be considerations like these that prompted President Nixon in 1971 to establish a new Council on International Economic Policy, which he chairs personally with the secre-

*The quotations immediately preceding and following are from an address given by Dean Starhl Edmunds of the University of California School of Public Administration at the U.S.-Japan Newspaper Editors' Conference, Honolulu, November, 1970.

tary of state as vice-chairman and Peter Peterson, a leading businessman, as executive director. The president declared, "This Council will provide a clear single focus for the full range of international economic issues at the highest level." With the new Council, and the Commission on International Trade and Investment, which is chaired by Mr. Albert Williams, it appears that the United States finally has come up with a machinery that can formulate a consistent and comprehensive foreign economic and trade policy and achieve a harmonious relationship between government and business. Indeed, many Japanese have the impression that a formidable "America, Inc." has now—if not previously—been born.

Costs of Vietnam

The tensions and conflicts between our two countries for these last several years have been caused mainly by U.S. economic frustration with Japan combined with Japanese political frustration with America. At the June 1971 Japan-U.S. Businessmen's Conference in Washington the American delegates bluntly warned: "The United States feels that the present inequities in Japan-U.S. economic relations must be corrected and that there must be full reciprocity in trade and investment opportunities." The U.S. side stressed the "urgency" of these problems and warned that "solutions would be applied in the political sphere if appropriate steps were not taken to relieve the economic pressures."

I feel these warnings should be taken seriously and Japan should respond to them with constructive action. At the same time the United States must realize that one of the reasons for the decline in its relative competitive strength in the world market since 1965 is the Vietnam war and that it is an absolute necessity for the United States to end that war as soon as possible. In February 1965 the Johnson administration escalated the war by bombing North Vietnam, which brought further massive U.S. involvement, causing enormous economic difficulties in the United States. It was said at the time that this was a war for freedom and for the security of Asia. However, since the disclosure of confidential Vietnam documents by *The New York Times* in June 1971 nobody any longer doubts that it is actually a dirty war that sullies the honor of American democracy.

Logically speaking, the inequities in Japan-U.S. economic relations that American businessmen complain of are a problem quite separate from the Vietnam war. But psychologically speaking, particularly from the Japanese point of view, it seems that the United States is demanding unilateral remedies from Japan to cure the economic curses that have been fundamentally caused by the Vietnam war. Naturally, the Japanese and Europeans resent the unilateral demand that they bear the "responsibilities of the surplus country," unless the United States is also prepared to fulfill the "responsibilities of the deficit country" by rectifying its unfavorable balance-of-payments situation. America can accomplish this either by pulling out of Vietnam or, as the late Dr. Karl Blessing, president of German Bundesbank, used to remark, "by putting her house in order."

Japan's frustrations with the United States are mainly political and psychological, having to do with Vietnam, Okinawa, and China. The policy of military containment of China which Washington has pursued for twenty years and is only now beginning to abandon always made Japan feel as though its hands were tied in what might well be a fluid situation. Every Japanese remembers how the Japan-Formosa Peace Treaty was forced through by Secretary of State Dulles against the will of Premier Yoshida.

Still, the Japanese people feel a strong affinity for the United States, as well as a devotion to Western democratic values, market economics, and human rights. The assassination of the two Kennedys and Martin Luther King, followed by black and student riots, did, however, shake some of our confidence in American democracy. These events were a tremendous blow to the United States' image among the Japanese public. Vietnam, China, Okinawa, and your "benign neglect" of the responsibilities of a key currency country—all these conglomerate irritations have reduced our confidence in you. In their hearts the Japanese retain much affection for America, but we have been frustrated and shaken by unilateral American policies and actions.

As the Vietnam war de-escalates, the competitive position of U.S. industries should improve, easing some of the tensions between us. President Nixon's plan to visit Peking is another welcome change, though the style of his announcement—without any prior consultation with Japan—was shocking and humiliating to Japanese minds. We have to be cautious, however, not to be too optimistic about the prospects. As President Nixon correctly declared,

Each of the major powers of the Pacific region—Japan, the USSR, the People's Republic of China, and the United States—is faced with difficult decisions in adjusting its policies to the new realities of East Asia. And the decisions they make will, in themselves, centrally affect the international situation in the region. The future structure of East Asia is, therefore, not clear. It depends on decisions not yet made. But it is clear that it will not be subject to the dominant influence of any one state.

The time for healthy readjustment and redefinition of the U.S.-Japanese relationship, looking to the 1980s, is definitely ripening. Both sides need to discuss, dispassionately, the complementary economic responsibilities of the "surplus country" (Japan) and of the "deficit country" (the United States). And both should seek, in closer consultation, ways to normalize relations with China, guided by one overriding consideration: that for both Japan and the United States their relations *with each other* are more important than the otherwise desirable and timely effort to improve relations with Peking. The U.S.-China accommodation should not be made at the expense of Japan. And, more specifically, a series of actions on the economic front could do much to improve our relations.

In the Economic Field

Despite the announcement of a New Economic Policy in August 1971 our international trade must be governed by the common spirit "not in protectionism but in a context of expanding trade and liberal payment" (as Treasury Under Secretary Paul Volcker put it last June). With an expanded EEC joined by Britain in sight, it is important that the world not retreat into regionalism with protectionist tendencies. Japan will do her best to implement the Eight Point Program for liberalization, announced by the Japanese government in June 1971. In summary, that means the following things: first, accelerating import liberalization so as to promote further reduction in the case of the remaining forty "residual import restriction" items this year; second, generalized tariff preferences for the exports of the developing countries, which took effect August 1; third, voluntary tariff cuts, particularly on imports of consumer goods, and advocacy of another round of general tariff reductions; fourth, accelerated capital liberalization—we will expand the list of 100 percent liberalization industries (those able to receive foreign direct investment) and lessen the number of nonliberalized industries to less than 10; fifth, abolition of nontariff trade barriers—for this purpose the present Automatic Import Quota System (AIQ) and the Automatic Approval System (AA) should be reviewed; sixth, improvements in the quantity and quality of Japan's foreign economic aid expenditures; seventh, establishment of more orderly export marketing practices—export financial incentives should be suspended or abolished, specially favorable financial treatment of exports by the Bank of Japan should be reviewed, and the financial emphasis of the Export and Import Bank of Japan should be changed from the export sector to the import and investment finance sectors; eighth, expansion of total demand so as to reduce export pressures and stimulate imports.

Immediate and drastic action by Japan to implement this Eight Point Program, together with the reasonable multilateral realignment of major currencies, including the U.S. dollar and Japanese yen, is necessary not only for improving U.S.-Japanese economic relations but also for Japan's own sake. These are the emergency measures for the immediate future. For the longer term, Japan will have to put a new economic and foreign trade policy into effect. Japan needs to change her economic policy radically in order to emphasize improving the quality of life rather than promoting exports. This requires a drastic reallocation of her national resources. Japan is now suffering a rapid rise of consumer prices and shortage of infrastructure, including home building and sewage systems. Even with the projected huge investment for infrastructure, amounting to $473 billion (at 1965 prices) for the coming ten years, Japan's per capita infrastructure in 1980 will only be equivalent to that of the United States in 1968.

Recommendations presented in May 1971 by the Industry Structure Council to the minister of international trade and industry are harbingers of these new policy changes. These recommendations strongly suggest that Japan, in the 1970s, has to shift the emphasis of her economy from "how to achieve" a high rate of growth to "how to utilize" what is already achieved for improving the quality of life and for promoting more harmonious international economic relations. The Council proposed six new policy objectives that Japan should pursue in the 1970s: first, shorten the work week about 12 percent to thirty-five hours, five days a week, in nonagricultural sectors, by the end of the decade; second, increase sharply social infrastructure investment to achieve the same per capita level in Japan in 1980 as the United States reached in 1968; third, accelerate investment to prevent environmental pollution; fourth, sharply increase investment for education and manpower development; fifth, similarly increase research and development investment; sixth, accelerate economic development expenditures in the developing nations—$7.5 billion is projected for this purpose by 1980.

American Policy

Turning to U.S. economic, trade, and industrial policies that we Japanese would like you to pursue, I would point to five areas.

First, I hope there is wide realization in America that, in a return to protectionism, we would all end up losers. Trade expansion and liberalization should continue to be our common goal. I sincerely welcomed the statement made by former Under Secretary of State George Ball to the Senate Finance Committee in May 1971, when he declared,

The pressures that our own government [has] recently brought on the Japanese government and Japanese industry have been directed with far more vigor to persuade the Japanese to limit certain of their exports to the United States than to open their market to our goods and investment. Sooner or later, if we are ever to succeed in persuading our Japanese friends to achieve that degree of liberalization required by an expanding trading world, we must cure ourselves of such schizophrenia. That our efforts should be directed toward liberalization rather than further restriction seems to me beyond question.

Second, the United States should take all necessary domestic measures to rectify its deteriorating balance-of-payments position and to curb inflation. This, in part, you seem to be doing under the New Economic Policy of President Nixon. As Treasury Secretary Connally has said, "This is a time for the private sector to do everything possible to hold down the rise in labor costs, to avoid unnecessary increases in interest rates, and to speed the return to price stability." Close co-operation between your government and business leaders is desperately needed.

Third, to keep the American economy abreast of the ever-changing world economic situation, the United States has to be courageous enough to pursue an industrial adjustment process instead of sticking to the status quo. Because many vested interests and pressure groups exist in a democracy, it is particularly difficult to let basic adjustments in the economy take their natural course. A commitment to liberal trade policy and the free market, however, does imply a comparable commitment to industrial adjustment: to letting more efficiently produced imports drive less efficient domestic producers out of business. To alleviate the unnecessary socio-economic hardships caused by such adjustment, well-planned government assistance measures are imperative, in close collaboration with business and labor. Some reasonably common formula for this purpose should be carefully studied and formulated among the major industrial states within the OECD and the GATT.

Fourth, present U.S. antimonopoly laws ought to be revised to meet the needs of the time. In a conflict like the present, unhappy U.S.-Japanese textile war, it would be preferable for both countries to handle this problem by direct negotiation between the two textile industries, leaving the governments to act as supervisory "honest brokers" to police the industry agreements and see that they are consistent with the law. U.S. textile firms avoided direct talks with their Japanese counterparts under rigid U.S. antimonopoly laws. Thus the problem turned into a political issue and attracted more attention than it essentially deserved. Also, your "extraterritorial" laws which conflict with foreign sovereignty should be amended so as to remove a further cause of international discord.

Fifth, we wonder why you do not feel any necessity to agree to international rules to control the operations of your giant multinational corporations. Is it wise to let these corporations operate freely, not subject to any internationally agreed-upon rules of behavior and restraint? As of March 1970 the number of Japanese-owned manufacturing enterprises in the United States was only twenty-six, compared with a total of 326 U.S. subsidiaries operating in Japan, with annual sales of more than $4.8 billion. In 1969, according to a survey of the U.S. Commerce Department, the net profit of all U.S. subsidiaries in Japan came to $1.7 billion, for an earning ratio of 16 percent per annum. These U.S. corporations received 60 percent of Japan's royalty payments of $350 million in 1969.

In a word, we would like to see the U.S. pursue realistic policies, which have often been promised but rarely acted on in the past. The three major requirements are: first, stepped-up international coordination of national economic policies, particularly among the industrialized countries; second, the formulation of a comprehensive program for assisting U.S. industries to adjust adequately to changing international competitive conditions; and last, but most importantly for the U.S. trade position, the pursuit of policies that will moderate internal inflationary forces in the context of a growing economy. For these purposes the New Economic Policy of August 15 seems to us rather disappointing. The New Policy almost wrecked the existing international trade and monetary order and thus was an invitation to protectionist tendencies in and out of the United States. The import surcharge should be abolished right away, and some kind of instrumental brake should be created in the international monetary system so that the United States, still as a key currency country, will be forced to abide by monetary discipline.

The Political Side.

As Henry Owen has written in *The Washington Post*, "There is a curious parallel between the current crisis in U.S.-European and in U.S.-Japanese relations." In each case, Mr. Owen believes, economic disputes have flared to expose security problems, and "these problems will persist until underlying economic issues are resolved—which will require political initiatives looking to more, not less, interdependence." I agree with Owen that "the issue is not whether one side can gain marginal economic advantage over the other but whether these industrial areas can work together in building a viable world order."

The important problem between the United States and Japan in an age of adjustment is what kind of "viable world order" we want to have, not only among the industrialized nations but also in the Asian-Pacific region, and what kinds of roles we should expect to play to preserve the peace and security of Asia. In this respect, we were dismayed by the U.S. failure to include Japan in any prior consultations over your China policy of July 1971 or your world trade and currency policy of August 1971. We welcome détente between the United States and the People's Republic of China as a first step to alter the present abnormal cold war power structure in East Asia. The Japanese people are definitely determined not to become a military power armed with strategic or tactical nuclear capability, even though Japan may have to modernize her self-defense forces with conventional weapons.

The consensus of public opinion in Japan is that NATO-type monolithic collective-security arrangements are not appropriate in Asia. Our security problems are best dealt with, we believe, not by "hard structure" scenarios but by "soft structures"—overlapping regional cooperation in many forms without rigid security pacts. This belief, together with the antiwar clause of the Japanese Constitution, is why the Japanese people are strongly opposed to making any military contributions to the Southeast and Northeast Asian countries. Japan instead has been earnestly contributing to various economic and political regional organizations, such as the Association of South East Asian Nations (ASEAN), the Economic Commission for Asia and the Far East (ECAFE), the Ministerial Conference for the Economic Development of Southeast Asia, the Asian Development Bank (ADB), and the World Bank. As an Asian country we think that Asian security problems should be resolved by political, economic, and cultural means, rather than by taking a narrow military point of view. Japan's decision to implement generalized preferential tariff reductions for all developing countries last August and the sharp increase of its textile imports from developing countries in Asia (currently running at $150 million) are two examples of this policy emphasis.

Even with living standards still relatively low compared with those of the United States, the Japanese people are courageously going through agonizing industrial adjustment processes and are determined to fulfill their responsibilities as an industrialized nation. They aspire to occupy an honorable place in the world community. They believe that Japan, along with such important and decisive nations for the future as West Germany and the People's Republic of China, should be made a permanent member of the U.N. Security Council.

We Japanese are prepared to try our best to further the peace and prosperity of the world, in cooperation with our American allies. We must strive for better collaboration, bearing in mind that events since July 1971 have produced two bitter lessons for both of us: Japan should not and cannot take the United States for granted in economic matters; and, at the same time, the United States should not and cannot take Japan for granted in political affairs.

COMING TRADE WARS?
NEO-MERCANTILISM
AND FOREIGN POLICY

by Harald B. Malmgren

Commercial and financial issues are starting to replace traditional diplomatic and security questions as the main stuff of
foreign policy. This shift in priorities is in part a consequence
of the receding threat of war between the superpowers. But,
just as important, a sweep of worldwide economic adjustment is also under way, changing the framework of international politics.

Two-thirds of the world's people live in the developing nations, and by the year 2000 this ratio is expected to rise to
about five-sixths. The political outlook for these countries
and their relations with the developed world depend heavily
on economics. For the political issues of development are
mainly economic issues. Income growth is the developing
world's political imperative, affecting the fate of its political
leaders, bringing about changed trade and financial flows,
and dominating diplomacy between rich and poor countries.

More immediately, there is a fundamental change in economic relationships among the major powers. The United
States is no longer the world's largest trading unit, for the
European Economic Community (EEC) has surpassed it, even
excluding internal trade among the six members. If Britain
and others join the EEC, economic power relationships will
shift more quickly and massively. Meanwhile, Japan is moving up fast. World trade is growing faster than Gross National
Product, and investment flows are altering the shape of national interests. Trade itself is becoming increasingly sensitive to changes in national economic conditions. As Richard
Cooper wrote two years ago, "Transportation costs have fallen somewhat, tariffs and other barriers to trade have fallen
much more, 'horizons' have broadened to provide greater re-
ceptivity to foreign goods." Cooper added,

. . . the accumulation of capital and the international transmis-
sion of technical knowledge have caused a convergence in the

"Coming Trade Wars? Neo-Mercantilism and Foreign Policy" was published
originally in *Foreign Policy*, Number 1, Winter 1970-71.

potential structure of production in industrial countries so that national advantages arising from climate, resources, or unique technological skills are less successful in insulating a country from foreign competition than they once were.*

These trends have made trade and financial questions more politically explosive. National economies increasingly depend for adjustment upon international mechanisms that can help them to weather shifting patterns and levels of trade without having to resort to extraordinary restrictions.

Many governments have not yet faced up to these slowly evolving but powerful forces of economic change. In the U.S., contrary to the theorizing of the American New Left, international economic issues rarely hold the high-level attention of those who make foreign policy. Foreign economic policy is still considered a tedious and technical subject in the upper reaches of Washington officialdom. The broad policy consequences of economic actions are hardly ever considered by secretaries of state. Presidents never give international economics anything like the time and attention they devote to military and diplomatic problems. This lack of attention to shifting economic forces at a high policy level has already allowed some major problems to erupt into conflict, while others fester. It has also permitted, and even encouraged, the strengthening of domestic special interest groups which work against international cooperation. One current example is the Japanese textile crisis.

The breakdown in 1970 of U.S.-Japanese negotiations on textile trade followed by a flurry of congressional activity to shape restrictive import legislation, was not a minor technical slippage in our commercial machinery. It was a confrontation in basic foreign policy which arose over economic issues. The textile trade had become a political hot potato in Japan months before the breakdown. Parliamentary debate and public discussion in Tokyo focused on such questions as whether Japan should again, as so often in the past, capitulate to U.S. pressure, whether doing so put an unacceptable strain on Japan's export economy, and whether Japan should not reduce its ties to the United States and turn more toward the Asian sphere and China. Two key politicians, Foreign

---

*Richard N. Cooper, *The Economics of Interdependence* (New York: McGraw-Hill, 1968), p. 80.

Minister Aichi and International Trade and Industry Minister Miyazawa, threatened to resign over the U.S.-Japanese confrontation.

The American position was that Japan must limit its exports of textiles to the U.S., even though this was a violation of Japan's rights under the international trading rules of the General Agreement on Tariffs and Trade (GATT). The reason: President Nixon had committed himself during the 1968 election campaign to provide import relief for the American textile industry.

Spokesmen for the United States explained that there was no problem with imports from Europe and that therefore there was no need for restrictions in that quarter. The problem lay in Asia, more specifically in Japan, Taiwan, Korea, and Hong Kong. In the long run it was expected that such countries as Singapore, Malaysia, and the Philippines would also fall into the problem category. Consequently, the issue blossomed into a yellow-skin discrimination question, further inflaming Japanese opinion.

The issue was a major one in Tokyo, but Washington hardly seemed to notice. For the U.S. president a minor campaign commitment was at stake. For his foreign policy bureaucracy it was a boring trade problem that somehow had to be solved in order to get on with more important issues, such as when Japan was to get Okinawa and under what conditions.

When the bilateral talks reached an impasse, President Nixon endorsed legislative import restrictions on textiles. Congress, given license to indulge its protectionist mood, then began to move on a trade bill. As legislators considered erecting new trade barriers not just for textiles but also for many other products, editorialists evoked the specter of the high Smoot-Hawley Tariff of 1930. Part of the reason for this was frustration with the import and foreign investment restrictions of the Europeans and the Japanese, which have an adverse effect on the United States. Much of it reflected growing congressional concern over unemployment, especially over the possible labor-displacing effects of imports from low-wage countries. In textiles, the allegation was that labor in the South, especially black labor, would be damaged by imports from Asia. Our regional economic and social policies required, it was said, protection of the U.S. textile industry. The same argument was then made for protection of the shoe industry and many others.

This problem was more general than it appeared. In the past year the AFL-CIO, altering its historic position, came out against free trade in many product areas. The unions even voiced opposition to the free movement of capital, criticizing U.S. government policies toward multinational companies as too permissive. Labor fears that large American companies may move their production facilities to Asia and other developing nations to obtain cheaper labor (the "runaway mill" problem). Even where companies stay home, there is apprehension that labor-intensive imports will slow the expansion of investment in creating new jobs.

This turnabout has pitted a labor problem, a vote problem, and a political commitment problem on the U.S. side against an issue of national importance on the Japanese side, reopening for discussion the foreign policy orientation of a major ally. The European countries, now strong enough to take an independent stand, have tended to side with Japan, warning the United States of the serious consequences of evading the GATT legal framework. Over time, they argue, as restrictions are piled upon restrictions, the U.S.-Japanese dispute could escalate to a trade war with many countries. Europeans interpret the U.S. position as an attempt to pass along to other countries a domestic electoral debt.

Neo-Mercantilism

What we are witnessing today is the fundamental clash of national policies that are primarily oriented toward solving domestic political and social problems. These policy clashes also existed in the past, but were softened by at least two mitigating factors. First, there was a continual effort after World War II to negotiate internationally in trade and monetary affairs, which produced a series of successful agreements to reduce trade restrictions and to improve monetary cooperation. Second, the political impact and attention toward foreign policy of interest groups such as organized labor and farmers was minimal. These limiting circumstances no longer exist. Multilateral discussions are at a standstill. There has been a rise in mercantilist sentiment in most of the world, while the present and future role of labor, farmers, and special interest groups has become increasingly important. Now businesses, workers, and farmers in all countries expect their governments to manipulate national economies to ensure full employment and prosperity. Where conflict arises with another country's interests, the domestic economic requirements are expected to prevail.

Historically, mercantilism is associated with preindustrial Europe, though as a guiding doctrine it was practiced in many states for centuries.* It was a conception of the role of the state that involved manipulation of the economy, but manipulation through reducing imports, stimulating home production, and promoting exports. It was thus a highly nationalistic conception of how governments should act. Its historic strength and support was finally balanced, if not toppled, by the advent of laissez-faire philosophy and internationalism.

Today we are seeing a resurgence of mercantilism, whereby governments meet domestic economic demands with conscious policies of manipulation, passing the costs of these policies as much as possible onto other countries. This neo-mercantilism is a profoundly disruptive force in international relations. It takes many forms.

The Common Market Wall

In Europe, the Six have managed to forge a reasonably effective economic union. Their major achievement, however, is not in establishing new political institutions, but rather in consolidating European agricultural policies. This has been no mean achievement, for until recently farm policies varied widely from government to government. European agriculture had become a serious social and political problem in certain regions. Any economic program had to include policies for caring for the needs of rural families engaged in farming. The answer was found in a new and ingenious system called the Common Agricultural Policy (CAP). Incomes were to be maintained and increased by supporting prices at high levels, without any production controls. Then, to prevent imports by cheaper suppliers from spoiling this supported market, import levies were to be assessed in an amount sufficient to bring the price of imports up slightly above domestic price supports. Imports thus became residual, filling needs in excess of domestic supplies.

Since EEC price supports were extremely high relative to world market levels (roughly twice as high for the major com-

*The classic study is the two-volume work by Eli F. Heckscher, *Mercantilism* (London: Allen & Unwin, 1935). My description of mercantilism here is highly simplified.

modities), and since technological change relentlessly pushed up productivity, production was stimulated. To avoid or reduce enormous surpluses in some commodities it was necessary to export, but exporting was out of the question at these high internal prices. Therefore the system had to provide export subsidies to the extent necessary to meet world competition at world market rates. The import levies were used to finance the export subsidies. The result was the ultimate in mercantilism: decrease in imports, stimulation of home production to substitute for imports, and increase in exports.

The reason for building this mercantilist machine was simple enough. Economic union would not be possible without a deal between France and Germany. France had farm programs in need of support, and Germany had industrial products it wished to sell in France. Germany was willing to pay in agriculture for better industrial access; besides, German farmers were very strongly in favor of high prices for their products. Thus internal political problems of social policy and rural and regional development were solved. To the rest of the world, particularly to efficient farm producers like the United States, the impact of the system has been costly. One effect has already been a drop of 40 percent in U.S. exports of CAP-protected products to the EEC over the last three years. The CAP system began to function in 1966-67, and protection now is roughly triple what it was at the beginning of the 1960s.

The direct economic damage to others goes even deeper. The highly subsidized prices of the EEC have become a source of intense downward price pressure on other agricultural exporters. This has caused great economic and political pain to smaller exporting countries like Denmark and New Zealand, and the beginnings of real trouble for larger ones like the United States. The new EEC agricultural system is a throwback. It is an explicit commitment to mercantilism as a way of life, having broad policy consequences for all trading nations. Even major importing countries are affected, as their own farmers feel the increased pressures of imports diverted from other markets to their own and sold at depressed prices.

Agrarian Reformers

The EEC is not alone in its tendency toward further trade distortions in agriculture. The Japanese, protected by a series of quantitative import restrictions inconsistent with the GATT, and holding to a support level for rice triple the world market price, are faced with a rapidly increasing rice surplus and mounting budgetary costs. This creates pressure to maintain import restrictions on other temperate commodities in order to stimulate diversification. Japan is now trying to unload some of its mountain of high-cost rice in the form of food aid, disrupting the rice markets of developing country exporters. Denmark, squeezed by widespread subsidization in world markets, has adopted a Home Market Scheme, a euphemism for export subsidies of its own. Australia and Canada have felt similar pressures, particularly in declining wheat prices during the last year (witness the political turmoil in Canada's western provinces). This was a result, in part, of past unwillingness by the Canadian and Australian governments and wheat producers to recognize that they must share in controlling world production by restraining their own output, or else face general deterioration in world grains prices, in spite of the International Grains Agreement provisions to the contrary.

The United Kingdom has also turned toward increasing protection, justifying each move in terms of balance-of-payments considerations. Both political parties in the United Kingdom advocate increased self-sufficiency in agriculture. An Economic Development Committee for Agriculture was established to develop import-saving policies which stimulate home production. Introduction of an EEC-type protection system is imminent. While there have been some difficulties in moving toward more self-sufficiency, and the costs are high both to the government and the consumer in the United Kingdom, there is no doubt about the direction of British policy.

The entry of Britain into the Common Market will almost certainly reduce imports from third countries and provide a new market for the painful surpluses of the Six, easing any pressure for reform at least for a time. The entry of Denmark, a strong agricultural exporter already, will compound the difficulties for third countries.

These developments in the major commercial markets come at a time when the developing nations are finally able to step up their rates of agricultural growth as a result of the Green Revolution in rice and wheat. Some of these nations are not only becoming self-sufficient, but are also pinning hopes on potential commercial exports. This is happening at the very time when the developed countries are pressing each other's prices downward through protectionism, artificially stimulated production, and export subsidization.

The director-general of the GATT said recently, "The situation now seems to have reached alarming proportions and to be already out of proper control." He was speaking of the whole of world agricultural trade. Recent trends bear out this bleak assessment. What are the political implications?

Most U.S. farm organizations are export minded and therefore supporters of freer trade. They have for many years exerted effective pressure to block protectionist moves in the U.S. and have been a crucial element in every coalition that has fought for trade liberalization. Alienation of the farm bloc, in addition to the recent shift of the AFL-CIO, means the end of the political balance in America that used to favor outward-looking trade policies. This erosion of the domestic political base has significant side effects. Agricultural export problems disturb men in Congress who must also vote on overseas defense expenditures. The export question hits them directly because it harms their constituents and gives them a sense of insult added to injury: Europe not only does not pay its own way in defense, but also artificially undercuts America's best export growth performers, agricultural commodities. The sentiment has a certain logic and powerful implications for the future of Atlantic relations.

Another political implication of EEC farm policy is its effect on the policies of other countries. Recently the Mediterranean nations have all found it necessary to negotiate special discriminatory, bilateral trade agreements with the EEC to insure access for certain products, particularly in agriculture. This adds to an already considerable network of special bilateral arrangements between the EEC and most of Africa, Greece, and Turkey. Even Israel is inside the discriminatory system.

Geo-economics

The EEC-Mediterranean preferences have damaged some U.S. citrus exports, but the basic policy problem cuts deeper. Preferential, discriminatory trading arrangements have been concluded for the self-admitted reason that they seem politically necessary. The most serious problem they raise is the precedent they set for the future. As EEC enlargement takes place, the question will arise as to treatment of the remaining EFTA* countries, and of the Commonwealth, and of U.K. dependencies (for example, the Caribbean). The tendency will be to negotiate even more special arrangements. Growing like Topsy, a geo-economic system that favors members and damages outsiders will be formed—a special system that is no longer so special. That it leaves Latin America for the United States to look after is only one problem. An even greater difficulty lies in the exclusion and eventual alienation of Asia. This European system will dominate world trade statistics, leaving the rest of the world to become a series of "special cases."

Taking into account the likely trade damage to the U.S. if European policies move further in their present direction, the traditional American support for European enlargement and unification is bound to be reassessed. A united Europe has been a long-time objective of U.S. policy, but the purposes of this unity were to help stabilize international relations, share the burdens of Western security, cooperate in managing the world economy, and assist in the development of poor countries.

In 1966 J. Robert Schaetzel, our ambassador to the Common Market, wrote:

> Over the full range of contemporary foreign affairs, American policy toward Western Europe has been marked by durability and rare continuity. The change of neither Presidents, Secretaries of State, nor political parties has altered the lines of basic policy. The government marches with American public opinion, for that ubiquitous man in the street still feels deeply that Western Europe is vital to the United States.**

This view expressed itself in the 1960s in the policy of "partnership," the goal of close cooperation between transatlantic equals. A spokesman for this course, Schaetzel warned that it would not always be a smooth one: "The sheer magnitude and novelty of the task of unifying Europe will preoccupy the Europeans. Caught up in these affairs, their governments will be less inclined, at least in the short run, to give attention

*European Free Trade Area (present members are: Austria, Britain, Denmark, Norway, Portugal, Sweden and Switzerland).

**J. Robert Schaetzel, "The Necessary Partnership," *Foreign Affairs* (April 1966).

even to what they would agree are common problems, or to give an equal priority to urgent international questions." What was not adequately foreseen was that Europe all the while was tending to consolidate an enormous economic club that not only ignored but actively discriminated against the United States, and even against most of the developing countries. By conscious design or otherwise this is how the Grand Design is evolving today. Trade discrimination may be a way for Europeans to demonstrate the end of U.S. tutelage, the answer to the U.S. dollar domination through direct investments. Whatever the motives, the consequences are highly disruptive and damaging. American diplomacy in the 1960s never really coped with these problems but focused instead on NATO political-military issues, which were of declining interest for most Europeans.

On the western side of the Atlantic, when outward-looking economic policies and multilateal initiatives to head off discrimination are urgently required, the United States instead seems to be reverting to a neo-mercantilism of its own. The symptoms first revealed themselves in the balance-of-payments program of the 1960s, which was aimed at earning more while paying out less abroad. Many of these Kennedy and Johnson administration measures were crudely mercantilistic, but they probably did not have great impact in practice (although the investment controls did relieve some apprehensions in Europe about American investment domination). The countries most affected were the developing countries, through aid-tying, "additionality," direct-investment restraints, and the decline in congressional appropriations for foreign assistance.

From Beef to Steel

During the Kennedy Round, the greatest trade liberalization effort in history, protectionism was held back by the momentum of international negotiations authorized by the 1962 Trade Expansion Act. In 1967, when the negotiations were concluded, protectionist sentiment in Congress suddenly rose sharply. From that time to this there has been a major push to restrict imports of textiles, shoes, steel, beef, and many other products. International political relations have been strained by U.S. diplomatic pressures on other countries to limit their exports voluntarily in order to head off restrictive trade legislation. Beef exporters in Australia, New

Zealand, and Latin America have accepted such informal limitations. In steel, foreign governments have turned a deaf ear, but foreign companies proved less stubborn and a steel producers' voluntary export restraint agreement has emerged "spontaneously." Pressures for greater textile restrictions continue. In dairy products, a tight import quota system keeps imports from exceeding 1 percent of the total American market.

These developments and others have angered our trading partners. The situation seems, no doubt, surrealistic to some American diplomats. After all, export of beef or of milk is not a major issue of foreign policy—or is it?

The Australian government answered the question by pointing out that its troops in Vietnam cannot be paid for if Australia is not permitted to earn its way in exports. When Nelson Rockefeller visited Latin America on his 1969 mission, the major political issue raised throughout the continent was that of American trade restrictions, particularly in beef and textiles. More recently, Brazil has been threatening to reassess its entire economic relationship with the United States if we insist on restraining its quite modest cotton textile exports. In steel, the Commission of the EEC has been furious that a nongovernmental restriction program was established at U.S. instigation, in disregard of international rules and of political relations between governments. In agriculture, most countries have agreed that our dairy quotas are so excessively strict as to be absurd, which undermines our case against the damaging agricultural policies of others. Finally, the failure of Congress for such a long period after the Kennedy Round to repeal the infamous American selling price legislation, even though it was negotiated as a separate trade deal during the Kennedy Round, made many Europeans feel that negotiating with Americans was basically a waste of time.

The political repercussions of these neo-mercantilist policy changes spread slowly, but they spread inevitably. Because they involve special interest groups, companies, workers, and farmers, their political effects are far-reaching and persistent. Unless high Washington policymakers start paying more attention to economics, the problems ahead will be amplified.

The Rich and Poor

They will be especially painful in relations with the developing world. At the close of the 1960s a number of reviews of the progress of the developing countries were set in motion. For preparation of Development Decade II, the group of "Wise men" under Professor Tinbergen was formed. For the World Bank, the Pearson Commission prepared a report. For the Inter-American Development Bank, Raul Prebisch completed a survey of Latin American problems and prospects. In Washington, the president's Task Force on International Development made its recommendations.

This many-faceted appraisal revealed several fundamental problems. During the 1960s the developing countries performed, on the average, better than anyone expected, growing at 5 percent per year. In the face of population growth, however, their per capita income grew by only half as much, and the income gap between rich and poor countries widened. The reports concluded that growth could be somewhat accelerated if the external flow of aid resources was increased. Among the recommended measures were that official aid should be raised in each donor country to 0.70 percent of GNP (Pearson) or 0.75 percent (Tinbergen), and private investment flows should also be raised. The greatest stress was placed on trade: "The first requirement for rapid international development is continued vigorous expansion of world trade."* Since trade accounts today for nearly 80 percent of total foreign exchange resources (aid and investment adding up to only 20 percent), trade will have to provide the engine for further growth.

The obstacles to improved trade performance are numerous. The developing countries themselves have tried for a time to follow mercantilist policies, keeping imports tightly restricted, stimulating home production, and subsidizing exports. Their efficiency by world standards is consequently low, with home-produced parts and materials more costly than imports and investments distorted toward less efficient sectors. They find themselves competing with each other's mercantilist policies as well as with the aids to exports provided by some developed countries for their own trade.

*Partners in Development: Report of the Commission on International Development (New York: Praeger, 1969), p. 14.

Even in agriculture, where the Green Revolution has raised productivity and expectations in a number of developing countries, there are problems. The farm price-support levels for these countries are often set at twice the world market level to stimulate production and provide higher rural incomes. Thus the Philippines has been able to export rice, but only by means of heavy subsidies.

Poor-country access to rich-country markets, where the demand is, and where hard currencies could be earned, is hampered by many obstacles. The tariff structures of the rich countries tend to work against the production prospects of developing nations. Tariffs against raw materials are low, or zero, but against processed products they are high, in order to protect processors in the rich countries. Moreover, the relative competitive position of most developing nations is weak because of their own distorted economies, unrealistic exchange rates, and marketing inexperience.

The Shadow of UNCTAD

The 1964-69 UNCTAD* confrontation of rich and poor on this issue eventually resulted in 1968 in an agreement by the developed countries to grant general tariff preferences for the manufactures and semimanufactures of developing nations. The United States reluctantly ended its opposition to the concept of general preferences, primarily because this seemed the only answer to the proliferation of discriminatory preferences negotiated by Europe. While agreeing in principle, the developed nations ran into numerous difficulties in finding a common approach for implementation. Impasses developed for a time over two issues: the types of safeguards to be maintained against excessive or disruptive imports from the beneficiary nations, and the principle of nondiscrimination itself. The former problem reflected U.S. desire for a common system providing equal conditions of access in all countries. The latter problem arose over the U.S. policy objective that existing discriminatory arrangements be ended, particularly those involving "reverse preferences" granted by developing countries to some products of some developed countries. The United States favored one general system applicable to all developing nations equally, as a one-level departure from Most Favored Nation (MFN) tariff rates. Washington essentially lost on both these issues, because political sentiment for maintaining the special deals

*United Nations Conference on Trade and Development.

was too strong both in Europe and in the African beneficiary countries. As for safeguards, each country agreed to go its own way.

Now the signatories are preparing to move ahead with implementation. But the political outlook for this is not good. The United States Congress must pass implementing legislation and in its present mood may extract a heavy price in the form of new trade restrictions. Beyond that hurdle lies one more fundamental. The Asian countries have been the most successful exporters of manufactures. Textiles are their greatest industrial success. The reaction in Europe, Canada, and the United States has been to insist on "voluntary" import restrictions, penalizing Asians because of their successes. Using the international agreement on cotton textiles under the GATT, the United States has restricted many countries, and it is now pressing to broaden the product coverage of restrictions to other forms of textiles.

The problem is not limited to textiles. Any labor-intensive products that achieve a high level of export success appear to be labor-displacing to the recipient countries. These effects are especially felt, or at least feared, in low-wage, high-unemployment regions of the developed countries. Pressures exist continually for new "voluntary" restrictions on more and more products. Since the developing nations have no real bargaining leverage and little power to retaliate, they are easily convinced of the wisdom of voluntary export restrictions by threats of worse treatment if they fail to cooperate (voluntary restrictions are always less harmful than legislated quotas, they are told).

Mushrooming Trouble

One small example of the kind of trouble they face is the story of what happened to Taiwanese canned mushrooms in 1968. The Taiwanese had built up in two or three years an enormously successful export business to Germany and the United States. Then the Germans imposed import restrictions. The U.S. industry had not been hurt, due in part to very careful marketing by the Taiwanese to avoid intrusion on existing American sales channels. The prospect of possible diversion of extra quantities of canned mushrooms from Germany to the U.S. was, nonetheless, too much for the American mushroom industry to bear. Certain members of Congress and the secretary of state were quickly mobilized to force Taiwan to roll back its export plans and hold to "voluntary" export targets. Taiwan protested in vain that a large number of workers would be affected and that these restrictions would make investors wary of further development efforts in other export fields. Despite the complaints, export quotas were quietly established.

Though this is a tiny example, it is not unique, and it is not limited to the United States. In Ottawa, Paris, Bonn, the same pressures arise. If broad textile restrictions are in fact negotiated internationally, we may expect other labor-intensive products to be next in line.

The agricultural import restrictions, tropical products taxes, and other nontariff barriers in all of the developed countries add to the trouble. These forms of protectionism are in fact far more significant in trade volume than any possible benefits flowing from tariff preferences. Moreover, if preferences actually begin to work, drawing in foreign investment to produce for preferred access to the markets of developed countries, other kinds of trade restrictions could well result. Labor unions will certainly complain about runaway mills. Success in any export line will breed restrictive reactions. In this psychological context the incentive to produce for export is not very great, and it is not surprising that the governments of developing countries have trouble encouraging private investment in the export business.

While these problems are brewing, foreign aid has not only stagnated, but actually begun to fall off. In real terms, the total flow from developed countries has dropped significantly in the 1960s.* The Europeans and Japanese have picked up a bit, but the United States aid levels are falling dramatically.

In overall outlook for the developing countries, then, the prospects for accelerating trade and stepping up aid are not at all good. This will have international political implications. Until recently the main export earnings of developing nations have come from commodities, in agriculture, minerals, and fuels. For products like cocoa and coffee it is a handful of landowners who directly feel the ups and downs of international markets, and government bureaucrats who get excited about world market injustice. In minerals, the big multinational companies dominate.

*See the comprehensive analysis of J. N. Bhagwati, *Amount and Sharing of Aid* (Washington, D.C.: Overseas Development Council, 1970).

Exports of manufactures have been gaining in recent years. Their growth rate is more than double that of commodity exports. Thus, their share is moving up steadily. Some degree of industrialization is necessary for overall development in most of the developing nations, and much of this will turn on export opportunities for manufactures. Unfortunately, there will be numerous frustrations for these kinds of exports. They will encounter restrictive policies abroad, and the economic losses caused by trade restraints will hit different kinds of people from those affected in the past. In manufactures they will often hit local business investors and managers, workers finding regular employment for the first time in the cities, families dependent on salaries and not on food raised on small rural plots, some of which could be stored for eating in bad times. When these people are denied the success they have earned and are living together in concentrated areas, their frustration seems bound to generate intense pressure on their governments and politicians. These pressures will be even more intense than the constituent pressures on the local level we already experience in the rich countries. The international problem will become jobs here vs. jobs there, votes for me vs. votes for him.

The foreign policy stakes must inevitably rise in this context. What was once a question of working out a frustrating technical problem in cocoa prices internationally, among bureaucrats, now becomes a frustrating political problem of satisfying the urban workers and voters that the great industrialized countries cannot tell them what to do.

Millions Unemployed

The dimensions of this problem are growing steadily because the employment outlook in the developing nations is extremely bad. The population problem is inexorably becoming an unemployment problem. As the labor force of the poorer countries grows steadily, new job opportunities fail to keep pace. Even if population growth were slowed dramatically tomorrow, unemployment would grow for decades afterward. The problem is further compounded by migration from rural areas to cities, so that it becomes concentrated politically, with no rural family system to provide basic "social security." The dimensions of this situation are not yet fully understood, and there are a number of urgent studies under way around the world. According to the Pearson Report:

Progress must be made in solving the unemployment problem if social and political turmoil is not to arrest the development process. For it is in the volatile cities of the developing world that agricultural stagnation and industrial unemployment combine to produce their gravest consequences. Urban growth is almost universally twice as rapid as the growth of the population in general, and some of the largest cities have even higher rates of expansion. Rural stagnation stimulates a flow of migrants from the land, and urban death rates are often lower than those in the countryside while fertility remains high.

It must be asked whether urban trends can be left to be the by-product of other forces in society. If present trends continued, the largest city in India would have over 35 million inhabitants by the year 2000.*

In such cities the amount and rate of unemployment will be staggering. Prebisch gave some idea of the problem in his 1970 report, concluding that this was now the number one problem of Latin America. He pointed out that the proportion of the labor force employed in manufacturing had actually gone down from 35 percent in 1950 to 30 percent today. To break out of this explosive situation, more industrial job opportunities must be created. But this requires more exports of manufactures either to the developed countries or to other developing countries or to both. Although trade with one another offers hope for the developing nations, their attempts to improve trade relations among themselves have tended to run afoul of the extreme mercantilism that each country practices.

Even though the main ingredient to relieving unemployment must lie in domestic policies that favor extensive use of labor, politicians will tend to blame foreign protectionism whenever there are riots of unemployed urban workers. This political aspect will be accentuated whenever a particular factory has to lay off workers or slow down working hours to accommodate export restrictions.

While these problems grow, the debt-service problem will be unfolding relentlessly, putting ever tighter constraints on some of the developing nations as a consequence of the steady increase in loans to sustain their development plans. This mix of circumstances can no longer be dismissed as a series of technical side issues.

*Partners in Development: Report of the Commission on International Development, pp.60-61.

The Politics of Economics

In other words, economic issues will increasingly be the mainstream issues of foreign relations in the closing years of this century. Economic issues involve the internal domestic interest groups and politics of each country. Particularly in the developing countries, where a broadening of popular participation in economic development is taking place, economic questions will steadily rise to the top of political priorities.

One easily senses the major political importance of specific economic issues in the course of international negotiations. In the heat of negotiations those closest to these specialized problems express freely the intense political pressures upon them. Country delegations divide even among themselves, with the hardest, most painful negotiations occurring *within* countries or blocs. Being specialized and highly political, the issues tend to be handled by a small number of people; that is to say, they are frequently referred to ministers, cabinets, and even heads of state. And, of course, this means that they bypass the normal bureaucracies in the inevitable negotiating crunches.

It is not widely known that even in the United States relatively small trade and international corporate business issues often rise all the way to the president for quiet decision. The reason is not that the interagency committees below him are inadequate, or filled with stubborn bureaucrats, but rather that potent domestic and international issues can only be reconciled by a political decision at the very top. But despite the fact that such issues reach the president's desk, they are rarely conceived and decided in terms of broad foreign policy. Each problem that comes along is handled as an isolated issue.

The interconnection of the domestic and foreign interests of the United States will become even more pronounced in the next few years. The prosperity of our farm sector is increasingly dependent on our world trade position. The prosperity of our multinational companies is increasingly dependent on the interaction of domestic and foreign policies on trade, investment, taxation, and antitrust laws. American labor has already begun to reassess its entire view of economic policy, as I have mentioned earlier, because it recognizes the direct linkage of its own interests with international policies and commitments.

In the European countries private commercial interests have less apparent influence on their parliaments than U.S. businessmen exert on our Congress. Nonetheless, whether in London or Brussels or Rome, domestic economic blocs are a large factor in politics. In Europe and Japan, power is concentrated in the hands of ministers of economics and finance or chancellors of the exchequer—generally the number two position in the cabinet. The men who hold these posts usually aspire to party leadership and therefore treat balance-of-payments problems with utmost seriousness. Thus economic questions receive high-level attention, even though special interests and parliamentary lobbies are somewhat more muted than in America.

The Need for Reappraisal

To cope with the complex and dangerous problems of this new decade, there is need first of all to recognize that domestic economics has great impact on international relations, while foreign economic developments, as never before, are coming to have a crucial influence on domestic politics. This is true of all countries, large and small, developed and developing. Our American decision-making process treats each economic issue as essentially isolated from other major questions and tries to resolve it on its own merits or in response to the special domestic pressures it generates. This process should be replaced with a conscious attempt to consider integrally the major political and economic policy questions and to frame guidelines for dealing with them in continuum rather than in vacuum.

A major policy reappraisal should begin with awareness of the growing power of mercantilism. As pointed out earlier, the neo-mercantilism we see today in every country is at heart an attempt to pass on to other countries some or all of the economic and social costs of domestic adjustments. In the case of the Common Agricultural Policy, for example, the Europeans have taxed imports, thus reducing import sales while gaining revenues. The revenues are used to push domestic surpluses onto world markets, further taxing the exports of competitors by depressing their potential profits elsewhere. All exporters thus end up paying part of the cost of Europe's social program for its rural population. The American textile restriction program has a similar effect. It penalizes Asian exporters and American consumers in order to provide special benefits to Southern mills in areas of low wages and high availability of black labor. Neo-mercantilism, sector by sector, whether aimed at industry relief or rural poverty, must inevitably repress the interests of other countries, in particular sectors, in particular regions.

This neo-mercantilism takes other forms as well, such as the continuation of the range of economic policies that bring persistent balance-of-payments surpluses to Germany and Japan. Sometimes other countries confronted by temporary balance-of-payments problems resort to arbitrary trade restriction measures, bypassing the internationally agreed-upon rules without a second thought, as have Canada, the United Kingdom, and France in recent years. Without better international mechanisms in the future, we can expect payments crises to lead to more such disruptive, inefficient policies. Resistance to making really fundamental changes in the international monetary system, or to developing effective institutional arrangements for economic policy coordination, is symptomatic of this worldwide mercantilistic trend.

Passing along to others the costs of one's own special problems does, of course, make home politics easier in the short run. It also allows the building of intimate ties with selected countries on the basis of discrimination against the rest of the world. In the long run, however, it works to the detriment of all, rupturing foreign relations, stirring antagonisms, misallocating resources, and serving special rather than general domestic interests.

International initiatives that have major economic consequences require active domestic support. The outward-looking domestic forces in our society need to be mobilized, their objectives pursued in concert. Where the United States might once have accepted some damage to its international economic interests as the price to pay for a political objective, we must now treat foreign economic policy as essential to the viability of any foreign policy at all. This is simply good politics. For if government is to "march with American public opinion," it must respond to the pressures of that opinion, which generally are expressed through economic interest groups. American opinion today is becoming less abstract, less concerned with dreams of unity, and more caught up with the question of how to ensure that we and Europe can cooperate and avoid harming each other while Europeans get on with their internal affairs.

To stress the primacy of economics and the need for multilateral cooperation in the years ahead is not to preach economic imperialism or to let the profit motive control social policy. To put it that way is to miss the real shared benefits to be gained in a shift away from today's mercantilist trend.

The Asian Future

Consider, for example, the developing countries of Eastern Asia, now moving ahead economically at great speed. They are being caught in an increasing dependence on Japan, their growth spurred by the phenomenal rise of the Japanese GNP. Growing more than 10 percent annually (discounting inflation) year after year, Japan already has the world's third largest GNP, after the United States and the Soviet Union. The Japanese, spurred by American pressures, are intensifying their foreign aid effort in Eastern Asia. An Asian Co-Prosperity Sphere is in effect being raised from the dead, with the unconscious encouragement of the United States to help it along.

The United States has poured into East Asia vast expenditures, in addition to arms and men, which, diffusing throughout the economies of the area, have stimulated another great part of Asian economic growth. Our military disengagement from the Far East, now begun, is bound to have economic consequences that increase political stress in the region.

Our political objective could probably be best defined as preventing the domination of Asia by any one power and doing so by encouraging new national and regional centers of political and economic strength able to keep power in balance. To achieve that objective and to ensure reasonable conditions for the economic future of friendly countries, we should have comprehensive economic policies ready for implementation as the U.S. military withdrawal proceeds. The Far East is potentially the strongest economic growth area of all the developing world, and if the United States retains no strong economic presence there, Japan will be left alone to dominate the region. That is almost certainly a prescription for increased political tension in Southeast and Eastern Asia.

Our present neo-mercantilist policies toward Asia run counter to American foreign policy objectives. We have military strategies and policies but no coherent economic plans. The other half of President Nixon's Guam doctrine is missing. This reflects an unawareness of the importance of international economics. Offending the budding Japanese giant and the other free nations of Eastern Asia by indelicate handling of trade issues seems profoundly bad foreign policy. Trade problems are an essential ingredient in our overall Asian political posture, and the more we disengage militarily, the more we bring economics to the fore.

Problems Ahead

In Europe our economic policies have been relegated to technical-level discussions, while policymakers concentrate on reviving the tired NATO defense debates of earlier decades. Europe is moving ahead toward its own objectives, convinced that the Americans are not much concerned about the major shift in transatlantic economic structure that is inevitably occurring. No significant effort is being made to put Atlantic relations on a course that is relevant to the issues of the 1970s and 1980s. Such a course requires new and improved institutions and consultative frameworks to regulate policies toward multinational companies, toward pollution control, toward the harmonization of balance-of-payments trade policies, toward economic relations with Eastern Europe. These are the issues that will concern Europe in the next two or three decades, because Europe is unifying along economic lines.

More generally, we need to develop international agreements, codes of conduct, and modes of cooperation that tackle the neo-mercantilism problem directly. This means directly addressing the problem of how to carry out domestic programs without passing the costs on to other countries. It means gradually revising past laws, regulations, and policies that manipulate the interests of other countries for the benefit of small domestic lobbies.

One application of this principle was embodied in the General Agreement on Tariffs and Trade. In certain cases the GATT provides that when a nation restricts trade for domestic protection reasons, it must compensate other countries or accept retaliation from them. This particular provision relates to a highly technical set of precedents and procedures, but its broad legal sense is an example of one way of dealing with the problem.

Many types of difficulties cannot be resolved so simply as this. With multinational companies the problem is to provide some common set of guidelines for intracompany pricing, taxation, antitrust, and the sovereignty rights of governments. Perhaps the most complicated problem in economic cooperation lies in the field of government regulation of pollution and environmental adjustment. If each nation goes its own way, some will be lax and others strict; some will require costly investment programs, and others none at all. In the absence of any framework of agreed-upon procedures, this in itself will tend to disrupt world trade, investment, and production. Cooperation in such areas, where the problems are pressing and growing, could have a high political payoff.

To grapple with the economics of the future, some governments may have to restructure themselves. This is a particularly pressing need in the U.S. government, where international economic issues are handled in highly compartmentalized fashion. Coordination and policy guidance are provided by more than a dozen different interagency committees (each with subcommittees) and numerous high-ranking officials in many cabinet departments and agencies and on the president's personal staff. In this bureaucratic setting it becomes nearly impossible to mesh economics with the other aspects of foreign affairs.

Not just in Washington, but in the universities as well we need analyses and proposals for new foreign policy departures, recognizing that economic questions will be the most potent element in the world politics of the next two or three decades.

More and more political leaders in the years ahead may find themselves asking the question "Growth for what?" Governments may increasingly try to manipulate national economies toward desirable social ends. If we travel in this direction, as I think we shall, the danger of disruptive trade wars and other neo-mercantilist clashes will loom ever larger.

Our ability to look ahead and begin to grasp the foreign economic policy issues that are now upon us will directly affect American economic interests and the interests of every other major country. The consequence of an inactive foreign economic policy, and a heavy reliance on military-related discussions and institutions, is to evade most of the political forces at work in the world today. Such evasions will ultimately come home to haunt politicians, for failure to promote external economic interests will eventually produce domestic reactions.

Finally, and most important of all in the long run, are our problems in dealing with that two-thirds of the world's population living in the developing nations. The politics of the Third World is and will be primarily economic. The developed nations cannot block that inevitable trend, which seems likely to dominate world politics through the close of this millennium. Relationships with the poor nations will be a function of the degree of neo-mercantilism in the rich countries. There may be wars, heavy pressures, new dependencies on one or another great power, but in the end economics will be the driving force that brings presidents, dictators, and ministers up—and brings them down. Economics in the years immediately ahead will be powerful politics. Neo-mercantilism will be its scourge, driving nations into international conflicts, as have ideologies and military imbalances in the past.

Intense effort to seek, step by step, area by area, more positive policies, and international codes of conduct in economic relations, is the direction we should now travel. Yet the basic forces at work today, the structures of governments, the disdain of diplomats and political theorists for these issues, all seem to portend worsening problems among the rich and heavier repression of the weaker nations. If trade wars come, they will come hard.

TRADE POLICY IS FOREIGN POLICY
by Richard N. Cooper

A distinction is sometimes drawn between "high foreign policy" and "low foreign policy," with the former concerning matters of national security and survival and the latter concerning a large number of secondary issues that arise in relations among countries. Low foreign policy requires many more man-hours of attention in governments, but receives far less high-level attention. Foreign trade and investment policies are traditionally regarded in the category of low foreign policy—the same is true of monetary and financial relations among countries—although this tendency is more pronounced among students of international relations than it is among high government officials.

Is this classification any longer tenable? Trade and monetary issues dominated the front pages of newspapers in the fall of 1971. They were overshadowed by the opening of China in the winter months, but the underlying issues raised in late 1971 were by no means settled then, and they will continue to require high-level attention well into the 1970s. Complications are likely to arise from conflict over trade policy.

Before turning to contemporary trade issues, however, it is worth asking whether the intrusion of trade problems into high foreign policy is a new phenomenon, and if so, why. To treat this question satisfactorily would require an excursion into history beyond my present scope and purpose, so instead of stating a definitive, thoroughly documented position I will simply advance a hypothesis on the question, a hypothesis that I recognize has a particularly American slant, with the objective of provoking response from those with a different perspective or with a deeper knowledge of history. I emphasize that the focus here is on transatlantic relations and not on relations *within* Europe or between the industrialized world and less developed countries.

The hypothesis is this. Historically trade issues frequently intruded into, and occasionally even dominated, high foreign policy among countries. But this intrusion was successfully suppressed during the past twenty-five years by the postwar

"Trade Policy Is Foreign Policy" was published originally in *Foreign Policy*, Number 9, Winter 1972-73.

agreements, notably the Bretton Woods Agreement and the General Agreement on Tariffs and Trade, governing economic relations among countries; they enabled trade to be relegated to a low-level issue. The establishment of a "world economic order"—a pretentious but not inappropriate term—kept trade issues off the agenda of high diplomacy except when governments deliberately put them there for reasons of high policy. In other words, trade issues per se did not intrude into high policy, although high policy did occasionally, and in important ways, intrude into trade relationships—for example, in formation of the European Economic Community and in proscriptions on trade with Communist countries.

The establishment of rules governing international trade permitted trade issues to be discussed and resolved in their own realm without intruding into other areas of policy; it created what might be called a two-track system, with trade issues traveling along their own track, not interfering with traffic elsewhere. A similar development occurred, under the aegis of the International Monetary Fund (IMF), in the monetary area, which by and large was also kept separate not only from general foreign relations but also, and sometimes undesirably, from trading relations.

It is worthwhile to recall the "world order" in international trade, as it was embodied in 1947 in the General Agreement on Tariffs and Trade (GATT). This agreement contained three broad features. First, it laid down general rules governing trading relationships among nations. Second, it included a general commitment by all adherents to lower barriers to trade, especially import quotas and tariffs. Third, it provided an orderly procedure for the discussion and resolution of trade grievances or misunderstandings among countries, including if necessary the controlled use of trade sanctions. Put very generally, the rules and the procedures amounted to recognition by all adherents that national actions influencing international trade were matters of *mutual* concern, not merely, as before World War II, matters of purely domestic policy.

The commitment to eliminate quotas and to reduce tariffs reflected a general view that international commerce was both economically and politically beneficial and that artificial barriers to trade should gradually be reduced to foster these benefits. Most significantly, trade concessions by one country were to be exchanged for trade concessions by its partners, *not* for political concessions in other areas of contact between nations; similarly, withdrawals of trade concessions—for which allowance was made—could be compensated by new *trade* concessions by the country withdrawing them or could trigger internationally controlled *trade* sanctions (withdrawal of concessions) by its trading partners. Bargaining on trade issues was to be kept within the arena of trade, the whole system designed to inhibit bargaining across different arenas of contact—in short, to keep trade on its own track.

The general rules laid especially heavy emphasis—it comprises Article 1 of GATT—on Most Favored Nation (MFN) treatment. Each adherent is to treat all other adherents on the same basis, with stated exceptions arising largely from pre-existing preferential arrangements. The United States, in particular, attached great importance to this provision for nondiscrimination in international trade. The rules also covered the use of quotas, increases in tariffs, the use of export subsidies, transit trade, and a host of other questions bearing on international trade.

It should be clear that GATT was never universal in coverage—at its inception in 1947 it had only twenty-three "contracting parties," although these covered the most important non-Communist trading countries except Japan. This number has subsequently grown to over eighty, but only because many exceptions to the rules have made the GATT acceptable to the new (largely less developed) membership, a matter to which we return below. (The far more ambitious and comprehensive Charter for an International Trade Organization failed to gain acceptance even in the cooperative euphoria of the immediate postwar period, nominally falling at the hands of the U.S. Senate, but on the stated grounds that Britain was unwilling to give up its Imperial Preference System and that at the insistence of many poor countries the Charter was so riddled with exceptions that it was robbed of its general applicability.)

The Separation Erodes

It should also be made clear that this postwar trading system was highly successful in a number of respects. National barriers to trade by industrial countries were greatly reduced; world trade and national economies grew at an unprecedented rate; and by and large trade issues *were* kept on their own track, at a low level of international relations, until the mid-1960s. It would be going too far to say that foreign trade issues were "depoliticized," since the formation of the European Coal and Steel Community and the European Economic Community, both involving foreign trade, were highly political acts. But it is accurate to say that trade issues intruded relatively little into high foreign policy. There were no great squabbles over access to materials (except briefly during the Korean War) or over access to markets, no serious charges of monopoly exploitation by international cartels operating under the protection of national governments, no trade wars—all of which had characterized earlier periods and especially the interwar period.

The arrangement that kept trade issues largely on their own track began to erode in the mid-1960s, and the erosion has recently accelerated. The identifiable sources of the erosion are several, and consideration of them involves going into the present sources of trade friction among the major industrial countries, a somewhat technical but nonetheless necessary prelude to further discussion of the relationship between trade issues and foreign policy in the next decade.

From the American point of view, the major sources of friction have been the Common Agricultural Policy (CAP) of the European Economic Community (EEC), the preferential trading arrangements established by the EEC, various nontariff barriers to trade in all major countries, and the persistence of quotas blocking imports into Japan. From the viewpoint of the rest of the world, the major sources of friction have been various nontariff barriers of the United States plus the rapid spread of so-called voluntary export restraints, largely at the instigation of the United States. Unlike in the monetary arena, however, where dissatisfaction is centered in Europe, dissatisfaction with the existing state of affairs in trade seems to be greatest in the United States.

Common Agricultural Policy: The CAP is in many ways the most important irritant, in part because of its links with other issues. The CAP represents both a gross distortion of trade flows and a gross violation of the international trading rules and commitments, the latter especially with respect to the variable import levy (instead of a fixed tariff) as a protective device and with respect to the subsidization of agricultural exports. These features in turn create pressures in other

countries, hurt or potentially hurt by the EEC's high protection, to seek preferential access to the European market and,
where EEC exports are in competition with those of other
countries, to respond by introducing their own export subsidies—a new kind of trade war that is already evident.

The CAP arose from a genuine need of the European
Community to bring diverse national agricultural policies into
line if a truly common market was to be achieved. This problem raised two quite separate questions: what was the
agricultural support system to be, and what was to be the level of support? The level of support has the greatest bearing
on actual trade flows, but it is the system of support that is
most important for its effects on world order in international
trade. At present, about one-sixth of EEC imports of agricultural products are covered by the system of variable
levies—the share would, of course, be much higher in
absence of the levies—the remainder coming in over
conventional tariffs (although in the case of tobacco and
wine, influenced by state procurement agencies or other restrictions). As their name implies, the protective effect of
these levies varies from time to time, and it also depends
upon the level of support chosen by the Community. The
levies have ranged as high as 300 percent of world prices.
Since no controls are imposed on production, high price
supports lead to production in excess of what can be consumed within the Community, and the surplus is exported to
the world market under subsidy. From 1962, when the CAP
was first introduced, to 1972, EEC imports subject to variable
levy *declined* by about one-third, during a period in which
total world imports nearly trebled and total U.S. agricultural
exports increased by over 50 percent.

Most of the increasingly acrimonious debate has focused on
the trade effects, with the EEC pointing out that *total*
American agricultural exports to the Community have risen
during this period. But from the viewpoint of foreign policy
this focus on trade flows misses the point, which concerns a
violation of the rules and spirit of trade cooperation by one of
the leading participants in world trade. This issue is complicated by the fact that the United States never formally raised
the question of violation in the GATT, although when in the
Kennedy Round of trade negotiations it tried to get CAP on
the table, the EEC responded by saying that it was nonnego-
tiable. Its broader implications have not been missed, how-

ever. Harald B.Malmgren, a leading U.S. official in the area of trade policy, has written that "the new EEC agricultural system is a throwback. It is an explicit commitment to mercantilism as a way of life, having broad policy consequences for all trading nations."* It was originally the United States, however, not the European Community, that took the lead in excluding agricultural products from effective discussion and consultation under the GATT, when it insisted in 1955 on a blanket waiver for its own domestic agricultural programs.

Europeans sometimes cite American agricultural support policy in defense of their system. It is worth a brief digression to explain why the comparison is not generally relevant except for sugar and dairy products, where the United States is culpable on similar grounds. The comparison is not generally relevant because for many agricultural products the United States would, in the absence of price support and production controls, be a major exporter at prices well below its domestic support prices. This is in contrast to Europe, which for most agricultural goods would be a major importer in the absence of price supports and import protection. Thus the American agricultural support system places the burden very largely on the American consumer and therefore represents an internal redistribution of income, while the European system, in addition to burdening the consumer, imposes major costs on residents of *other* countries and thus represents an international redistribution of income. The European system has a much greater international impact.

Furthermore, as social policy, American farm programs based on price supports and acreage controls have been ineffective. They have not succeeded in protecting the low-income family farm, one of their stated objectives. Thus they hardly serve as a model for European farm policy with similar social objectives.

It is noteworthy, finally, that national security considerations have not been used to justify European policy. These would lead to a self-sufficiency ratio considerably less than 100 percent and hence would result in no export surpluses.

Preferences: The second major contentious issue is trade preferences. These started in 1958 as an extension to the Community as a whole of France's trade preferences with its

* See pp. 22-45.

African colonies, soon to become independent. But others soon followed, so that by 1971 the EEC had preferential trading arrangements with most of the countries bordering the Mediterranean Sea and several others as well. Some of these preferences arose out of the CAP, at least indirectly, for the high agricultural protection within the Community hurt traditional suppliers and they appealed for relief. Rather than reduce the level of protection, the EEC provided relief on a selective basis, to the point at which for some commodities the EEC now has four tariff rates, depending on source. These arrangements represented a flagrant violation of the principle of nondiscrimination in the GATT. Moreover, although the EEC has occasionally used the argument that through its tariff concessions it is merely providing foreign aid to poor countries, that position can hardly be reconciled with the fact that the Community has extracted preferential tariff concessions from those countries for European exports. American officials have found these so-called reverse preferences particularly offensive.

Europeans have often been puzzled by the vehemence of American objections to these preferential trading arrangements, particularly since so little U.S. trade is affected, and they therefore attribute the response to the domestic political power of the Florida Citrus Association and similar pressure groups in the United States (as Ralf Dahrendorf did recently in *The World Today*). But this bemused perspective misses the central issue, which is not so much trade diversion in the particular case as the violation of a leading principle, some would say *the* leading principle, on which postwar international trading relations are thought to have rested. If the violation goes unchallenged, it is likely to spread to countries, such as the EFTA (European Free Trade Association) neutrals,* where American trade interests are much greater. Moreover, when the world's leading trading area treats the basic ground rules so cavalierly, those rules can no longer be used to resist protectionist pressure within the United

*An arrangement with the EFTA neutrals would conform with Article 24 of the GATT if it were a free trade area covering substantially all trade. But the numerous exceptions in the draft agreements suggest that a considerable amount of trade diversion will take place, that is, EFTA suppliers will be favored over outsiders, but will not be treated on a par with Community suppliers. Even if this were not true, Americans can hardly be pleased with an arrangement that holds out no broader promise, as the EEC originally did, for political unification of Europe.

States, or indeed in any other country. Former U.S. Secretary of Agriculture Hardin expressed American irritation and anxieties forcefully when he observed that

the European Community is now openly derisive of GATT-MFN (Most Favored Nation) requirements. The grave danger is that as a result of the present plans for enlarging the Community, European and African nations will have created a trading area sufficiently large to enable them to depart entirely from MFN treatment and will plunge the rest of the world into a trade jungle in which special deals become the practice rather than the exception, and in which spheres of trading influence will develop as a matter of course.*

Quotas: Trade problems perceived by Americans are not exclusively with the European Community. Japan maintained extensive quotas on imports until recently, in direct contravention of GATT; moreover, some American firms argue that investment (for example, in servicing facilities) is necessary to export competitively and therefore that Japan's tight controls on inward investment indirectly block imports of manufactured goods. (The United States—perhaps even more than Japan—has also taken exception to European restrictions on the importation of Japanese goods, technically legal under the GATT since they were entered as reservations at the time Japan adhered to the GATT.)

Export Restraints: At the same time, other countries have winced at the U.S. lead in promoting so-called voluntary export restrictions. When applied by an adherent to GATT, these also contravene that agreement; and when they are encouraged by the United States, that represents a clear and flagrant contravention of its purposes and spirit. These restraints started with the Long-Term Cotton Textile Agreement of 1962, but since then they have been extended to a long list of commodities—the United States now has over seventy such agreements on industrial goods, compared to only seven in 1962. They include such diverse products as steel, beef, mushrooms, and most recently synthetic and woolen textiles. These restraints are not aimed mainly at Europe, although some, like steel, directly involve European exports. But they create anxiety among some Europeans, just as European trade preferences do among Americans.

* Testimony before the Williams Commission, *United States International Economic Policy in an Interdependent World*, papers, (Washington, D.C.: Government Printing Office,1971), volume 1, pp.799-800.

Nontariff Barriers: Some mention must be made of non-tariff barriers to trade, an important issue in the mid-1960s that has now subsided somewhat. Close study of such barriers suggests that for the most part they are less tractable but also less important than they were once thought to be, the major exceptions being agricultural policies and government procurement practices. Some, such as border tax adjustments, reflect misunderstanding all around, on both sides of the Atlantic. Others, such as the American selling price, have (rightly) taken on symbolic value far in excess of their trade implications. Clearly future trade negotiations must take up nontariff barriers, but on a case-by-case basis within some broad framework of negotiation. This will be low-level foreign policy.

Finally, it should be mentioned that some segments of the American public feel they have been cheated by the whole postwar trade regime, for despite the clear commitment of the GATT to nondiscrimination in international trade and to the reduction of trade barriers, at no time since 1945 have dutiable American products had nondiscriminatory access to most Western European markets. Postwar discrimination against dollar goods on balance-of-payments grounds had not yet been completely phased out before the inauguration of the European Community and the European Free Trade Association in the late 1950s. There were, of course, at each moment persuasive reasons why discrimination was necessary, but the capacity of U.S. officials to rationalize this rather striking continuity to the American public has worn increasingly thin.

To sum up, the rule of law in international trade is under serious threat. Such basic principles as nondiscrimination and a ban on export subsidies have been badly eroded, to the extent that one may wonder whether they really inhibit violations any longer. The U.S. government's move in 1971 to give special tax treatment to profits of export corporations illustrates the erosion.

Moreover, even the procedural aspects of GATT have been eroded. The EEC has refused to acknowledge that the preferential areas are in violation of GATT, and discussion of the questions has stalemated, leaving in abeyance the whole compensation procedure. GATT procedure has been further eroded, in practice, by the adherence of many less developed countries, which have come in under blanket exception to some of the rules and have interpreted the exceptions broadly, refusing, for example, to request waivers for preferential trading arrangements clearly not in conformity with Article 24. Yet there are limits to the capacity of any organization to tolerate wide exceptions for some members while still holding the line effectively on others.

Effects of the Erosion on Foreign Policy

The two-track system implied effective separation of trade issues from general foreign policy except at the discretion of governments for overriding and persuasive reasons, such as the use of a common market to promote the political integration of Europe. Loss of confidence in the rules of order will eliminate this separation and thereby will lead to much greater intrusion of domestic economic interests, through trade policy, into general foreign policy. Once the rules break down or cease to be regarded as fair, they cannot be used effectively by governments to block particularistic pressures within their own countries. Therein lies a major danger for international relations, especially for the United States.

The domestic political coalition in support of liberal trade for the United States has broken down, partly in response to the perceived erosion of international trading rules cited above, partly in response to other developments in the national and international economy. The disillusionment of American agriculture has already been mentioned. With the notable exception of dairy farmers this sector has traditionally been a strong supporter for liberal trade. It still has a strong stake in liberal trade and leans in that direction, but with considerably less conviction than previously. Former Secretary of Agriculture Hardin has asserted that U.S. agriculture gained nothing from the Kennedy Round, and his view is widely shared.

Organized labor as represented by the dominant AFL-CIO has switched its allegiance from liberal trade to virulent restriction, concretely in support of the Burke-Hartke bill, calling *inter alia* for import quotas on virtually all industrial goods, designed to reduce imports substantially (by about one-third) from existing levels and to assure that imports grow no more rapidly than domestic demand, product by product, exporter by exporter. Organized labor's ire has been directed especially at the import quotas of Japan, and at the restrictions maintained by European countries on imports from Japan, which are believed to direct Japanese sales efforts to the American market. But its general disillusionment with liberal trade is also influenced by the perceived erosion of the international trading rules to the disadvantage of the United States and, even more, by the rapid growth of American investment abroad in a fashion that labor believes displaces U.S. exports and augments U.S. imports. The actual merits of these claims involve complicated analysis beyond the scope of the present paper; but they clearly reflect prevalent protectionist attitudes.

The business community is still ambivalent on the question of liberal trade, an ambivalence that reflects in part divergent interests within the business community, but also reflects a failure by some firms and industries to see their general interests clearly. Moreover, the possibility of foreign investment blunts the position of a number of firms on trade liberalization, since mobile firms can continue to sell in protected markets by investing there. Their ardor for liberal trade is thus diluted, particularly when a strong liberal stance might antagonize business colleagues or even, in some cases, make more difficult the continuation of their existing pricing and market-sharing practices.

The Intrusion of Trade

As noted above, the United States has not in fact enjoyed nondiscriminatory access to most major markets at any time since World War II. This fact was successfully rationalized by the American government on a variety of grounds, principally the need for rapid postwar recovery in the face of severe dollar shortage, followed by the overriding political case for the integration of Europe. These rationalizations are no longer persuasive as we enter the 1970s, particularly since European countries, in American eyes, have interpreted their license for trade discrimination far too freely.

The breakdown of the old coalition in support of liberal trade, and the failure to replace it with a new one or by a persuasive rationalization for the present state of affairs, is likely to result not only in more protectionism of a clear and straightforward kind but also in a greater intrusion of foreign trade issues into general foreign relations. Of the three "body blows" delivered by the United States to Japan in 1971—announcement in July of President Nixon's visit to China, introduction in August of the New Economic Policy (with its 10 percent surcharge on imports), and extension in October of an ultimatum on trade in noncotton textiles, an issue that had been discussed inconclusively for two years—two were economic, threatening, or appearing to threaten, Japan's vital trade interests. Throughout the preceding two years the U.S. government showed extraordinary insensitivity to the internal political difficulties within Japan created by U.S. demands for Japanese restraints on exports of synthetic and woolen textiles, to the point at which this became a leading issue in Japanese relations with the United States. Japan's failure to respond to U.S. demands on this issue in turn threatened to derail senate ratification of the treaty returning to Japan jurisdiction over Okinawa, another leading issue in Japanese-American relations.

Cavalier U.S. treatment of Japan in 1970 and 1971, largely on economic questions (and in turn reflecting U.S. irritation at Japanese trade practices), cannot avoid affecting the credibility of U.S. policy in other areas. In particular, if the United States cannot be relied upon in the economic arena, how reliable are its security commitments to Japan? Japanese doubts of this type may have far-reaching and profound implications, even tilting the balance toward the adoption of nuclear weapons.

Similarly, disillusionment of the farm bloc and others in the U.S. Congress with the trade practices of the European Community may well garner support for the Mansfield Resolution calling for the withdrawal of U.S. troops from Europe, an action that would have profound repercussions on the future course of European diplomacy and military policy.

In short, when trade relations sour, they infect other areas of policy, even "high policy," via domestic political attitudes and pressures. As public antagonism in the arena of trade mounts, it erodes the president's freedom to pursue constructive actions toward other countries in other arenas as well as trade. Middle America strongly supported Treasury Secretary Connally's tough stance against America's trading partners; this is a danger sign for foreign relations, going well beyond commercial and monetary relations. Schelling has put the issue well:

Trade policies can be civilized or disorderly. U.S. trade policies can antagonize governments, generate resentment in populations, hurt economies, influence the tenure of governments, even provoke hostilities. . . . Aside from war and preparations for war, and occasionally aside from migration, trade is the most important relationship that most countries have with each other. Broadly defined to include investment, shipping, tourism, and the management of enterprises, trade is what most of international relations are about. For that reason trade policy is national security policy.*

It is now also clear that trade actions by *other* countries can similarly antagonize the American government and generate resentments in the American public, with correspondingly ominous influences on other arenas of international relations.

What Can Be Done?

Somehow the leading nations of commerce must restore harmony in their trading relationships if further unraveling is to be avoided. Three possible courses of action come to mind:

1. Reaffirm the existing trade rules, as embodied largely in the GATT, extend the rules to cover loopholes that have developed in violation of the spirit of the GATT, and alter actual trading practices to conform with the reaffirmed position.

2. Acknowledge the irreversibility of some of the actions that have been taken in recent years but attempt to set down a new set of rules and procedures that will govern trading relations in the future, perhaps abandoning the commitment to nondiscrimination in a way that is clear and accepted by all.

3. Bypass the sharp discrepancy between rules and present practices by affirming an objective of completely free trade, combined with a common policy for agricultural support, within the definable future.

None of these courses of action will be easy, and some observers may be tempted to say that all are impossible. The problem of discriminatory trading arrangements is especially thorny. Reaffirmation of the principle of nondiscrimination requires that the existing discriminatory arrangements be successfully rationalized or phased out. On the other hand, finding a clear alternative principle, one that permits some discrimination but still appears reasonable and places limits on "unreasonable" arrangements, is extraordinarily difficult.

*T. C. Schelling, "National Security Considerations Affecting Trade Policy," Williams Commission, op. cit., p. 737.

The attempt to accomplish this with respect to less developed countries through generalized tariff preferences by all industrial countries for all less developed countries has so far proved disappointing, with the European Community having adopted a niggardly scheme that preserves preferences for those countries that have special relationships with the European Community, and the United States having adopted no scheme at all.*

Reaffirming the MFN principle among industrial countries could be done if all the relevant countries agreed to a gradual, specified phasing out of their preferences (including reverse preferences), just as the U.S.-Philippine preferential arrangement has been virtually phased out on a preestablished schedule. This would involve raising some tariffs to the MFN level and might cause problems for countries such as the EFTA neutrals that have been engaged in free trade with certain other European countries for several years.

Alternatively, MFN tariff levels could be gradually reduced to the preferential tariffs levels, eliminating the discrimination in that way. This course would be subsumed under a general commitment to move to free trade and would imply eventual free trade in many industrial commodities, though not in agriculture. The advantage of a general commitment to free trade, to be implemented even over a relatively long period of time (for example, ten to fifteen years), is that it could be used to bypass direct confrontation over a number of the rules, notably the principle of nondiscrimination, since discrimination would perforce disappear under free trade. Indeed, it is difficult to see why the European countries should not agree to such a course of action, since enlargement of the Community combined with extension of duty-free treatment to industrial products of the EFTA neutrals plus generalized tariff preferences for all less developed countries means that Canada, Japan, and the United States would be the only important trading countries with products dutiable in Europe—a rather blatant form of discrimination, bound to be offensive to the American public. Whether Canada, Japan, and the United States would readily undertake such a commitment, however, remains more questionable.

*For evidence on the niggardly nature of the EEC scheme, see my "The European Community's System of Generalized Tariff Preferences: A Critique," *Journal of Development Studies*, July 1972.

Such a strategy must in any case be supplemented by some reexamination of the rules, for certain issues would be made more rather than less salient by a move to free trade. The three most important areas concern measures to deal with "market disruption" (including so-called voluntary export restraints), domestic agricultural policies, and government procurement practices. Existing rules in these areas are deficient or nonexistent and need to be further developed.

There are some recent signs that governments are willing to grapple with these problems. A high-level group (the Rey Committee), established by the Organization for Economic Cooperation and Development (OECD) in June 1971 to reexamine trade relationships among the member countries, recommended that trade liberalization "should be pursued in all fields—tariffs, quotas, and other nontariff barriers—and cover trade in both agricultural and industrial products." And in February 1972 the United States, the European Community, and Japan all agreed to an extensive review of trade relationships with a view to establishing the basis for major trade negotiations in 1973.

One troublesome practical question that is likely to arise with increasing frequency is the locus of world leadership, or initiative, in establishing and fostering an appropriate trading system for the 1970s. During the past two decades the United States has generally provided the leadership for major changes on a global scale in the realm of economics as well as in security. This role will be increasingly difficult for the United States to sustain, for several reasons. First, within the United States there has been some loss of self-confidence in its capacity to carry on a leadership role, with a self-fulfilling reduction in such capacity. Second, partly for that reason, more importantly out of pride in its own postwar achievements, there is less willingness in Europe to follow the lead and greater interest in a show of independence. Third, however, there is still no effective capacity within Europe to take on a position of global "system oriented" leadership. The European Community is still far too involved in putting itself together and still too uncertain about the final relationship between Community and national states to be able to take up the mantle, as European response to the monetary crisis of late 1971 testified, even though by quantitative logic that mantle in the economic arena should pass to the European Community, now the world's largest trading unit. Furthermore, there remains the possibility that leadership in system-wide changes cannot be compartmentalized by subject, with Europe taking the lead in trade while the United States retains it in matters of mutual security. The consequence of no leadership would be stalemate, not of a kind perpetuating the status quo, but one in which *ad hoc* responses to particularistic pressures within and between nations would worsen the world trade climate substantially.

There is, unfortunately, historical precedent for the passage of leadership from one nation to another with a major fumble in the course of passage. The United States first surpassed Britain as the world's leading trading nation about the time of World War I, after nearly a century of British predominance and initiative in matters of world trade. The 1920s and 1930s represented a period of uncertainty and confusion in trade policy, as Britain abandoned its global orientation for the Imperial Preference System, but the United States refused at first to accept the position of leadership that its trading position warranted. It took a number of years of chaos in trade policy (admittedly abetted by, but also contributing to, the Great Depression) before the United States accepted leadership and initiated negotiations under the Trade Agreements Act of 1934. It would be far better to learn from this experience than to repeat it. The United States should not be hasty in shedding its responsibility for leadership in the system as a whole, and the Community should strive to develop a global orientation rather than merely a European one.

INTERNATIONAL MONETARY ECONOMICS

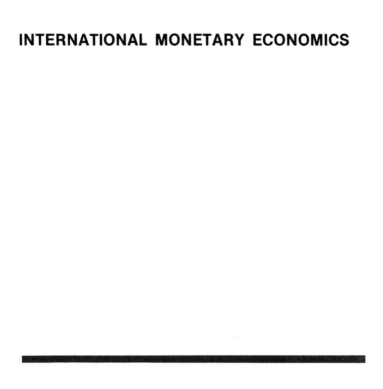

HOW THE DOLLAR STANDARD DIED
by Harold van Buren Cleveland

The dollar standard, like the British Empire, was created in a fit of absence of mind. Until recently, it did not even have a name, or rather it was miscalled the "gold-dollar system."

That designation was highly misleading, because it implied that the dollar's usefulness as international money derived from its link to gold. It implied, more precisely, that the dollar was subject to the discipline of gold—that the U.S. commitment to convert foreign official holdings of dollars into gold on demand was a significant check on the ability of the U.S. Federal Reserve System to supply dollars at will to the rest of the world.

There was, in fact, no such external discipline. Yet the belief in its existence helped to conceal the politically unpalatable fact that the use of the dollar as international money gave to the United States unilateral power to influence monetary conditions throughout the trading world.

The system that the architects of the postwar monetary order had in mind was very different. It was neither as centralized nor as open, nor did it include the rigidity of exchange rates that was to develop under the dollar standard. The Bretton Woods blueprint, in fact, foresaw a decentralized and relatively flexible system in which each country would enjoy a high degree of autonomy in the management of its own money supply. Equilibrium among national monetary systems (balance-of-payments equilibrium) was to be assured in part by national controls on international capital flows but mainly by domestic monetary and fiscal measures and by adjusting exchange rates.

Indeed, the Bretton Woods Agreement implied that parities would be changed readily, as evidenced by the fact that its draftsmen showed little concern about international liquidity. New gold production was assumed to be sufficient to supply the world's need for international reserves. The only provisions made for increasing liquidity artificially were modest quotas in the International Monetary Fund.

"How the Dollar Standard Died" was published originally in *Foreign Policy*, Number 5, Winter 1971-72.

In common with other American charters for the postwar world, the Bretton Woods Agreement was essentially Wilsonian. It presupposed an identity of national interests in maintaining an open and harmonious international monetary system. Countries were assumed to be willing—and politically able—to accept the stern discipline of gold for the sake of keeping their currencies convertible and their economies open.

The political realism of this optimistic conception was never put to the test. The system that actually developed imposed no such discipline and involved no such presumption of readiness to subordinate domestic economic policies, or exchange rates, to the requirements of payments equilibrium. On the contrary, it made such generous provision for international liquidity as largely to obviate, for most of the industrial countries, serious conflict between domestic economic objectives and external balance.

The dollar system had two defining characteristics. One was the general use of the dollar by foreign governments and central banks as a reserve asset. The other was the presumption that the parities of major currencies were not simply pegged temporarily but actually fixed—that is, unlikely to change. This presumption applied with particular force to the dollar. It was generally assumed, in other words, that the effective exchange rate of the dollar would never change either through a deliberate devaluation initiated by the United States or by virtue of a general upvaluation of other important currencies.

In combination, these characteristics of the system assured for a time the rapid expansion of world trade and production in an open international environment with an expansive monetary climate. The assumed invulnerability of the dollar's parity made it possible for the United States to expand its domestic money supply without much regard for the effect on the balance of payments. And this, in turn, kept the entire world monetary system liquid, sometimes too liquid. For it enabled other major countries to follow expansive domestic monetary policies, while at the same time keeping their currencies convertible on current account, liberalizing controls on capital movements, and continuing to build their international reserves. In short, the system eased the balance-of-payments constraint on domestic expansion not only for the

United States but for most of the other industrial countries as well. Britain was the only consistent exception.

The system worked successfully precisely because domestic economic policies were *not* subject to balance-of-payments discipline. With its relatively self-contained economy the United States could not, politically, have lived with a fixed exchange rate for the dollar on any other basis. Nor would the other large industrial countries have found it easy, or even possible, to keep their payments in equilibrium without exchange controls if they had been forced to do so by a shortage of international reserves. Yet everything depended on the United States. In combination, these economic and political changes have made the hegemony of the dollar an anachronism.

Understood in this way, it is evident why the dollar standard contained the seeds of its own destruction. For in the last analysis it depended for its proper functioning on a political relationship between the United States and the other major industrial countries that made the overtones of dollar hegemony acceptable. The immunity of the United States to balance-of-payments discipline, coupled with the sheer economic weight of the United States and the rigidity of exchange rates generally, meant that the U.S. Federal Reserve operated as a supranational central bank, exerting a large influence on monetary conditions in other countries and setting the tone of the world's monetary climate.

Anachronistic Hegemony

The dollar standard was acceptable as long as Europe and Japan felt dependent, politically and strategically, on the good will of the United States—so long, too, as the accumulation of unwanted dollars in official reserves was not too large and there seemed to be a chance that the outpouring might one day cease. But these conditions could not long endure. The European economies (or most of them) and Japan were catching up with the U.S. economy. Changes in the world political system (the relative decline of U.S. and Soviet power, China's rise, and Europe's growing sense of power and identity) reduced Europe's feeling of dependence on the United States. In combination, these economic and political changes made the hegemony of the dollar an anachronism.

Furthermore, the increasing mobility of money internationally (due in part to the internationalization of American corporations and banks and the growth of the eurocurrency markets) tended to sharpen the issue from Europe's standpoint.
Although it contributed to Europe's economic growth, it also
increased the interdependence of national monetary systems, rendering the dominant monetary position of the
United States more irksome.

The rapid buildup of dollar holdings, official and private, in
Europe also helped to convince the money markets that the
central premise of the dollar standard—the dollar's immunity
to devaluation—was in doubt. The Common Market decision
in 1971 to proceed with monetary unification reinforced this
perception, for it suggested that European currencies might
soon be upvalued collectively against the dollar.

Finally, the war in Vietnam and the consequent failures of
U.S. domestic economic policy also played a part. The inflation in the United States, resulting from budgetary deficits
financed by excessive monetary expansion in 1965 and
1967-68, helped to weaken the U.S. competitive position on
trade account. And the Federal Reserve's erratic, stop-go
monetary policy all through the period 1965-70, in conjunc-
tion with the high international mobility of short-term funds,
aggravated the pressures on European exchange rates and
brought sharply to the consciousness of Europeans the extent of their monetary dependence on the United States.

The final breakdown was precipitated by the Federal Reserve's massive expansion of the U.S. money supply in Janu-
ary-July 1971. By helping to cause an accelerated outflow of
short-term funds from the United States and to undermine
remaining confidence in the dollar, this policy played an important part in the timing of the crisis. The timing was also
influenced by the unexpectedly sharp deterioration of the
U.S. trade balance—a development that made clear how
much the U.S. competitive position had deteriorated and
convinced the markets that the dollar's turn to be devalued
had finally arrived.

Although it will doubtless live on in the Western Hemisphere
and the Pacific area, the dollar standard is now history so far
as Western Europe is concerned. After the massive flight of
funds from the dollar into European currencies in 1971, it
will not again be possible to convince the money markets

that the dollar's parity vis-à-vis European currencies is beyond question. Nor will the major governments of continental
Europe again be willing to support the dollar against massive
speculative attack. As their present actions show, they would
prefer to let their exchange rates rise or to check the dollar
inflow by exchange controls.

The situation created by the breakdown of the dollar standard
is fraught with extreme danger to the openness and efficiency of the international economy and, indeed, to the political
harmony and security of the Western world. The present pattern of managed currency floats—"dirty" floats as German
Economics and Finance Minister Karl Schiller picturesquely
called them—along with proliferating financial controls is
not the birth of a new order but the onset of monetary anar-
chy. A new kind of system, more consistent with an open
world economy and less conducive to political conflict, is urgently needed.

So much is generally agreed. But how this is to be accomplished is far from clear, for there are deep conflicts of interest involved, particularly between Western Europe and the
United States.

Looking Backward

In their search for a model of international monetary order
relevant to present circumstances the Common Market governments seem to be thinking about a system of relatively
fixed parities. The dollar's role as a reserve asset would be
phased out in favor of gold or Special Drawing Rights (or
both). As the Common Market's resolution of September 13,
1971 concerning monetary reform put it, there should be "a
gradual decrease of the role of national currencies as reserve
instruments" and "in the future, all countries or organized
groupings of countries [should] respect without exception
the obligations and constraints of adjusting their balance of
payments and put the appropriate internal policies into
effect."

But such a model looks backward to Bretton Woods rather
than forward to something genuinely new. Indeed, it would
impose a balance-of-payments discipline even stricter than
that implied by the Bretton Woods blueprint, for it emphasizes internal measures for balance-of-payments adjustment
and does not seem to contemplate the ready adjustment of

parities originally foreseen at Bretton Woods. Nor would it provide sufficient international liquidity to make the discipline bearable.

A Wilsonian system of this kind has never been a real possibility. It would clearly be politically unworkable today. It is illusory to expect the United States, with its large and relatively self-sufficient economy, to give a high priority to balance-of-payments considerations in the conduct of its domestic economic policies. Nor would the larger European countries accept the external discipline over domestic policies that this model involves. Perhaps European officials and central bankers have lived so long in an inflationary world of ample or excessive international liquidity that they have forgotten how painfully deflationary a reserve shortage can be.

In their own search for monetary order U.S. authorities also appear to be looking backward. The Nixon administration seems to believe that, given a more balanced pattern of exchange parities, the system can be reconstituted on the basis of relatively fixed exchange rates and the dollar standard, although with Special Drawing Rights (SDRs) providing a larger part of international liquidity than in the past. A model of this kind is probably still workable within a "dollar area" that would embrace the Western Hemisphere and the Pacific countries, including Japan. But the Common Market governments will never again accept the kind of system that implies an open-ended obligation to hold dollars that are not freely convertible into gold or other reserve assets, such as SDRs.

Exchange Rate Flexibility

There is one and perhaps only one constructive way out of this impasse. Both Western Europe and the United States will have to acknowledge that an attempt to return to relatively fixed exchange rates between the dollar and European currencies is a dead end. A restoration of international monetary order requires that the task of maintaining payments equilibrium between the dollar and European currencies be accomplished mainly by adjusting exchange rates. For the alternative is neither a return to the fixed-rate dollar standard nor a move to a fixed-rate gold-*cum*-SDRs standard but rather a proliferation of financial controls, trade warfare, and rising political tension.

By "flexibility" is not meant a world of currencies floating individually and separately in the classical sense long advocated by academic economists. According to economic theory, if all countries allowed their exchange rates to float freely without sustained "one-way" intervention by central banks, international payments would stay in balance without the need for controls on capital movements. Countries would also be free to follow whatever domestic policies they wished, since the free movement of the exchange rate would always maintain payments equilibrium.

But the present condition of the international monetary system stands in ironic contrast to this model. Instead of allowing their exchange rates to float upward freely in response to market forces, the European countries and Japan and, to a smaller extent, Canada have resisted the appreciation of their currencies by intervening in the exchange markets and by imposing new controls to cut down financial inflows. The objective has been to avoid the larger adjustments in trade balances that would otherwise occur and thereby to prevent the internal economic dislocation these adjustments might entail.

The lesson taught by this experience is that exchange rate flexibility, whether in the form of floating rates or simply frequent changes in parities, is not a real political possibility for small and medium-sized countries* that have a relatively high ratio of foreign trade to national production. For such countries, exchange rate changes have a major impact on domestic prices, employment, and income distribution. Thus they will normally be resisted, by controls if necessary.

For such countries, indeed, there is relatively little to choose between a fixed rate system without ample international liquidity and a flexible or floating rate system. Either system is likely to involve external pressure on domestic economic policy, or on the exchange rate, which is too damaging to national economic interest to be tolerable politically.

*Canada, which has lived comfortably with a floating exchange rate for long periods, is the exception that tests this generalization. Canada could do so because it has normally so conducted its domestic monetary policy as to stabilize its floating rate vis-a-vis the U.S. dollar. In this way Canada has normally been able to avoid the internal troubles referred to in the text, but at the price of subordinating its monetary policies to those of the United States. In effect, the Canadian economy has worked under a floating rate about as it did under a fixed rate and with about the same economic consequences.

The corollary is that, for a very large country with a low dependence on foreign trade, a flexible or floating rate system is more conducive to freedom of external transactions than a fixed rate system, in the absence of ample international liquidity. Thus, for the United States in its monetary relations with Western Europe, rate flexibility makes sense.

The same reasoning applies *mutatis mutandis* to the European Economic Community, if it is able to achieve sufficient capacity for joint decision making in the area of exchange rates and the collective creation of reserve assets usable among members. For an enlarged Common Market would also have collectively a low dependence on external trade.

Movement along this road involves serious political problems and conflicts of economic interest within the Community, as the current disagreement between Germany and France shows. Yet it is nevertheless a likely outcome, because the alternative is a breakdown of the Common Market itself.

The dollar standard originally made the creation of the Common Market possible. The ample international liquidity it provided made relatively fixed rates possible not only globally but also within the Community. And fixed rates were an essential precondition of the removal of tariffs and exchange control within the Community and for the establishment of its Common Agricultural Policy. Now that the dollar standard is finished, for Europe at least, the Community can be expected to find its own substitute. For the Community's customs union and agricultural arrangements could not survive an indefinite continuation of the present disorder, which afflicts monetary relations among its members as much as or more than their relations with the United States.

A New Regionalized System

If this analysis is correct, it implies that the global monetary system will tend to divide into two great regional groupings, one centered on the United States and the other on the enlarged Common Market. Within the "dollar area," which would embrace the Western Hemisphere and the Pacific area, including Japan,* currencies would normally be pegged to

*Ultimately Japan may seek to form a "yen bloc" which would include Pacific countries that are critically dependent on trade with and investment from Japan. The Japanese might be prompted to do so by regional trade preferences in Europe-Africa and the Western Hemisphere. But the political prerequisites of this development are lacking today.

the dollar. Essentially, the dollar area would be a residuum of the old, global dollar system. Countries other than the United States would normally hold their reserves mainly in dollars, and payments deficits within the area would be settled in dollars.

The Common Market would attract to itself those European, African, Middle Eastern, and sterling area countries with primarily European trade relations and political orientation. Such countries would peg their currencies to the European currencies—or to the strongest of them. They would tend increasingly to hold their international reserves in the stronger European currencies rather than in dollars.

Between the two blocs exchange rates would normally be more flexible than within them and the need for reserves usable for interbloc settlements would be correspondingly small—necessarily so, since the availability of such reserves (gold and SDRs created in the International Monetary Fund, for example) would be limited.

A regionalized monetary system of this kind would not be as open or as politically harmonious as was the dollar system in its heyday. The conflicts of interest between the blocs over exchange rates and new trade policy might be serious. Already evident tendencies toward regional trade preferences would be confirmed and strengthened. Yet this regional ordering of international monetary relations would probably be preferable to the realistic alternative—a continuation of present anarchic tendencies.

The outcome depends critically on the spirit and style of transatlantic economic diplomacy and on the Common Market's ability to pull together. If the United States continues to play Texas poker, if France continues to block the efforts of Germany and the European Commission to achieve common flexibility against the dollar, and to insist that European monetary cooperation take mainly the form of common external exchange controls—the outlook is grim. But if reason and moderation prevail in Washington and if the Community eventually reaches agreement on some kind of "common float," a regionalized monetary system of the kind envisaged here should work well enough.

No iron law of international finance decrees that a more unified world monetary system is bound to work better than a less unified one. For unity presupposes a political consensus

on who is to lead and who is to follow. Where no such consensus exists—and this is why the dollar standard has come
to an end—a partial separation may achieve greater harmony
than a unity that has outlived its time.

THE FUTURE OF THE DOLLAR
by Richard N. Cooper

The international monetary system has been in almost continuous turmoil for the past four years. The situation is thus superficially in a high state of flux. In the meantime, we hear statements to the effect that the international reputation of the dollar reached its peak in the mid-1950s, or that the international *position* of the dollar peaked in late 1971, when the world formally accepted a de facto dollar standard. As the dollar's position improved, its reputation declined. And it is asked: how long will the decline in stature continue? how far will it go?

Questions like these leave the economist uncomfortable. The questions themselves are not precise. Even if they were, the context in which they are to be answered is not well defined. To discuss the future of the dollar requires specification of some framework. Is the discussion to be positive or normative: what will happen or what should happen? If it is positive, should it be conditional on other events, or unconditional—that is, a straight forecast of the future? Economists are generally much more comfortable with conditional forecasts, "if . . . then . . ." propositions that must meet certain standards of internal consistency, and occasionally even of plausibility, but not of certainty or even high probability. If the conditions are not fulfilled, they are neither surprised nor troubled that the "forecast" turned out to be wrong.

A straight unconditional forecast gives the economist further difficulty because it involves forecasting political actions as well as economic events; economic forecasting is at least conditional to that extent, and more often it is further conditioned within an economic framework.

These observations are highly relevant to a discussion of the future of the dollar, for that is deeply tied up with the future of the international monetary system, and that in turn is highly dependent on decisions strongly subject to political motivation and political will. There is no generally accepted framework in which the future of the dollar can be discussed unconditionally, in part because economists have generally treated governments as exogenous agents, acting on the

"The Future of the Dollar" was published originally in *Foreign Policy*, Number 11, Summer 1973.

system from outside it. This perspective marks a sharp difference from analysis of the firm or the household; the distinctive lesson of classical economic analysis is that it shows that an apparently autonomous agent is in fact tightly constrained, at least in the long run, by the economic environment in which it operates. This perspective has only recently been extended to governments, and then only in a limited context and largely to local rather than to national governments.

In spite of these difficulties, partly to provoke discussion and partly to provoke the self-denying effect (whereby a prophecy sets in motion avoidance mechanisms), I will make an unconditional forecast about the future of the dollar for, say, the next decade.

It is this: at the end of a decade the position of the dollar will not be very different from what it is now. The dollar will continue to be suspect and the struggle to find acceptable ways to rein it in will continue, but generally they will fail and the dollar will still be widely used both as a private international currency and as an official reserve currency. By then Europe will have greatly reduced its dependence on the dollar for intra-European transactions, probably with a clearing arrangement providing for intervention in European currencies, but with final settlement in dollars, and linked to the dollar for non-European transactions. Other national currencies, and especially the German mark, will play a greater relative and absolute role as international money. While the dollar will therefore have rivals, and the rivals will create new problems of financial stability, the dollar will continue to dominate all of them in importance. The private international role of the dollar will continue to grow.

The basic reason for this forecast is simple: there is at present no clear, feasible alternative. The numerous plans for international monetary reform that have been put forward do not deal satisfactorily with the structural problems inherent in the present situation, and (partly for that reason, but only partly) the relevant governments are still very far apart in what they regard as desirable in an international monetary system. Failing to agree on an alternative perpetuates the evolving status quo. In addition, while there will be progress toward European monetary unification, it will be sufficiently slow to prevent the development of a serious rival to the dollar at the global level. Europeans themselves will resist strongly the evolution of one of the existing European currencies, especially the mark, into a position of dominance, but they will find difficulty in constructing and introducing an adequate substitute.

Furthermore, the behavior of the American economy is likely to be very creditable compared to the economies of other industrial countries. The balance-of-payments problem, as it is now perceived, will not be entirely solved, but price developments in the United States compared with those of other countries will give the dollar a favorable image abroad. There will be great pressures on the U.S. trade balance as a result of rising demands for energy and other raw materials, but that will be true of other industrial countries as well; their continued more rapid growth may in this respect compensate for the fact that in the United States imports will be necessary not only for growth but also, in some cases, to substitute for dwindling domestic supplies. Long-term capital outflow from the United States remains a potential problem, since the United States is still a relatively capital-rich country with correspondingly lower returns to capital for any given technology. But the gap has narrowed substantially already, and capital outflows will remain under enough political control (for example, through the passage into law of some of the provisions of the Burke-Hartke bill) that the outflow will not become embarrassingly large, except of course during periods of speculation against the dollar. And foreign investment in U.S. markets will grow rapidly, compensating for some of the outflow.

The forecast of a single individual is not terribly interesting, especially when it is made without high conviction but merely with more conviction than can be applied to major alternative outcomes. But once some assumptions are stated, an unconditional forecast shades over into a conditional forecast, and that can give rise to dispute over the assumptions and over the alleged link between the assumptions and the forecast.

To provide perspective on the assumptions and on the link between assumptions and forecast, this essay will review briefly how the dollar got to its present position, the structural tensions inherent in the present condition, some proposed solutions and possible outcomes arising out of those tensions, and the deficiencies of the proposed solutions.

A Short History of the Dollar

The dollar emerged as a strong currency after World War I. The U.S. economy had been stimulated by the war, while European economies were set back. Also around this time a truly national capital developed in the United States, a co-alescence of earlier regional markets. The capacity of the country to export capital (after having been a large net im-porter in the nineteenth century) became evident, and, by the late 1920s, 55 percent of all foreign bond issues were being made in the United States, denominated in dollars. The polit-ical turmoil of the 1930s, especially in Europe, reinforced the attractiveness of the dollar as a currency of refuge. By 1940, $2.5 billion were held by foreigners in American bank depos-its and other liquid claims, and even more were held in Amer-ican securities. Central banks also held over $1 billion. At the end of World War II, in 1945, foreign central banks held $4 billion in liquid dollar claims. This compared with $10 billion equivalent (at the overvalued exchange rate of 1 £ = $4.03) held in sterling, although admittedly most of the holdings of sterling were really long-term war debts to India, Egypt, and other members of the British Empire, held in liquid form.

The story thereafter is well known. The world economy grew apace, and the U.S. dollar, "as good as gold" and convertible into gold at a fixed price of $35 an ounce, provided the de-sired growth in international reserves. World reserves grew by 26 percent between 1945 and 1960, of which 10 percentage points were in the form of new monetary gold and 14 percentage points were in the form of U.S. dollars. Gold re-serves held by the world excluding the United States grew faster than total gold reserves, since other countries added to their gold holdings also by buying from the inordinately high U.S. gold stocks; only two-thirds of their additional gold holdings came from new production; one-third came from the United States.

By 1959 the growth in dollar reserves of a few European countries ran ahead of their desire for additional dollars, and the United States became increasingly fearful about sales of gold from its stocks. During the 1960s the growth in foreign official dollar holdings increased, so that by the end of 1970

End of Year International Reserves

	1945	1960	1970	1972
	($ billion equivalent)			
Gold	33.3	38.0	37.2	38.9
U.S. gold holdings	20.1	17.8	11.1	10.5
Foreign Exchange*	14.3	18.6	44.6	100.3
U.S. liabilities	4.2	11.1	23.8	61.3
U.K. liabilities	10.1	6.3	6.6	8.2†
Other**	—	3.6	10.8	16.3
Total Reserves	47.6	60.2	92.5	155.5
Addendum: World exports during the year	34.2	113.4	280.3	368.0

*Reported assets differ from U.S. and U.K. reported liabilities by minor differences in concept, by measurement error, by official holdings of foreign exchange other than dollars and sterling, and (mainly) by official deposits in the eurocurrency market.

**Special Drawing Rights (SDRs) and reserve positions in the IMF.

†September.

Sources: *Federal Reserve Bulletin*; *International Financial Statistics*.

there were over $30 billion in dollars in official reserves, amounting to around a third of total international reserves (see chart).*

Since the mid-1960s, and especially since March 1968, when the price of gold in the London market was allowed to rise substantially above the official price of gold, it has been said that the world has been on a dollar standard, because the dollar was de facto inconvertible. This is not strictly true. There were in fact many conversions of dollars into gold at the United States Treasury during these years, and indeed in 1970 alone more than five dozen countries converted a total of $630 million into gold. To be sure, most of these were associated with the increase in International Monetary Fund (IMF) quotas that year. But forty-six countries had converted dollars into gold in 1969, and a dozen countries converted

*There is some ambiguity about how many dollars were held in international reserves at this time, for a substantial discrepancy had developed between liabilities reported by the United Kingdom and the United States, on one hand, and foreign exchange assets reported to the International Monetary Fund (IMF) by all central banks, on the other. The bulk of the discrepancy was presumably dollars held in the eurodollar market, hence not recorded as liabilities to official holders by the United States. But some of the discrepancy was also explained by official holdings of currencies other than the dollar and the pound.

dollars into gold in 1971, before suspension of convertibility. What was true is that total dollar assets held by central banks exceeded U.S. monetary gold by enough to raise serious questions about the continuation of convertibility.* Large holders of dollars knew that they could not convert substantial amounts of dollars into gold without threatening the U.S. capacity to maintain convertibility, hence the system itself. This restraint on conversions was made formal only in the case of Germany, which in 1967 agreed not to convert dollars into gold. Belgium, France, the Netherlands, and Switzerland among Group of Ten countries all converted some dollars into gold in 1971.

The "de facto inconvertibility" of the dollar into gold was made formal in August 1971 when President Nixon announced his New Economic Policy, which among other things involved the imposition of a freeze on wages and prices and a 10 percent surcharge on many imports as well as the declaration of nonconvertibility. This declaration followed large outflows of dollars from the United States, and the magnitudes of world dollar holdings increased radically in 1971 and 1972. Official dollar holdings rose by over $40 billion, more than doubling official foreign exchange holdings. The U.S. payments deficit, which on a liquidity basis had averaged around $3 billion a year for nearly a decade, suddenly rose to $22 billion in 1971 and $14 billion in 1972. The United States had actually run a surplus on official settlements in 1968 and 1969, but this became a large deficit of nearly $10 billion in 1970 and nearly $30 billion in 1971, dropping back to $10 billion in 1972.

Reasons for Change

The reasons for these sharp changes are three. First, the U.S. trade balance gradually deteriorated following the Vietnam war boom of 1966, but the extent of the deterioration was masked in 1969-70 by a weakening economy. Second, monetary policy turned from being contractionary (with very high interest rates) through the first half of 1970 to being

---

* The term "convertibility" is here used to mean convertibility of the dollar into gold at a fixed official price. This is only one of many possible meanings of "convertibility," and one of the least important. The dollar continues to be convertible into other currencies without restriction, either at a relatively fixed price or at a fluctuating price. For various distinctions and their relative importance, see Gottfried Haberler, *Currency Convertibility* (Washington, D.C.: American Enterprise Institute, 1954).

expansionary (with much lower interest rates, especially on short-term securities) in late 1970 and 1971 (tight money explains the official settlements surpluses of 1968 and 1969), and heavy American borrowings in the eurodollar market began to be repaid after the change. These in turn were converted into other currencies in which higher yields were available. Finally, in late spring 1971 speculative movements of funds began to augment other outflows in a major way, and the outflows then became mutually reinforcing. Much has been made of the drawing power of Japan and Germany, and indeed between them these two countries added over $20 billion to their reserves in 1971 and 1972. But that still left an additional $40 billion that was well distributed among other countries. All industrial countries and many less developed countries experienced substantial increases in their reserves during this period.

In short, the legacy of the last several years is huge official dollar holdings widely spread around the world. In addition, there are large and not wholly explained private dollar holdings outside the United States. And over $15 billion of the increase in official foreign exchange reserves in 1971 and 1972 cannot be accounted for by the U.S. deficit, indicating cycling through the eurodollar market and the growing use of the mark, the yen, and possibly other currencies as official reserves.

The Smithsonian Agreement of December 1971 devalued the dollar (in terms of gold) for the first time since 1934 and revalued the mark and the yen. U.S. officials were not really satisfied with the extent of those negotiated exchange rates and were reinforced in this view when (not suprisingly, in view of the long response lags inherent in modern commercial transactions in sophisticated products) the U.S. trade balance did not improve in 1972. They therefore took the occasion of some currency disturbances to devalue the dollar again fourteen months later.

Deficiencies in the Present Monetary System

Analyses of the ailments of the present international monetary system have now become conventional: they revolve around the tensions that arise out of international use of a national currency and out of imperfections in the balance-of-payments adjustment process. The former tensions arise because the reserve currency country ceases in practice to be under any balance-of-payments discipline once it becomes clear that its capacity to convert outstanding holdings of its currency into other reserve assets cannot be tested without breaking the entire system. The latter difficulties arise because discrete changes in exchange rates, the principal and ultimate adjustment measure under the Bretton Woods system, invite large-scale, disruptive speculation in anticipation of such changes. They also impose major shocks to foreign industries in close competition with industries in a country the currency of which has been devalued. Moreover, the system has the additional weakness that countries in balance-of-payments surplus are under no strong pressure to alter their exchange rates even when such alteration would be desirable.

While there is now official recognition of the weaknesses of the present system, the emphasis of such recognition varies markedly from country to country. In particular, the United States has concentrated its attention on the deficiencies in the adjustment process, and especially on the unwillingness of surplus countries and (as the U.S. government perceived it, at least before February 1973) the inability of the United States to change exchange rates when necessary, while in contrast "Europe" (which, however, doesn't really speak with one official voice on these questions) has emphasized of late the weaknesses of a system that uses the dollar extensively as an international currency. The United States calls for effective control over its exchange rate, while "Europe" calls for a resumption of convertibility of the dollar. This strong difference in emphasis threatens a total impasse in discussions of monetary reform unless a reasonable bargain can be struck that covers both areas. In the meantime, U.S. liquid liabilities to foreign central banks have grown to over four times U.S. reserve assets, which at the end of 1972 stood at $13.1 billion, including gold, Special Drawing Rights (SDRs), reserve position at the IMF, and small holdings of foreign exchange. Under the circumstances the United States simply cannot accept any obligations of convertibility and hence "discipline" on its balance of payments without greater assurances on its capacity for exchange rate adjustment than other countries are apparently willing to give. The position of European countries is complicated in considerable measure at present by their firm commitment and tentative steps to achieve monetary unification, although ultimately such unification should make payments adjustment vis-à-vis the United States easier.

Quite a number of possible futures arise out of the impasse noted above, but it seems useful to distinguish two broad classes of possibility. The first involves a disappearance of the reserve currency role of the dollar, or at least reduction to *de minimis* and geographically confined proportions. The second involves an entrenchment and reinforcement of the international role of the dollar, perpetuation of a "dollar standard."

The second outcome is said to be totally unacceptable to many European and some other countries, although apparently they were less troubled by the incipient dollar standard embodied in the Smithsonian Agreement of December 1971 than by the immediately available alternatives. Moreover, it has been argued that the world could do a lot worse than the dollar standard so long as the American economy is well managed, even when the criteria of good management are exclusively domestic ones, that is, concentrating on maintenance of full employment and reasonable price stability without explicit regard for the balance of payments.* The United States, as the balance wheel of the world economy, should stay on an even economic keel, and then other countries could adjust to the United States. Whatever might be said about this arrangement from the point of view of optimum economic management, it is clear that such an arrangement would continue to rankle and would induce a continual struggle to alter the regime. The regime therefore is allegedly unstable and would sooner or later degenerate into a dollar bloc of those countries that were not offended (or found the benefits sufficiently great to outweigh the offense) by a dollar standard and a rest of the world that could not accept a dollar standard and could afford to do without it.

Thus attention is turned to the first possible outcome, a drastic reduction or even elimination of the reserve currency role of the dollar and a move to a system in which the United States is treated with greater symmetry and must behave more like other countries in the context of international fi-

*See Ronald I. McKinnon, *Private and Official International Money: The Case for the Dollar*, Princeton Essay in International Finance No. 74, April 1969.

nance. The success of achieving this depends on an agreement that involves four components: (1) restoration of convertibility of the dollar into other reserve assets, (2) an agreement on how to handle the large volume of outstanding official dollar holdings, (3) an improvement in the adjustment process, especially as it affects the United States, and (4) arrangements to deal with the problems arising from extensive private international use of the dollar. Each of these points will be taken up in turn.

As noted above, the simple arithmetic of U.S. liquid assets and liabilities is against undertaking an obligation of convertibility without further changes, especially in view of the suspicion that not all the dollars are willingly held. This limitation also applies to "indirect" convertibility that is brought about by a U.S. obligation to support a given set of exchange rates by market intervention. Without adequate reserves the United States cannot sensibly agree to more than token intervention, no matter how hard French Finance Minister Giscard d'Estaing and other European officials press the point. So discussion shifts at once to the other areas.*

Consolidation of Foreign Exchange Reserves

A leading proposal, with numerous variants, is to consolidate all reserve currency holdings by converting them to an international claim of some kind, a special issue of SDRs or a new kind of deposit at the IMF. In the limiting case, the consolidation would be both compulsory and complete and would be accompanied by prohibition on further acquisitions of dollars by official holders. In other words, after the consolidation the dollar would become fully convertible and conversion would always take place. This represents the ideal, fully symmetric world sought by some reformers. Most proposals do not go this far and allow the retention of "working balances" of dollars for exchange market intervention and other limited purposes, but these working balances would be restricted in amount.** Still weaker versions call for establishing the pos-

*For a critical review of the conditions for resumption of convertibility of the dollar, with a presumption against it, see William Fellner, "The Dollar's Place in the International System: Suggested Criteria for the Appraisal of Emerging Views," *Journal of Economic Literature,* X, September, 1972, pp. 746-55.

**Robert Triffin, for example, has proposed that no more than 15 percent of a country's total reserves could be held in the form of national currencies. See his "International Monetary Collapse and Reconstruction in April 1972," *Journal of International Economics*, Vol. 2, September 1972, p. 387.

sibility of converting outstanding dollars into some special reserve asset but leave the option to the existing holders of dollars. Many outstanding dollars would presumably remain unconverted because of the interest yield they command or because of distrust of, or inconveniences associated with, the new asset. This version aims to satisfy those who reluctantly hold dollars now, by providing indirectly a form of guarantee on their international reserves. But it would not satisfy those who are concerned with the weaknesses of the present system, for it still leaves the dollar with a substantial reserve currency role and the United States without sufficient discipline on its capacity to run payments deficits.

Still other versions permit consolidation of outstanding dollar balances as of some fixed date but do not prohibit the subsequent acquisition of dollars. This proposal would start with a clean slate but would leave open the possibility of a repetition of the present difficulty in future years.

The link between convertibility of the dollar by the United States and the consolidation of outstanding reserve balances of dollars into some other, possibly new, reserve asset is clear and direct: the United States cannot undertake a convertibility obligation so long as the number of dollars subject to conversion so greatly exceeds the United States' capacity to convert. Moreover, without consolidation the United States might find its own reserves depleted over time even if it maintained balance in its international payments, taking one year with another. This possibility arises because countries in surplus might convert their dollar earnings at the United States Treasury, while countries in deficit would pay with dollars rather than with other reserve assets. The link also cuts the other way: without convertibility any consolidation is *ipso facto* only once-for-all, and the United States remains free to run payments deficits.

The Adjustment Process

Even a strong version of consolidation would not permit the United States to agree to reserve asset convertibility. Convertibility also requires that provision be made for adequate balance-of-payment adjustment and for dealing with large movements of foreign private dollar holdings. Without assurance that it can adjust its own effective exchange rate (that is, actually influence cross rates, not merely alter its parity in terms of gold/SDRs), the United States under convertibility would have to govern its domestic economy by the dictates of balance-of-payments requirements. Yet for the United States that could be exceedingly expensive in terms of underutilized labor and capital, or in terms of inflation, and incurring those costs would be in the interests neither of the United States nor of other countries. Thus, as perceived by the United States, an adequate adjustment mechanism must meet two conditions: (1) countries with substantial payments surpluses must adjust in one way or another so as to eliminate the surpluses, and (2) when many countries are in surplus, the United States must be able to change the exchange rate between the dollar and other currencies.

The Bretton Woods regime provides assurance on neither of these conditions. Adjustment of exchange rates is considered a last-resort device, with a presumption against it. And given the large and discrete nature of the changes, there are built-in inhibitions to using this device, as noted above. This being so, countries in surplus are under no serious pressure to change their exchange rates. The presumption must be altered so that a country in surplus is assumed to appreciate its currency, unless there are compelling reasons against appreciation.

The present system as it has evolved around the reserve currency role of the dollar also makes difficult an adjustment of the dollar exchange rate with any certainty, for inertial forces are on the side of preserving the exchange rate between other currencies and the dollar no matter what happens to the dollar/gold parity. The tortuous negotiations of December 1971 made clear how difficult an adjustment of the dollar exchange rate can be, even in the face of demonstrable disequilibrium. (The second devaluation of the dollar, in February 1973, in many respects went more smoothly. But even that followed a major and disruptive flow of funds from dollars into other currencies, leading to a closing of the foreign exchange markets.) Again, it is necessary to shift the presumption in favor of a change in the exchange rate of the dollar with respect to other currencies when the United States is in payments deficit and the surpluses are widespread. These presumptions would of course have to follow certain guidelines, to minimize the chance that exchange rate changes take place when they are unnecessary or undesirable. The guidelines should be agreed to and understood by all countries so all countries could be held accountable to them. Such guidelines, or presumptive rules as I have called them elsewhere,* would meet both the requirements of the United States.

Unfortunately, resistance to both points remains strong. Many officials do not like the idea of shifting the presumption to greater flexibility of exchange rates, and most financial officials do not at all like the idea of laying down rules, even presumptive rules that could be ignored in good cause, to govern changes in exchange rates. This is regrettable, but it is a present fact. For reasons that are obscure, the developing country members of the Committee of Twenty and the International Monetary Fund Executive Board seem also to have taken a strong stand against greater exchange rate flexibility. Their reluctance is thus added to the reluctance of many Europeans to move in this direction, a reluctance that is fortuitously but unfortunately reinforced at the present time by the assigned but exceedingly difficult task of proceeding toward European monetary unification on a relatively short timetable. Perhaps a few more financial crises will provide the required dose of persuasion. But in the meantime, an honest forecast is that the U.S. requirements for improvements in the adjustment mechanism will not be met.

Private Dollar Holdings

As if there were not enough other difficulties, there remains the problem of foreign private dollar balances. These have become huge: $20 billion in American banks at the end of 1972, augmented by an additional $60 billion or more in the eurodollar market, net of inter-European bank deposits. Some of the eurodollar deposits are official rather than private—perhaps as much as $10 billion—but to the extent that is so, the outstanding official claims on the U.S. reserve assets under a regime of convertibility have been understated above.** Even after allowing for official balances, the private

*See my "Gliding Parities: The Case for Presumptive Rules," in G. Helm, ed., *Approaches to Greater Flexibility of Exchange Rates: The Burgenstock Papers* (Princeton University Press, 1970). I there suggest that changes in international reserves above some minimum amount would provide the most defensible guideline, but other criteria might also be added. See also C. Fred Bergsten, *Reforming the Dollar: An International Monetary Policy for the United States* (New York: Council on Foreign Relations, September 1972), pp. 48-62.

**Data on the eurodollar market, while improving rapidly, are still unsatisfactory. Eight European countries report the eurocurrency claims and liabilities of their banks to the Bank for International Settlements, which in turn publishes summary information in its annual report. But a breakdown be-

balances are very substantial. To give some idea of the relative magnitude of these holdings, together they exceed the total domestic money supply of every country except the United States ($253 billion) and Japan ($101 billion). These large balances presumably reflect the need for international money in the world of private transactions, and the advantages of international banking. They may also reflect the competition of unregulated banks with domestic banks which in all countries are subject to numerous government regulations concerning reserve requirements, the payment of interest on demand and time deposits, restrictions on assets, and the like. Whatever the reason, large balances are held for transactions purposes and for short-term investment. These balances are highly mobile in times of impending financial disturbance, which in turn contributes to the disturbance.

How do these balances fit into the plans for international monetary reform? Should they be funded along with the official balances? Should restrictions be placed on the eurocurrency market so that the balances, once funded, do not simply reappear? Eliminating the private balances and restricting the eurodollar market could only be done at considerable cost to the efficiency of private international transactions. At least this is the dominant view in international banking circles, and it is probably correct. To the extent that the growth of the eurodollar market has taken place merely as an evasion of sensible government regulations of domestic banking systems, however, the cost of restricting the market would be lower, and might even turn into a benefit. The weighing of those costs and benefits will not be considered here. The point is, so long as the eurodollar market exists, it is a source of potential disturbance, and large movements of private dollars into official hands at some future time could easily undo whatever had been accomplished through consolidation of official dollar holdings.

To appreciate this, suppose that the adjustment process works well, in the sense of keeping payments in balance over a period of time, but that it works slowly. Then if large private dollar balances are converted into other currencies, what

tween private and official deposits is not available, and extensive activities by banks in other countries are not decomposed into bank and nonbank claims and liabilities, thus preventing a measure of the real size of the eurodollar market. For example, $11 million of the U.S. bank liabilities were to foreign banks, many of which are undoubtedly in the eurocurrency market. Thus some "double-counting" is involved in simply adding the two totals.

happens? Is the United States to be held accountable for converting the resulting official balances into other reserve assets? Unless there is some provision for accommodation of this contingency, the system will break down, that is, a convertible dollar will necessarily be declared inconvertible or be allowed to float freely in the exchange market. There is, to be sure, some self-correction in the eurodollar market. A large withdrawal of eurodollars will lead to a sharp increase in eurodollar interest rates, and this rise will tend to inhibit further withdrawals. But if eurodollar rates rise far enough, they will attract funds from the United States (or funds that otherwise would have returned to the United States), and this will be so even with restrictions on capital outflows from the United States; for such restrictions, unless they encompass *all* international transactions, that is, unless they represent a full panoply of exchange controls, are bound to be less than fully effective in the postulated circumstance. Thus the corrective adjustment in eurodollar rates will not be sufficient.

Moreover, the exposure to large movements of capital does not arise only from large private foreign dollar holdings. Other currencies are increasingly held by foreigners as well— the mark has already been mentioned—and these funds will be mobile as well, although their countries of origin are better supplied with reserves to cope with them than is the United States. More significant, *domestic* funds are also increasingly mobile and can be expected to move in ever greater volume across the foreign exchanges when profit-making opportunities present themselves. This is one manifestation of the growing economic interdependence among countries.

Lines of Credit

It is necessary to have large swap facilities or other large lines of credit to cover this contingency. But unfortunately such lines of credit may recreate the situation that consolidation of outstanding official dollar balances was designed to avoid. If the conversion of private dollar balances into other currencies is short-lived, the situation will reverse itself and no problem will arise. But if the conversion turns out not to be reversed, then some arrangement will be necessary for additional consolidation. The arrangement in the past to cover such contingencies has been for the United States to draw on its network of swap facilities, amounting now to nearly $12 billion, for credit for ninety days and possibly longer; but if reversal did not occur within a relatively short period of time, then the swaps would be repaid out of a drawing on the IMF, which in effect converted the swaps into a three-to-five year line of credit. But the present swap network and U.S. drawing rights (at $8.4 billion for the gold tranche and four credit tranches combined) at the IMF are totally inadequate for the potential exposure involved in conversions of private dollar balances. Moreover, U.S. drawing rights at the IMF are limited by the probable need for the IMF itself to borrow in order to honor a large U.S. drawing. This inadequacy has been masked in the past by a totally different mechanism: the willingness (however reluctant) of central banks to acquire and hold dollars without limit. Thus a "dollar standard" automatically provides the required line of credit to the United States: recycling is built into it. An alternative would be to endow the United States with a large initial allocation of reserves, say, in the form of SDRs, so that it could meet any convertibility obligations arising from massive conversion of private dollar holdings. But such an allocation could also be used to finance payments deficits. It would therefore be difficult to justify, especially in a period in which many developing countries are also laying down special claims for larger allocation of SDRs.

Freely floating exchange rates would of course avoid this whole problem—or, more accurately, they would transform it into a different but no less difficult problem, namely, how to avoid or mitigate the influence of speculative currency movements on exchange rates, which represent too important an economic variable for most countries to allow to move with complete freedom under all circumstances.

The best alternative would be to convert the IMF into a true lender-of-last-resort—a true central bank for central banks in the classic sense—by allowing it to lend any amount of SDRs necessary to permit member countries, and in particular the United States, to maintain their convertibility obligations in the face of large outflows of liquid funds. If currency conversions reversed themselves, the United States would repay the IMF immediately thereafter; if they did not, the United States would be committed to repay the IMF over a long period of years, and the dollar exchange rate would be allowed to adjust enough to permit the United States to run the requisite payments surpluses.

The IMF would have to be released from the present tight constraints both on its capacity to lend and on its authority to create SDRs, and this will of course give central bankers pause. But the lessons we learned to deal with financial crises at the national level years ago must now be applied, with appropriate modification, at the international level. The great and growing mobility of private funds requires it.

In summary, private dollar balances are the *pièce de résistance:* not to make allowance for them would jeopardize most of the reform plans advanced thus far. But to make allowance for them, for example, by offering a large special allocation of SDRs to the United States or by prohibiting foreign private holdings of dollars or by endowing the IMF with true central bank powers, calls for more drastic changes than have so far been contemplated by officials. This is the basis for my forecast at the outset of this paper: at the end of a decade the position of the dollar will not be very much different from what it is now.

While such a state of affairs may appear to be satisfactory, especially to Americans, that will not be so. For in several senses the system will not be a stable one. Rivals to the dollar, while not displacing it from position, will make larger, and more frequent, large-scale movement of funds from one currency to another in response to anticipated gains or losses; and these movements will be sufficiently alarming to monetary officials to prompt continuing pressures for tight controls on international transactions. Moreover, an international system that continues to be dependent on a national currency will not be accepted as a durable system, and this lack of acceptance will itself be a source of instability in the system, for attempts, individual and collective, to alter the system will be constantly in the air. The lack of acceptance of a dollar-dominated system can hardly avoid corroding other aspects of international relations as well.

Thus, it is devoutly to be hoped that the forecast proves to be too pessimistic, that those charged with monetary reform will cease dallying and press forward with the complicated and comprehensive changes that are necessary.

WHY EXPORTS ARE BECOMING IRRELEVANT

by Lawrence B. Krause

The economy of the United States is increasingly dominated by the production of services rather than goods. Forty-six million Americans are employed today in service-producing industries such as transport and public utilities, trade, finance and real estate, education and health services, and government. This is nearly double the number employed in goods-producing industries such as manufacturing, construction, mining, and agriculture. Two recent publications have noted this trend and some of its consequences.* In addition, the U.S. Bureau of Labor Statistics has published a study indicating that the trend toward relatively greater production of services than of goods will likely continue through 1980.** This phenomenon raises a series of new possibilities for U.S. international trade policy.

Economists for some time have been seeking a better explanation of the basic nature of international trade than is afforded by the well-known static theory of comparative advantage. Some of the most interesting recent research work attempts to explain the evolution of comparative advantages. The conclusion seems to be that those industries where productivity gains are above the average for a country will tend to produce products competitively for world markets, while industries advancing at less than the average rate are likely to suffer in international competition. Laggard industries can be expected to lose parts of their market in foreign countries through declining export sales and to lose parts of their domestic market through greater imports from abroad. The determination of which industries will capture more than average productivity gains has been related to the structure of domestic demand plus the evolution of scientific technology. It is these factors that one must explore to make some judgment about future comparative advantages.

*Victor R. Fuchs, *The Service Economy*, National Bureau of Economic Research, 1968; Sheldon W. Stahl, "The Service Sector—Where the Action Is," *Monthly Review*, Federal Reserve Bank of Kansas City, March 1970.

**U.S. Department of Labor, Bureau of Labor Statistics, *The U.S. Economy in 1980*, Bulletin 1673, August 1970.

"Why Exports Are Becoming Irrelevant" was published originally in *Foreign Policy*, Number 3, Summer 1971.

Agricultural and Nonagricultural Wage and Salary Employment, by Industry Division, 1947, 1969, and Projected 1980

(Numbers in thousands)

	1947	1969	Pro-jected 1980	Percentage Change 1947-69	Percentage Change 1969-80
Goods-Producing	26,373	27,766	30,014	5.3	8.1
Mining	955	628	550	—34.2	—12.4
Contract construction	1,982	3,411	4,600	72.0	34.9
Manufacturing	15,545	20,121	21,935	29.4	9.0
Durable goods	8,385	11,898	13,015	41.9	9.4
Nondurable goods	7,159	8,255	8,920	15.3	8.1
Agriculture	7,891	3,606	2,929	—54.3	—18.8
Service-Producing	25,399	45,980	59,515	81.0	29.4
Transportation and public utilities	4,166	4,448	4,740	6.8	6.5
Trade (wholesale and retail)	8,955	14,644	17,625	63.5	20.4
Finance, insurance, real estate	1,754	3,559	4,260	102.9	19.7
General services	5,050	11,103	16,090	119.8	44.9
Government	5,474	12,226	16,800	123.4	37.4
Federal	1,892	2,757	3,000	45.5	9.0
State and local	3,582	9,469	13,800	163.1	46.4
Total	51,772	73,746	89,529	42.4	21.4

Source: U.S. Department of Labor, Bureau of Labor Statistics, *The U.S. Economy in 1980*, Bulletin 1673, August 1970, Table A-22, pp. 53-56.

The U.S. Economy Today and in 1980

Despite the fact that the United States produces the most advanced and sophisticated manufactured products in the world, and a superabundance of agricultural products, and Americans consume more goods per capita than any other nation, more of our people are employed in the production of services than in the production of goods. The distribution of the American labor force by industry divisions is shown in the Labor Department table on page 93. One is struck by the increasing importance of services and the relative decline of goods-producing industries since World War II. In 1947 the labor force was roughly divided equally between goods producers (including agriculture) and the service industries. Between 1947 and 1969 there was a growth of 81 percent in employment in services, while employment in goods-producing industries increased by only 5 percent; thus, by 1969, 62 percent of the labor force was in services.

The important implication for international trade that is demonstrated in the table concerns the nature of the kinds of things Americans are demanding as their incomes rise. The most important growth area in terms of employment since 1947 has been in government services, most overwhelmingly at the state and local level. Educational service has been the area of fastest growth and represented 52 percent of state and local government activities in 1969 (as measured by employment). General services were the second fastest growth area for employment between 1947 and 1969. About 10 percent of general service employment is in private educational institutions. Thus, education as a whole—both private and public—represented 8 percent of total employment in the United States. The largest category of employment within general services, however, is medical and other health services, also an area of substantial increase in demand by Americans. The third fastest growth area for employment has been in finance, insurance, and real estate services. It is only in the fourth spot in the growth league that one will find a goods-producing industry, contract construction, which grew only slightly faster than wholesale and retail trade, another service industry. Looking at manufacturing, one finds the surprising result that employment grew by less than 30 percent from 1947 to 1969, much below the rate for the labor force as a whole.

This economic trend could have profound significance for U.S. international trade. If comparative advantages develop in areas with the fastest growth of domestic demand and U.S. domestic demand is becoming increasingly service oriented, then the export of goods may be becoming relatively less profitable for American producers. Indeed, the only goods-producing industry enjoying above average growth is contract construction, which by its nature cannot be exported as goods. The United States might well become more specialized in service exports; and the most important service export might be management services, which are a combination of education and capital inputs—both factors of relative abundance in the United States.

The generalization that the United States is likely to become less interested in the export of goods must be qualified in certain important respects. Agricultural employment has declined both relatively and absolutely in the U.S. economy; yet agriculture remains important in U.S. exports. The economic health of U.S. agriculture is, if anything, even more dependent on world markets today than in the past. The explanation of this lies in the fact that U.S. comparative advantage in agriculture comes from an abundance of fertile land that has no significant alternate use, from a desirable climate that does not get expended by use in agriculture, and from scientific inputs that are a function of educational services. Thus, U.S. agriculture has an enduring comparative advantage. In manufacturing, however, labor is the primary national factor (all other factors being more transferable internationally), and labor can be attracted to the expanding service sector.

Other enduring U.S. comparative advantages might be found in science-based industries where rapidly changing technology will give certain U.S. products a technological lead over rivals. While other nations will adopt the new technology, high levels of U.S. research and development expenditure should ensure that ever newer U.S. products will always be available for export. Furthermore, the overseas production activities of American based corporations will provide an enduring market for various intermediate manufactured products. The U.S. home operations are likely to remain the largest and most integrated of corporate activities, and they will be able to fill gaps in production abroad by exporting from the United States. But even after taking this into account, American firms are likely to serve their foreign markets mainly by direct production abroad.

This is not to suggest that exporting may not continue to be of great interest to a few goods-producing industries, or that exports will cease to hold the interest of our government policymakers. Agricultural trade will probably require substantial attention and much interest. But the overwhelming majority of U.S. economic activity by 1980 will be even less closely related to the export of goods than it is today, with the relative level already quite low.

The Labor Department table above foresees the continuation, if not an acceleration, of the trend toward service production through the next decade. By 1980 about one-third of the U.S. labor force will be employed in goods production. If one considers only tradable goods (excluding contract construction), the table anticipates only a 4 percent increase in employment as compared to a 12 percent increase in the entire labor force. On the other hand, it projects sharply rising consumer expenditures for medical care, education, and recreational services. Certain durable goods will be in heavy demand, but these will be mainly furniture and household equipment, which because of heavy transportation costs do not easily enter international trade. Thus, the export of goods is likely to be of declining interest to Americans. In 1980 the United States will have what could be called a "postindustrial" or a "service" economy.

In other words, the private U.S. economy during the 1970s will become even less oriented toward exporting goods than it has been in the past. Because all U.S. goods production will be in a state of relative decline as compared with services, a larger share of U.S. goods consumption might come from imports. Taken together, these two trends imply a strong deterioration in the U.S. trade balance. Since a trade balance deterioration for the United States must be offset by a reverse process in other countries, one must examine whether and how this trend will produce equilibrium from a worldwide point of view.

In fact, such a trend would appear to be desirable. American companies for many years have been investing substantial sums abroad, primarily by direct investments. These investments are now yielding large dividend and interest returns to their parents (representing a net of $5.8 billion in 1969), and such returns are likely to grow substantially during the decade of the 1970s. Larger trade surpluses by other countries will be required to make these payments possible.

The United States may well be on the road to becoming a mature creditor country not unlike Great Britain, France, and the Netherlands in earlier historical periods. The U.S. balance of payments in the future could record large trade deficits overcome by even larger service surpluses. The existence of two countering trends, however, does not guarantee that an equilibrium will come about. The maintenance of equilibrium requires a working price adjustment mechanism, namely, occasional exchange rate changes.

Three Commercial Policy Implications

If U.S. international commercial interests evolve as suggested above, then three policy implications can be identified. It would not appear that the United States would have much to gain by devoting diplomatic efforts to the further freeing of world trade. The world must look elsewhere for such initiatives, possibly to the European Economic Community. The welfare of American consumers, of course, can be improved if U.S. trade barriers are reduced, but this can be accomplished by unilateral American action. The sole exception—the one U.S. export industry that can be helped through liberalization—is agriculture. Thus, agriculture must be included in any further attempts to liberalize trade, if such efforts are to make economic or political sense to the United States.

A second implication concerns future support for liberal trade in the United States. Since the end of the Kennedy Round, organized labor in America has switched from the free trade to the protectionist camp. Some believe that this is a temporary aberration based on the unusual lobbying pressure of the textile unions. This optimism seems unjustified. As long as the economic policies of organized labor are directed toward furthering the interests of workers in goods-producing industries—who are the backbone of the labor movement today—then protectionist forces are likely to dominate. The labor unions are thus shedding their traditional mantle as the defender of consumer interests in the United States and are becoming instead advocates for narrower special interests. Of course, there is no inevitability about this. Many important unions are in the service sector, but they have let the goods-producing unions determine labor's commercial policy despite the fact that protectionism is counter to their own economic interests.

A third implication may seem somewhat paradoxical. It would appear that the American economy will be even more closely integrated in the world economy ten years from now than today. It is possible for a business firm to sell 5 to 10 percent of its output in foreign markets as exports and still not get deeply involved in economic developments abroad. The export sales department may be set off by itself, unable to attract the attention of top management, or the domestic sales department can fill orders as they are received from abroad without making any special accommodations to foreign customers. However, the operation of a foreign subsidiary abroad is quite another matter. For it involves interaction with foreign workers, suppliers, distributors, financial institutions, and governments. Foreign business and political conditions are important ingredients in business decisions that are taken at all levels of the overseas-based subsidiary. These factors, which already impinge on many U.S. firms, will continue to grow in importance as our companies expand abroad.

The conclusion, then, is clear and simple. The United States must begin to think of itself as a producer of services rather than as a producer of goods. Washington is paying much too much attention to commercial policy. The recent free trade versus protectionism debate in Congress is really an anachronism. The issues in that debate just don't matter a great deal in terms of employment in the United States, for only a small fraction of our labor force is engaged in production for export or in competition with imports. The most one can say is that protectionist interests have exaggerated and distorted reality more than their free trade opponents. Important foreign policy interests of a political character *are* at stake in the current trade controversies, but these have been lost sight of in a welter of misleading statements about economics. What is of even greater economic and possibly political interest to the United States than trade, however, is the treatment of earnings from our direct investments abroad. This neglected subject needs much greater attention. Countries investing heavily abroad typically become trade-deficit nations. That is what is meant by the very phrase "mature creditor country."

And that, unless the economic indicators are badly in error, is precisely what the United States is in the process of becoming.

RELATIONS WITH DEVELOPING NATIONS

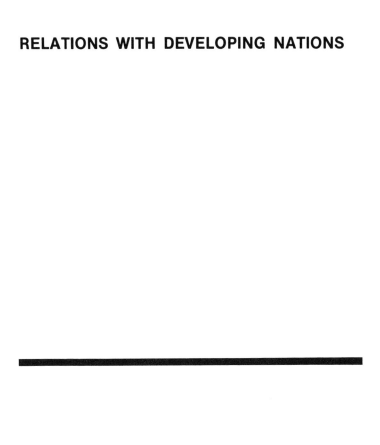

THE THREAT FROM THE THIRD WORLD
by C. Fred Bergsten

Present U.S. policy neglects the Third World almost entirely, with the exception of our few remaining military clients (mainly in Southeast Asia). This policy is a serious mistake. New U.S. economic interests, which flow from the dramatic changes in the position of the United States in the world economy and the nature of the new international economic order, require renewed U.S. cooperation with the Third World. New policy instruments, including—but going far beyond—foreign aid, are necessary for the United States to promote such cooperation.

Any generalizations about the Third World represent vast oversimplification. Indeed, there exists no clearly definable "Third World." I use the term only because it is widely understood as meaning all countries outside the "industrialized West" and the "Communist Empire." In those countries, four major patterns appear likely to dominate the decade ahead.

First, economic and social development is likely to be the overwhelming priority policy objective. Perceptions of the potential rewards from development are broadening and deepening throughout the world. So are realizations that such progress actually is possible. Desire for economic and social progress is thus increasingly likely to dominate internal politics.

Second, the economic goals of the Third World will go well beyond maximizing GNP. Most developing countries, along with most industrialized countries, have now learned that growth alone cannot guarantee the fundamental and politically central objectives of economic policy—full employment, relatively stable prices, equitable income distribution, and ultimately an enhanced quality of life.

Many less developed countries (LDCs) are disillusioned with both the results of the past and its simplistic focus on a single target. Despite the impressive growth rates of the aggregate Third World in the 1960s, unemployment exceeds 20 percent in many countries. The per capita income of the poorest LDCs, which now contain half of the world popula-

"The Threat from the Third World" was published originally in *Foreign Policy*, Number 11, Summer 1973.

tion, has been growing by only 1.5 percent annually. The gap between the income of the richest 10 to 20 percent and the poorest 20 to 40 percent within many LDCs has been getting wider. There are 100 million more illiterates in the Third World now than twenty years ago, and two-thirds of all children there suffer from malnutrition.

Third, the countries of the Third World will increasingly insist upon autonomous management of their own societies. They will reject dictation from outsiders of all types: foreign governments, international agencies, multinational corporations. This is partly due to the increasing self-confidence that has come from recent successes, as well as to the cadres of indigenous talent that are now becoming available. It is partly due to the shortcomings which they now perceive in external "assistance" and in the models of "development" offered them by outsiders. And it is partly due to nationalist desires in the Third World to overcome a feeling of dependence on the rich.*

Fourth, the Third World will continue to need outside help. Few LDCs will be able to meet their economic and social needs without steady infusions of foreign exchange.

The new policy targets of the Third World and its desire for independence, however, call for significant shifts among the modes of help and the manner in which that help is extended. Third World countries will place higher priority on trade than aid, because trade brings with it less foreign influence and, in many cases, creates more jobs. They will place higher priority on borrowing in the private capital markets than on seeking foreign direct investment, because they want more labor-intensive production processes and less foreign direction than frequently accompany multinational firms. They will focus more heavily on international monetary policy because of its critical importance for the achievement of a liberal trading regime and for a freer flow of private portfolio capital, and because it offers new opportunities for development finance without strings. Most of them will seek increased multilateralization of official aid to maximize their own roles in the decision-making process.

*As Isaiah Berlin has suggested, "It is lack of recognition that, more than any other cause, seems to lead to nationalist excesses." "The Bent Twig: A Note on Nationalism," *Foreign Affairs*, October 1972, p. 30.

The Response of the Rich

At present, the industrialized countries are responding inadequately to these Third World needs.

The Third World needs increased access to world markets, perhaps more than anything else, but protectionism is accelerating. Indeed, the attitude of the industrialized world toward LDC exports of manufactured goods has totally reversed in a remarkably short period of time—from supporting tariff preferences *for* them a few years ago, to serious contemplation of new "orderly marketing safeguards" aimed largely *against* their "low wage" products now. The level of real aid is stagnant, and the debt servicing of some LDCs has reached the point where they are now net exporters of capital to the industrialized world. The quality of aid is declining as most terms harden; tying alone reduces the real value of aid by 10 to 30 percent below its nominal value. There is no progress toward stabilizing commodity prices or toward helping LDCs gain access to private capital markets.

The United States is the least responsive to Third World needs of any industrialized country at this time. U.S. help is small in quantity and getting smaller. Its quality is declining. It often runs directly counter to the central objectives of the LDCs just outlined. It lags far behind the policies of Europe and Japan. The administration and Congress must share in the indictment.

The United States regards developing countries, both large and small (for example, India and Chile, not to mention Indochina), solely as pawns on the chessboard of global power politics. Rewards go only to the shrinking list of explicit collaborators. Economically, the United States has been increasing its trade barriers as Europe and Japan have been lowering theirs. Europe and Japan have been extending tariff preferences to the LDCs since 1971, but the United States has yet to make good on its commitment to do so. U.S. development aid, as a percentage of national GNP, is now next to last among all industrialized countries. The United States delayed its latest contributions to the International Development Association and Inter-American Development Bank for over a year, inhibiting their flow of current lending. The United States has failed to contribute anything to the soft-loan window of the Asian Development Bank. It has sought to bilateralize multilateral aid instead of multilateral-izing bilateral aid, as called for in President Nixon's reform proposals of September 1970 and April 1971, by blocking loans from the multilateral lending institutions to countries that have expropriated private investments, even when those countries (*unlike* Chile or Peru) have compensated U.S. firms under international law. At the Stockholm environment conference in June 1972, the United States was the only major country that opposed additional assistance to LDCs for financing antipollution equipment, which their plants need to meet the environmental safeguards imposed by—among others—the United States itself.* It has even abandoned its own initiative to achieve multilateral untying of bilateral aid.

Despite this catalogue of shortcomings, it must be noted that some of the present LDC focus on U.S. inadequacy is unjustified. Many people around the world continue to expect the United States to take all of the major international initiatives, even though the era when the United States could or should do so is now over. And U.S. performance is not all bad: it has taken the initiative to reform the international monetary system, and it is attempting to launch a new round of international trade-liberalizing negotiations. Healthy economic relations among the industrialized countries are critical for the fortunes of the LDCs, so these U.S. efforts to restore such relations promote major LDC interests.

But numerous clashes have already developed between an increasingly self-confident but still needy Third World and a decreasingly responsive industrialized world. Such clashes are likely to become far more serious in the future. The desire for progress in the Third World, and indeed the expectation that it *will* occur, is great. Failure to achieve it will almost certainly produce major frustrations, which could in turn produce highly emotional and even irrational responses across the globe. If the frustrations are caused in significant part by the recalcitrance of the industrialized countries, or even by widespread perceptions that such recalcitrance exists, much of the response may be aimed in their direction. If any particular industrialized country is widely perceived to be the leading recalcitrant, especially if that country is the United States, it could bear the major share of that response. What risk does this involve for the United States?

*See Edward P. Morgan, "Stockholm: The Clean (But Impossible) Dream," *Foreign Policy*, Number 8, Fall 1972.

The Third World and U.S. Economic Interests

The Third World retains some importance for U.S. security. But its new, major impact on the United States is economic.

Much of the impact, however, relates to the position of the United States in its triangular economic relationship with Europe and Japan. The pervasive and growing economic interpenetration among these three industrialized areas is increasingly important to the welfare of key groups in each. At the same time, it threatens the welfare of other key groups. Severe political tensions thus arise. The foreign economic policies of each area are increasingly politicized and increasingly polarized, and have become potentially explosive. They could easily come to dominate the overall relationships among the areas if new ways are not soon found to resolve cooperatively the disputes that inevitably arise. They have already done so on particular occasions, as when the British prime minister refused to meet with the president of the United States to talk about high politics in late 1971 until the United States initiated steps to end the international economic crisis triggered by its New Economic Policy.

Such an outcome is now possible because the security blanket that had previously smothered such economic disputes is being steadily nudged aside. Serious intra-alliance disputes over economics could brake the progress toward East-West détente by breaking the solidarity of the "West" on which détente in part depends. Economic conflict could thus leave us further from, rather than nearer to, a true generation of peace.

But the acceleration of international economic interpenetration, with its complex sets of costs and benefits, is not limited to the industrialized world. It is global. The U.S. stake in the Third World is growing, and the leverage of the Third World to affect the United States is growing.

Natural Resources

First, the United States is rapidly joining the rest of the industrialized countries in depending on the Third World for a critical share of its energy supplies and other natural resources. For oil alone, annual U.S. imports are expected to rise by $20 billion by the end of the decade. But it is not only much-publicized oil; accelerating imports of other raw materials will raise these figures significantly.

Four countries control more than 80 percent of the exportable supply of world copper; they have already organized and have already begun to use their oligopoly power. Two countries account for more than 70 percent of world tin exports, and four countries raise the total close to 95 percent. Four countries combine for more than 50 percent of the world supply of natural rubber. Four countries possess over one-half the world supply of bauxite, and the inclusion of Australia (which might well join the Third World for such purposes) brings the total above 90 percent. In coffee, the four major suppliers have begun to collude (even within the framework of the International Coffee Agreement, which includes the main consuming countries) to boost prices. A few countries are coming to dominate each of the regional markets for timber, the closest present approximation to a truly vanishing resource. The percentages are less, but still quite impressive, for several other key raw materials and agricultural products. And the United States already meets an overwhelming share of its needs for most of these commodities with imports, or will soon be doing so.

A wide range of Third World countries thus have sizable potential for strategic market power. They could use that power against all buyers, or in a discriminatory way through differential pricing or supply conditions—for example, to avoid higher costs to other LDCs or against the United States alone to favor Europe or Japan.

Supplying countries could exercise maximum leverage through withholding supplies altogether, at least from a single customer such as the United States. Withholding is a feasible policy when there are no substitute products available on short notice and when the foreign exchange reserves of the suppliers become sizable enough that they have no need for current earnings.

The suppliers would be even more likely to use their monopoly power to charge higher prices for their raw materials, directly or through such techniques as insisting that they process the materials themselves. Either withholding or price-gouging could hurt U.S. security. The threat of either could pressure the United States to compromise its positions on international political and economic issues. Either would hurt U.S. efforts to combat domestic inflation and restore equilibrium in our international balance of payments.

The price and balance-of-payments effects on the United States of withholding or price-gouging by suppliers of raw materials could not be attacked through conventional policy instruments. Domestic demand for raw materials could be dampened only at the cost of additional unemployment. Foreign suppliers are outside the jurisdiction of U.S. price controls. Substitution of domestic resources would also raise costs significantly. Stockpile sales help only for a short time. Devaluations make resource imports more costly without much dampening their volume. Such actions could thus cause major new problems for the U.S. economy and international position.

Such Third World leverage could have a double bite on the United States if used discriminatorily against it, thereby benefiting the competitive positions of Europe and Japan. Such discriminatory action, triggered either by the suppliers or by our industrialized competitors, is by no means impossible. It was attempted in oil by some Arab countries in 1967 and has been actively sought at least by Italy and France in the recent past. The spectre of "cannibalistic competition" among the rich for natural resources is unfortunately a real possibility which suggests that the owners of those resources have tremendous clout.

The Third World suppliers could also cause major problems by the way in which they use their huge export earnings. Oil earnings alone could rise to at least $50 billion per year by the end of the decade. It is hard to see how more than $20 billion of the total can be spent on imports. These countries could thus add to their portfolios $30 billion *per year*—seeking profitable (or mischievous) outlets. They could use the money to disrupt international money markets overtly, and we have already seen that they generate great monetary instability, perhaps without consciously trying, by pushing the world toward a multiple reserve currency system. Aimed specifically at particular currencies, they could seek to force the United States (or anyone else) to adopt policies that clashed with its national objectives of the moment—as a few Arab countries, from a much weaker financial base, attacked the United Kingdom by converting sterling balances in June 1967 and again in 1971.* At a minimum, the uncertain destination

*Feeling no responsibility for the system, they hold their assets in whichever national currency appears most likely to appreciate in value and/or has the highest yield at the moment—switching rapidly among currencies (and

of these huge resources will add to the already formidable problems faced by the international monetary system, which can affect the United States quite adversely.

The oil situation is, of course, the prototype. The concerted action of the Organization of Petroleum Exporting Countries (OPEC) in raising oil prices has raised energy costs throughout the world and dramatically increased their revenues. Such extortion by the oil producers—including such "normal" LDCs as Nigeria, Indonesia, Iran, and Venezuela—is likely to continue. This economic pressure is unlikely to be reduced as a result of the OPEC countries' taking over the production facilities from the international companies,* because the OPEC countries themselves—including "opposition" politicians in each—have well learned from the companies that *each* benefits from getting the highest possible price for *all*, and that price cutting by one would be counterproductive, because it would quickly be emulated by the others to preserve existing market shares. Equally important is the fact that OPEC has shown other countries how to do it. Oil may be merely the start.

To be sure, each of the specific commodity situations presents different and complex problems. There are serious obstacles to concerted supplier action: the economic option of using substitutes for some of the commodities, the political problem of achieving adequate cooperation among the suppliers, and the risk of overt retaliation by the industrialized world (or just the United States).

But the two obstacles specific to commodity action can be largely overcome within the Third World itself. Subtle pricing and marketing strategies could boost consumer costs and producer gains significantly without pushing consuming countries to the development of substitutes, which requires heavy initial investments and start-up costs. Concerted action by copper, tin, and bauxite producers would sharply

even buying gold in the free market) as the situation changes. Some of those oil countries that are members of the International Monetary Fund (IMF) have even opted out of the Special Drawing Rights (SDR) scheme, which was a first step toward reducing such problems. For the problems involved, see C. Fred Bergsten, "Reforming the Dollar: An International Monetary Policy for the United States," Council on Foreign Relations Paper on International Affairs No. 2 (New York: Council on Foreign Relations, September 1972), esp. pp. 9-13.

* As argued by Theodore H. Moran, "Coups and Costs," *Foreign Policy*, Number 8, Fall 1972.

reduce the risk to each that cheaper aluminum or tin could be substituted for higher priced copper, or vice versa. An alliance among the producers of coffee, cocoa, and tea could preempt a similar substitution. Objective calculations of the benefits to all producers could provide a basis for "equitable" division of the spoils.

All that is needed to permit political cooperation is increased knowledge of the market and the potential gains from concerted action, self-confidence, and leadership. Whether such action actually eventuates would seem to depend quite importantly on the policy milieu of the future. The countries involved will certainly be more likely to act if the industrialized world frustrates their efforts to achieve their goals more constructively, and if they are barred from participating effectively in global decisions that vitally affect their own destinies. They are more likely to act against the United States alone if the United States is the most obstinate or neglectful of all. Even a perception of such obstinacy or neglect, sufficiently plausible to be widely believed in both the Third World and the industrialized countries themselves, could trigger action. It would seem far better for the United States, and for all the industrialized countries, to try to preempt such risks by taking initiatives to help these countries fulfill their aspirations by more stable means.

Investment and Trade

Second, a number of Third World countries exercise major leverage over U.S. investments. The book value of U.S. direct investments in the Third World exceeded $23 billion at the end of 1971 (about $14 billion excluding oil), and the real market value is at least twice as large. About 5 percent of U.S. corporate profits now derive from these investments. Many jobs relate directly to them. Even excluding oil, they provide over $1 billion annually for the U.S. balance of payments.

Earnings on foreign investment are particularly important to the United States because of their strategic importance for its balance of payments. Many observers expect the United States to move into a structural trade deficit of growing size by the end of the decade, with the huge flow of investment earnings paying (in foreign exchange terms) for its net imports, overseas government expenditures, and continued net outflows of private capital. Any significant cutback in investment earnings would thus require new measures to compensate elsewhere in the balance of payments, levying new costs on us. Cutbacks in imports or subsidies of exports, perhaps by further devaluations, would again raise U.S. prices and costs. New constraints might emerge for U.S. foreign policy, perhaps far more costly than the actions suggested here to avoid negative Third World action. Effective controls on capital exports to help the balance of payments in the short run would cut future income from abroad, including income on investments already made, and hence produce the same constraints in the future.

Confiscation of its investments in the Third World could thus create major costs for the United States. Much of this investment is in the same raw materials just discussed, so Third World action could affect the United States doubly (as it already has in oil) by both raising our costs and reducing our earnings. It is often argued that any foreign confiscations would eliminate new U.S. investments in the confiscating countries, along with the return on old investments, so there would be no net cost to our balance of payments. This argument of course ignores the negative effects of such action on domestic jobs, profits, and perhaps even prices.

But it is also almost certainly wrong for the balance of payments over the longer run, since virtually all foreign investments return more income to the United States—and hence provide financing for net imports of goods, and so on—than they cost us capital at the outset. In the short run it is not clear that takeovers of one U.S. investment place a halt on new U.S. investment even in the same country; major U.S. endeavors have continued in Peru despite the takeover of the International Petroleum Company. Given the focus of multinational firms on growth and market shares, it is quite likely that investments in alternative foreign locations would supplant investments that would have taken place otherwise in the expropriating country—perhaps a little less efficiently, with lower eventual returns to the United States. It is thus highly likely that the net effect of foreign confiscation on the U.S. balance of payments would almost always be negative.

Third World countries could also adopt a variety of measures against U.S. investment, far short of confiscation, that would hurt U.S. economic interests. Expropriation with compensation would, of course, eliminate future earnings and could

cut U.S. exports and jobs. Requirements that the local subsidiaries of U.S. firms export enough of their output to meet
targets determined by the host government, reinvest some
sizable share of their earnings, or limit their imports, could
all reduce the value of the investment to the United States.
The investment area provides unique opportunities for Third
World action geared specifically to the United States, in view
of our dominant share of foreign investment.

Third, Third World countries could undertake massive repudiation of their debts to the industrialized world if it became
unwilling to negotiate "fair rescheduling" thereof. U.S. government claims on LDCs totaled about $25 billion at the end
of 1971, and private claims other than direct investment
added another $15 billion. Foreign payments of principal and
interest on these U.S. assets were well over $2 billion in 1971.
In the wrong policy milieu, the severity of the debt burden
faced by many of these countries—many of which have
become net capital exporters—could propel them to action to
evade it. The effects on individual U.S. financial institutions,
on our overall money markets, and on the U.S. balance of
payments, could all be severe. Repudiation has already been
threatened by a number of countries and has been avoided
only because each one has succeeded in getting its debts re-
scheduled as a result.

Fourth, Third World countries could create additional economic difficulties in the industrialized world by deliberately
cutting the prices of their manufactured exports. The United
States is already seriously concerned about the effect of
imports, particularly from "low wage countries," on U.S.
jobs. But these countries might feel forced to compete even
more vigorously if they were unable to receive cooperative
treatment for their output in major international markets, or
otherwise meet their need for jobs and foreign exchange.
They would, of course, do so subtly enough to avoid early
detection and clear "blame," and only in instances where
they could expand output sufficiently to take advantage of
the price cuts in the short run and where foreign demand was
adequate to make the strategy pay over the long run.

Again, the United States might not be able to respond
through conventional measures. Antidumping duties might
be inapplicable, because the foreign market would so dominate internal demand in the Third World that the suppliers

would simply use the export price at home as well. Suppliers could also avoid countervailing duties, even under the elastic definition of "export subsidies" now applied by the Treasury, by using devaluations (including multiple exchange rates) to effect the price cuts. The United States could always react with import quotas, but quotas would almost certainly levy high costs on the United States by limiting trade with "innocent" countries, as well as the aggressive price-cutters, and in turn trigger retaliation or simply market-induced cutbacks in U.S. exports.

Fifth, LDCs could expand their exports by becoming "pollution havens." They could ignore pollution concerns in their production processes, and perhaps even foul the world environment in the process. Some major LDCs (Brazil, for example) are in fact already inviting those industries most heavily restricted by new antipollution standards in the United States to come to their countries with a promise that they will be free from the antipollution measures that are raising production costs in the United States.

These are some of the negative steps through which countries in the Third World can seriously hurt the United States. Each of these steps has already been tried and, in particular cases, has succeeded. The United States can always adjust—but the costs of doing so will become increasingly significant.

The United States also has numerous theoretical means to retaliate against such moves. Many have already been mentioned: import quotas, denial of new private investments or foreign aid, including blockage of loans by international financial institutions in which the United States has effective veto power, even overt military intervention in cases of blatant withholding of energy supplies for purposes of political blackmail. But most of these responses are only theoretical. Any LDC that undertook such actions would do so with sufficient subtlety so that tough U.S. responses would be difficult to mobilize, especially since some domestic interests (importers, consumers, exporters, other private investors) would be hurt as a result. The thought of military intervention seems remote after the domestic divisiveness of Vietnam. And, perhaps most importantly, other industrialized countries will usually be waiting in the wings with money and long-term purchase contracts—in the same way that the Japanese and European companies wasted no time entering Chile in the wake of its nationalization of U.S. firms. Neither gunboat nor dollar diplomacy will work very well for the United States in the 1970s.

Thus it is no longer clear that the United States would emerge "the winner" in confrontation with the Third World. Even if it were economically irrational for other countries to trigger such confrontations, however, this by no means rules them out. Individual LDC governments might be forced into such a posture by internal political imperatives even if the outcome was unfavorable to their "true" national interest. But the main point is that the United States would suffer significant costs even if, in some sense, it "won" a confrontation—by substituting high-cost shale oil for lower-cost Persian Gulf crude, or South Carolina cotton goods for Korean synthetics. In the long run, there will be no winners. Since the policy framework of U.S. relations with the Third World is likely to go far in determining whether such events occur, or even threaten to occur, U.S. interests would be greatly served by creating a framework in which they will not occur.

Management of the International Economic System

In addition, the United States needs positive help from the Third World on a number of issues. Achievement and maintenance of an effective international monetary system is critical to U.S. economic and foreign policy interests. Agreement among the industrialized countries is central to achieving such a system. But a majority of the Third World must also agree to any changes in the Articles of Agreement of the International Monetary Fund, because amendments to the Articles require a weighted majority vote of 80 percent and the support of 60 percent of all member countries—and the Third World holds about 27 percent of the weighted vote and well over one-half of the total membership. Beyond reform of the system, active cooperation from Third World countries will be needed to preserve its stability because of the financial power that they will wield in the future.

The United States also needs to move rapidly into a major new negotiation to reduce barriers to international trade, to promote its own export and anti-inflation interests, and to block the accelerating protectionist trend that may otherwise fill the trade policy vacuum. The LDCs are potential U.S. allies here, because of their urgent need for access to foreign markets. Yet the Third World as a whole could impede the effort by placing overriding concern on the fact that new tariff reductions on a Most Favored Nation basis would erode its own newly won tariff preferences. The large number of developing countries linked to Europe could do so to retain their own selective preferences in the Common Market. LDCs could be especially reluctant to support total elimination of tariffs, which would wholly eliminate their preferences, even though such a goal could prove necessary to dramatize the negotiations sufficiently to produce the needed political support to launch them.

Such attitudes would be a great mistake for most LDCs, since they stand to gain far greater access to developed country markets from even a modestly successful multilateral trade negotiation than from the niggardly preferences that now exist. Nevertheless, such a view could prevail unless the Third World was confident that its interest would be met sufficiently in such a global negotiation to offset the loss—for example, by giving them preferred treatment under any new "safeguard mechanism" that could otherwise choke off their new industries anytime they began to significantly penetrate a "sensitive" developed country market, and by providing generous preferences during the period when all tariffs were being phased out.

The United States should be seeking allies wherever possible on monetary and trade issues. It faces a stacked deck in the General Agreement on Tariffs and Trade (GATT), where the "one country-one vote" rule means that the European Community—the principal target of most U.S. attacks there—goes into every debate with a huge voting lead, given its own membership plus its numerous associated states. The LDCs have nine seats of the new Committee of Twenty. It should be possible to induce most LDCs to side with the industrialized world on oil and other resource issues, since they are heavy consumers who can afford price increases even less than we. Yet the LDCs can be expected to support U.S. interests only if the United States supports theirs. Even the toughest of recent U.S. negotiators have ignored these obvious sources of potential support for U.S. international economic efforts and have, indeed, launched policies that drove them to oppose us. Active engagement of the Third World in such global issues would pay the additional dividend of inducing them to accept a measure of responsibility for the functioning of the entire system, rather than leaping outside it to continue and even accelerate the policy of confrontation on "the big picture" symbolized by the creation of the United Nations Conference on Trade and Development (UNCTAD) as long as a decade ago.

The United States also needs the Third World to take more U.S. exports if it is to achieve the improvement now needed in its trade balance. Most of the other industrialized countries are basically mercantilist, unwilling to accept large enough shifts in their trade positions to accommodate the needed U.S. improvement, and strong enough to resist such shifts. Third World countries, on the other hand, can readily use additional imports as they pursue their development goals. Many of them can steer purchases to the United States—or away from us—if they want to, through their elaborate control machinery. They can only finance their additional net imports, however, through traditional forms of concessional development finance, access to private capital on terms that render neither their debt burdens nor sovereign control of their internal economies intolerable, and new modes of development finance such as the "link" to Special Drawing Rights (SDRs)—all of which require policy cooperation from the United States (and others). The two aspects of economic interdependence are here revealed most clearly: the interdependence among the various international economic issues of monetary policy, trade, and investment, and the interdependence among all countries, rich and poor alike.

Drug addiction is a critical problem in America today. Yet any of a number of LDCs can produce enough opium to easily supply the entire addict population of the United States and will find it politically difficult to avoid doing so unless their economies are successful enough to enable them to fully compensate their poppy growers. Further removed in time, yet perhaps as threatening to broad U.S. interests, is the need to avoid unbearable strain on our environment and resources by slowing the growth of world population—the vast bulk of which now occurs in the Third World, and which history demonstrates will be checked definitively only by the achievement of much higher levels of income. The list of issues goes on and on.

The Implications for U.S. Policy

There are thus a number of economic issues of critical importance to the United States on which it needs help from Third World countries; otherwise, these countries could seriously impede U.S. interests. If they are unable to achieve their own priority objectives in a constructive and cooperative milieu, they may well seek to use this emerging leverage in an atmosphere of destructive confrontation. They may even use their economic leverage to pursue political goals, exploiting their own comparative advantage, in bargaining terms, and hence intensify the potential costs to the United States of noncooperation.

Third World leverage is heightened by the possibility that they will be increasingly able to play on disputes among the members of the U.S.-Europe-Japan economic triangle in the future, as they have played on disputes among members of the U.S.-USSR-China political triangle in the past (and may again). The great economic powers will certainly strive to reconcile their most important differences and restore a stable international economic order. Even if they succeed, however, their relations will clearly be much more competitive than in the past—because Europe and Japan now compete with the United States as economic equals, because internal U.S. economic conditions will require the United States to continue to concern itself deeply with its external economic situation, and because there will be no overriding cold war issues to submerge such conflict. And it is, unfortunately, possible that the major powers will fail to resolve their differences, assuring bitter competition for Third World support.

Europe and Japan have long ago realized this fact of international life and have placed their relations with the Third World high on their list of foreign policy priorities. The Europeans are busily lining up allies throughout Africa, the Mediterranean, and the old British Commonwealth, and are even signing trade pacts in Latin America. They make no effort to hide the fact that the Third World is a focal point of their foreign policy. Japan, although hindered by its own colonial past in Asia, is making similar efforts.

In such a framework, the opportunities for discriminatory action by the Third World are magnified. They can play off one consumer of raw materials against another, one private investor against another, one exporter against another—wholly or partly in return for policies favorable to their own interests. Some of this has always occurred, some does today, and some always will. But it could become a major factor, with significant effects on the United States in the 1970s and beyond, if we continue to lag behind the rest of the industrialized world in this crucial policy area.

The United States needs to pursue its interests in the Third World through three types of policies. Their basically economic nature stems from my earlier conclustions: that the priority goals of most LDCs are economic, that the major threat to the United States from the Third World is likely to be economic, and that the policy tools with which we can respond to the Third World are primarily economic. Each would work best if carried out cooperatively by all of the industrialized countries together, to share the costs and present the strongest deterrent to aggressive Third World action.

One set of policies could include explicit or implicit hands-off agreements among the major powers in the security sphere and joint trade and aid liberalization in the economic sphere. A second type of cooperative policy, in the economic field, would aim at creating a joint defense by the industrialized countries against the potential LDC threats outlined in this article, such as a monetary system that could withstand speculative attack indefinitely by recycling footloose capital among central banks, and the presentation of joint fronts by countries that consume raw materials produced in the Third World—for a start, an Organization of Petroleum Importing Countries (OPIC) to counter the Organization of Petroleum Exporting Countries (OPEC). A third approach is to bring the Third World itself into active cooperation wherever possible and to induce it to accept the obligations that usually produce responsible behavior. U.S. policy should vigorously pursue all three approaches.

There are several different specific U.S. policies that can fit within this framework. Third World considerations should add to the U.S. interest, already strong for other reasons, for new reductions of international trade barriers. The United States should join Europe and Japan in extending tariff preferences. It should renew its effort of 1969-70 to liberalize all tariff preference schemes and go further by proposing preferential treatment for LDCs within developed country nontariff barriers. It could take the lead in expanding the scope of LDC textile exports in the coming effort to negotiate a multilateral all-fiber agreement. It should seek to improve the quality of aid by getting all donors to untie it from procurement from their own suppliers, ease its terms, and channel it through the multilateral lending institutions. It could support a "link" between world monetary arrangements and development finance,* new understandings and perhaps rules to govern the activities of multinational firms, and perhaps a higher level of concessional aid. It should get the industrialized countries to routinize consultation with the LDCs on the wide range of international economic issues that affect them directly, and consciously seek to thrust them into positions of international responsibility as rapidly as possible.

Most of these measures, especially if undertaken along with the other major industrial countries, would be very cheap. Tariff preferences would be unlikely to raise U.S. imports by more than $300 million per year; they would be temporary, anyway, if we succeeded in winning multilateral agreement to eliminate all tariffs over ten to twenty years, and we would get some offsetting additional exports in return. Our trade balance would probably benefit from multilateral untying of bilateral aid, especially now that our competitive position has been dramatically improved by the two devaluations. It makes little difference to the financing of the U.S. government whether our aid loans are for twenty-five years at 3 percent or for forty years at 1 percent. "Link" financing can be provided to the Third World with no cost to us.

Many of these steps have long since been agreed to in principle by the major countries. The Nixon administration has taken initiatives on many of them—global trade negotiations, liberal tariff preferences, untying of aid, multilateralization of aid. *The Nixon Doctrine explicitly envisages a process in which U.S. help for other countries would evolve from direct involvement through support for their own security capacity to general support for the economic base on which they can construct their own security capability, a close parallel to the process called for here. But the administration has attached inadequate priority to these issues, generally retreated in the face of domestic political opposition, and repeatedly demon-*

*The author's specific proposal was outlined in *Foreign Policy,* Number 10, Spring 1973, pp. 185-87.

strated its own structural bureaucratic weaknesses in dealing on a sustained basis with matters that it perceives to be of secondary importance. And the Congress has failed to counterbalance the absence of decisive administration leadership.

The rationale for U.S. involvement I have outlined suggests pinpointing some U.S. programs, such as bilateral aid and debt reschedulings, for those countries that could most affect U.S. economic interests. Doing this could lead to results opposite from the present pinpointing. For instance, Chile would be viewed, at least in part, as the world's major copper producer rather than as an ideological foe whose internal politics we disapproved of and which has confiscated U.S. property. Some other programs, such as trade policies and the distribution of international liquidity, could be applied to the Third World as a whole in an effort to create a constructive overall climate. The few oil "sinks" obviously need no aid, but several "normal" LDCs play an important role in the oil picture and even the "sinks" might well be susceptible to sincere efforts to provide them with roles of international responsibility commensurate with their wealth.

The main conclusion from this analysis is that the United States must, in its own national self-interest, adopt much more cooperative and responsive policies toward the Third World. This will clearly require cooperation on the part of the Third World as well, in which it accepts clear-cut responsibilities in return for the cooperation extended to it. But simple insurance principles suggest that the United States ought to spend a modest amount of resources in an effort to avoid the risks discussed above, particularly since these risks could deeply affect the great power relationships that seem likely to dominate future U.S. foreign policy.

The principles of *Realpolitik* lead to the same conclusion. U.S. leverage over countries with which it has a significant level of transactions is far greater than over those with which it has none or few. Both the stick of denial and the carrot of new assistance are then far more likely to be credible—as is abundantly clear whether we wish to negotiate about skyjacking with Cuba, naval piracy with Barbary pirates or North Korea, or terrorism with Palestinian guerrillas. We would be able far better to avoid the risks of confrontation, and to "win" confrontations if they did occur, if we had long ago taken some of the measures proposed here.

None of the specific steps suggested, nor even the whole set taken together, should be expected to guarantee a Third World hospitable to all U.S. national interests. The United States cannot buy economic concessions any more than in the past it could buy political allegiance. Indeed, hard bargaining on numerous specific issues is likely in light of the sharp increase in Third World independence and power. But U.S. policy must seek to contain such bargaining within a framework of generally cooperative relations rather than within a framework of confrontation and hostility.

In the early 1960s virtually all observers in the United States, and most abroad, erroneously projected the perpetuation of an American hegemony over the non-Communist world; this hegemony was, in fact, already being permanently eroded by the economic miracles of Europe and Japan. In the early 1970s most observers project an American-European-Japanese tripartite hegemony; yet because of the economic progress of the Third World, this hegemony, too, may become obsolete before it is ever enthroned. The future will not be so simple. It will encompass an array of actors whose significance differs across an array of issues. The Third World will play an important role in that world, and thus deserves a much higher place among the priorities of contemporary American foreign policy.

THIRD WORLD TARIFF TANGLE
by Richard N. Cooper

Along with the moon landing, the green revolution, and other major human achievements of the last decade should be included the fact that the poor countries* of the world began to grow rapidly. The criticism and complaints emanating from the United Nations Economic and Social Council, from the United Nations Conference on Trade and Development (UNCTAD), and from many foreign representatives of the poor countries leave the opposite impression, but during the sixties the so-called Third World did very well, modestly exceeding the 5 percent growth target ambitiously set at the beginning of the first Development Decade. Even after allowing for alarming increases in population, the poor countries achieved a growth in per capita income higher than the United States or the European countries did during any comparable length of time in their formative period of growth before World War I. A dozen or so poor countries did outstandingly well. We no longer fall into the simple error of equating economic growth with social development or with improvements in human welfare; but I take it for granted that economic growth in poor countries is a necessary, if not a sufficient, condition for both of these more basic aims.

This creditable performance is due in no small measure to the sharp increase in foreign aid that took place in the early sixties. But equally noteworthy is the performance of exports from poor countries; these grew by 7 percent a year in the 1960s, nearly twice the rate of 3.6 percent per year that prevailed in the 1950s. Trade thus complemented aid as a source of success.

Looking ahead, it is difficult to see how rapid growth can continue without a rapid increase in exports of manufactures, not from each and every poor country—for some of them will find it advantageous to concentrate on their tradi-

*In their search for inoffensive terms, the international agencies have progressed through "backward," "poor," "underdeveloped," and "less developed" to "developing countries" to describe the low income countries of the world, with "developed market economy countries" (DMEC) and "socialist market economy countries" (SMEC) to cover the other two groups. But "rich" and "poor" are more descriptive, so long as the discussion is clearly about income and not culture.

"Third World Tariff Tangle" was published originally in *Foreign Policy*, Number 4, Fall 1971.

tional exports, particularly in view of the increased demand for raw materials in other developing countries—but from the Third World as a whole. The press of rapidly growing populations on limited arable land will require a rapid growth in nonagricultural employment, and this points to industrialization, which is also desired both as a symbol of modernity and as an instrument for achieving it. Industrialization in turn simultaneously requires markets for its products and stimulates a demand for raw materials and for capital equipment, much of which will have to be imported. Foreign aid will assist, but it alone will be too little in quantity to satisfy the need for foreign exchange; and it has concomitant disadvantages, not least that it generates a burden of external debt. That leaves exports. Many poor countries will inevitably depend heavily on exports of traditional products for a long time to come, because they account for so large a portion— 85 percent—of present export earnings. But exports of these products will grow too slowly to do the job of financing needed imports and repaying burgeoning debt, so exports of manufactures must provide the necessary growth.

Against this background, what will be the role of tariffs in the development process? The question can be considered under two headings: tariffs in rich countries on imports of manufactures from the poor countries and tariffs in poor countries on imports of manufactures from other countries, poor as well as rich. The first of these has been the subject of intense official discussion during the last six years, in the form of a proposal for the rich countries to grant preferential tariff treatment to imports of manufactures from all poor countries. The second question has not received nearly the attention it deserves, but it has recently been the object of several careful studies in the World Bank and the Organization for Economic Cooperation and Development (OECD). I will take up first the question of tariff preferences by the rich for the poor, then the question of tariff policies of the poor countries, and will conclude by stating where I think the nature of "partnership in development," to paraphrase the title of the Pearson Report,* really lies in the area of trade policies.

Preferences for the Poor

The proposal for tariff preferences arises from the desire to stimulate exports of manufactures from the poor countries

*Lester B. Pearson (Chairman), *Partners in Development: The Report of the Commission on International Development* (New York: Praeger, 1969).

for the reasons given above, combined with an apprehension that the poor countries' exports cannot compete successfully in sophisticated markets with exports from rich countries. Tariff preferences would put manufactures from poor countries on an equal footing with domestic production in the rich markets and give them a competitive edge over exports from other rich countries.

A proposal for generalized tariff preferences—to supersede existing preferences within the British Commonwealth, between the European Community and the former French and Belgian colonies, and between the United States and the Philippines—was first advanced in the United Nations Economic Commission for Europe in 1961. Raul Prebisch listed it as one of the principal objectives of the first United Nations Conference on Trade and Development (UNCTAD) in 1964, but the proposal was then strongly opposed by the United States, Switzerland, Japan, and the Scandinavian countries. The idea simmered for several years and was subjected to study by experts. Then, at a meeting with Latin American presidents in 1967, President Johnson held out the prospect that the United States might alter its position. (This is an interesting example of how the need to say something positive at a meeting of heads of state can alter a national policy on an issue, even though the basic adverse substantive judgment has not changed.)

Attainment of generalized preferences became the rallying objective of the poor countries at the second UNCTAD, in 1968, in an effort to extract some positive achievement from an otherwise dismal proceeding. UNCTAD II resulted in a general commitment by the rich countries to develop a scheme, and by the fall of 1970 they were able to submit several proposals to UNCTAD's continuing committees.

The two major contending proposals were those of the United States and the European Community. The former called for duty-free entry of all manufactures from poor countries, except for textiles, shoes, and petroleum products, with the understanding that "escape clause" action would be used to restore tariffs on any imports that caused substantial injury to American producers. The European proposal, in contrast, was a tariff-free quota amounting, for each product, to the imports from poor countries in a base year plus 5 percent of the imports from other rich countries in the preceding year, with no designated exceptions such as those on the American list, but with certain reservations regarding cotton textiles, coir (cocoanut fiber), and jute products.

In the end, the rich countries were unable to agree on a common scheme. So each was left free to introduce its own preferential tariff treatment of imports from poor countries, subject to several general conditions. Preferences were to be temporary (ten years), and they were not to be considered binding commitments, that is, they could be reversed unilaterally at the insistence of the importing country. The European and Japanese schemes were put into effect in the summer of 1971; the U.S. scheme still needs to be submitted to Congress.

American Plan or European Plan?

An astonishing feature of this whole major effort to alter trade policy, now covering ten years, is the virtual absence of any serious analysis of tariff preferences in terms of their ultimate effects on economic development or even their proximate effects on trade flows. I know of only two detailed attempts—both made *after* the U.S. policy reversal—to estimate the effects of tariff preferences on the exports of poor countries. They differ in their methodology and in their degree of detail, but they both suggest that unlimited duty-free treatment of all exports of manufactures from all poor by all rich countries (excluding the Communist ones) would result in an increase in exports of manufactures by about 20 percent, on the generous assumption that output of manufactures in the poor countries can be expanded at constant costs. This expansion would amount to about $1.5 billion at 1970 trade levels, or about 3 percent of total exports from poor countries and about 12 percent of total net foreign assistance flows to poor countries. Somewhat more than half of this increase would arise from a net expansion of world trade, while a bit under half would represent the diversion of imports from other rich countries to poor countries.

This estimate, while small relative to total requirements, is nonetheless not negligible. But it is based on a scheme far more generous than those actually proposed. The exclusion of textiles, shoes, and petroleum products from all preferential treatment (that is, the U.S. scheme applied by all rich countries) would cut the estimated gains in half, while the

European tariff-quota scheme (applied by all rich countries) would amount *at best* to the passing back to poor countries of about $500 million to $600 million in tariff revenue now collected on the products. *At worst* (if the poor countries compete among themselves to get the limited tariff-free quotas) the European scheme might achieve nothing at all.

The European formula would achieve so little because it allows a rate of growth that is generally less than what imports from poor countries have been achieving anyway, except for those products, such as jet aircraft, for which poor countries are exceedingly uncompetitive (that is, for which they have a very small share of the market). European officials say privately that the quotas will not in fact be invoked for any but the most sensitive items, but since they can be invoked at any time, and presumably would be invoked on complaint from domestic interests, this assurance hardly provides the basis for expansion of export capacity in the poor countries, which is the immediate object of the whole exercise. Moreover, the scheme is designed to maximize trade diversion, since tariff quotas will generally prevent a fall in European prices. It thus assures that adjustment will fall on other rich countries rather than on home producers.

These remarks suggest some skepticism concerning the benefits from tariff preferences. But why not take whatever gains they make available, even if they are small? The answer is that there are also at least three costs associated with adopting a system of tariff preferences. The first arises from the cynicism revealed in the process of negotiating the preferences. Among the rich countries, only Britain favored a generalized system of preferences at the outset, and that transparently, because Britain was seeking to spread a burden that it felt itself to be bearing alone by readily accepting imports of light manufactures from poor countries in the Commonwealth, notably Hong Kong, India, and Pakistan. (In fact, both the United States and the European Community in 1961 were importing more manufactures from poor countries than Britain, and during the sixties British imports of manufactures from poor countries grew more slowly than did imports of other rich countries, with over half of the large increase in the total imports of manufactures from poor countries going to the United States alone.) Japan, as the rich country that found its own exports in closest competition with those from poor countries, understandably opposed the scheme strongly. Germany and the Netherlands were both attracted to the idea as a way to cope with French pressures within the European Community for extending preferences to an ever enlarging circle of countries in the Mediterranean area. They also had the political motive of gaining goodwill with poor countries at a time when their foreign aid programs were well below United Nations targets and below what most people thought appropriate for such important countries; such goodwill could be had cheaply so long as the United States maintained its doctrinaire opposition to preferences.

But as the poor countries increasingly made tariff preferences the acid test of a favorable disposition by the rich toward their aspirations and ambitions, thus reinforcing the search for symbolic and political gestures as opposed to solid achievements, the United States found itself increasingly isolated in opposition and increasingly uncomfortable in that role. As a result, the U.S. desire for goodwill, especially in a world more and more restive about the U.S. role in Vietnam, induced a switch in the American position, to the deep consternation of many Europeans and of Japan. But any such goodwill will be short lived when the poor countries perceive that they have been cheated, partly by their own exaggerated expectations, partly by the niggardly nature of the schemes likely to eventuate. The political gains from introducing preferences will backlash as the poor countries revert to acrimonious accusation.

A second cost associated with adopting a system of tariff preferences is that the introduction of them threatens the General Agreement on Tariffs and Trade (GATT), which laid down the basic ground rules for trade among nations in the postwar era. Tariff preferences are, of course, an outright violation of GATT's Article 1, which lays down the principle of nondiscrimination in trade and is to be set aside only in the cases of pre-existing arrangements, such as the United Kingdom Imperial Preference, and in new customs unions and free trade areas covering the bulk of trade among the trading partners. Members can collectively waive the requirement, but breaking the inviolability of the Most Favored Nation principle will open up the possibility of trade favoritism among countries unless a clear-cut and well-defined general tariff preference scheme is installed, a possibility that now seems remote.

More importantly, tariff preferences threaten to erode the restraints the GATT put on deliberalization of trade by its procedures for consultation, compensation, and controlled retaliation. The rich countries view tariff preferences as a burden, like foreign aid, and they want to waive the GATT principles on restoration of tariffs. This would be a dangerous precedent. The whole postwar effort of the GATT, largely successful, has been to internationalize trade policy, to make deliberalization difficult except under carefully controlled circumstances. But in this area the rich countries want to retain their individual freedom of action. There is even the possibility that the poor countries may end up worse than they would have been without preferences, since the rich countries might grant niggardly preferences in exchange for the removal of the GATT restraints on future import restrictions.

A third cost associated with adopting a system of tariff preferences is that, guided by noble sentiment and the politics of gesture, the rich countries have given up the principle of reciprocity as it applies to the poor countries, a gesture that is likely ultimately to redound to the disadvantage of those countries, for reasons to be discussed below.

Tariff Policy in the Poor Countries

Let us turn from this gloomy assessment of tariff preferences to the actual export performance of the poor countries during the past decade, which, as noted above, has been very good indeed. Their total exports have grown by nearly 7 percent a year, and their exports of manufactures, the object of the preferences, by over 13 percent a year, compared with less than 11 percent for exports of manufactures from the rich countries. Although some preferential arrangements between rich and poor existed during this period, the bulk of the growth took place without preferential access, while the slower but still impressive growth in exports of the rich countries was greatly stimulated by the formation of the European Economic Community and the European Free Trade Association.

It is easy enough to list the countries that have performed well and those that have performed badly: Korea, Taiwan, and Thailand are in the former category and Argentina, Brazil, and India in the latter. But is there a systematic explanation for the striking difference in performance among the poor countries?

It is an extraordinary fact that those large poor countries (over ten million in population) that have done best are generally those with only moderate tariffs on imports—20 to 40 percent on average—while those that have done badly have very high tariffs and other restrictions on imports. Moreover, there is an even stronger dichotomy between moderate and high tariff countries on other measures of performance more significant for development. The moderate tariff countries show higher rates of growth in per capita income, higher growth in agricultural output, higher growth in manufacturing output, higher growth in industrial employment, and more efficient use of capital investment. A simple unweighted average of the growth in per capita incomes in the 1960s for half a dozen moderate tariff countries was over 4.5 percent a year, compared with under 2 percent a year for an otherwise comparable group of high tariff countries. Agricultural output grew by over 4 percent a year in the former group and less than 3 percent a year in the latter.

At first blush it is perhaps surprising and merely coincidental that tariff levels are related to these diverse measures of economic performance, but, in fact, there are sound theoretical reasons why high tariffs on imports of manufactured goods should lead to these results.

The key point to recall is that the tariff discriminates in favor of certain domestic producers and that discrimination in favor of some segments of the economy automatically involves discrimination *against* other sectors. It might seem in the case of the tariff that the discrimination is against foreign suppliers, not domestic sectors. And so it is in part. But by raising prices of the tariff-ridden good, the tariff imposes a burden on all domestic users of that good. And by limiting imports of the good, the tariff leads to an exchange rate that is higher than would be required in the absence of the tariff. This second effect, in turn, both discourages exports that are not subsidized and encourages imports that are subject to lower than average tariffs.

Thus, tariffs on imports of manufactured goods will turn prices within the country in favor of manufactures and against agriculture and will encourage the importing of agricultural products—on both counts discouraging local agricultural output. And, in fact, those countries that have pushed hardest to achieve industrialization through high tariffs have generally experienced stagnation in the agricultural sector. Since the agricultural sector is so large in most poor countries, this stagnation has had a marked effect on overall growth. Recently, of course, technological changes associated with the green revolution have combined with changes in economic policy to encourage agriculture, and several countries have shown remarkable progress. But the tariff still acts as a drag. Similarly, tariffs on manufactures, by creating high cost industries and leading to a higher than otherwise exchange rate, have discouraged both exports of manufactures and exports of primary products. In some cases, to be sure, (for example, Colombia and Pakistan) extensive subsidies to nontraditional exports have offset the high costs and led to a substantial increase in exports of manufactures despite the high tariffs. But the restrictive tariff structure still discriminates against agriculture, and it biases economic activity heavily toward the misuse of capital and against the employment of labor in the growing industries.

Moreover, tariffs impede a mutually beneficial division of labor among the less developed countries themselves, virtually all of which have markets far too small to enjoy many economies of scale under competitive conditions without foreign trade. The world's sixth largest country in population, Indonesia, has a domestic market for manufactures smaller than that of Norway, for example, which has four million people.

Infant Industry: Growing Up Absurd?

Another feature of tariff policy in the poor countries frustrates the objective of achieving enlarged industrial employment. It is the practice of charging much lower tariffs on imports of machinery than on imports of other manufactured goods, the aim being to encourage investment. In consequence, the use of machinery is indirectly subsidized, encouraging capital intensive industries and leading to the substitution of machinery for labor in many activities, from construction and road building to production of manufactured goods and even farming. This helps explain the paradox in many poor countries that rapid increases in industrial output are associated with very low increases in industrial employment. The counterpart of this phenomenon is, of course, that capital is used inefficiently, in the sense that a lot of investment is required to achieve a given increase in output. Both of these developments—slow growth in industrial employment and inefficient use of capital—are especially prevalent in the high tariff countries.

I have put heavy weight on tariff policy in explaining the diverse economic performance of the poor countries. Are there other, more plausible, explanations? Three possibilities come to mind. One is close association with the United States, the protective covering of which provides a much more favorable climate for investment in some countries than in others. Moreover, U.S. imports of manufactures have been growing exceptionally rapidly in the past five years. Korea, Mexico, and Taiwan come to mind in this regard. A second factor, not wholly unrelated to the first, is the level of foreign aid and other capital inflows received by poor countries. Again, Korea and Taiwan have been especially favored in this respect compared with India, and Mexico and Israel have received large inflows of private capital in lieu of foreign aid. Finally, is it not possible that the chain of causation is the reverse of the one I have implied, from good performance to moderate tariffs, rather than the other way around?

These possibilities cannot be rejected summarily without substantial investigation. But if a special relationship with the United States is so important, why has not the Phillipines also done very well? It is, after all, the only country to receive tariff preferences from the United States (they are due to last until 1974). And if foreign aid is decisive, why has the performance of Algeria and Chile been so mediocre? These countries have received several times more aid per capita than the countries with outstanding growth performance. Finally, several countries, for example, Brazil and Korea, have lowered their tariffs from high to moderate levels (and reduced quantitative restrictions on imports), with a subsequent marked improvement in performance, suggesting that import policy does influence growth, even if there may also be some reverse causation as well.

I conclude, therefore, that there is tentative though overwhelming evidence that a relatively liberal trade policy fosters the stated economic objectives of the poor countries far better than a restrictive import policy. The conclusion is tentative insofar as alternative explanations have not been explored thoroughly; but it is overwhelming in the sense that if this view turns out to survive such exploration, the evidence for countries of moderate or large size is heavily one-sided—unlike the evidence so often produced on questions of economic and social policy.

Note that this evidence does not support a case for free trade (although the experience of Hong Kong and of other free trade zones suggests that free trade is not obviously mistaken), nor does it refute the "infant industry" argument for some tariff protection. It does suggest that tariffs in the range 20 to 40 percent on average are much more likely to be successful in achieving the aims of infant industry protection than are tariffs averaging 60 percent or above. Even such exponents of growth through import substitution—the principal objective of high tariffs—as Raul Prebisch now concede that the process has gone much too far in many countries, and therefore they urge that tariffs be lowered and rationalized.

Assurance of Market Access

I am suggesting that the economic policies of the poor countries, and especially their tariff policies, have much more to do with their economic performance than will tariff preferences, even under the best circumstances. With the wrong policies, they cannot do well even with preferences. During the past two decades Algeria, India, and the Philippines have all had preferential access to major industrial markets and this access was more generous than under a generalized scheme, for many other competing countries were excluded from the arrangements. Nevertheless, those three countries did quite badly in economic growth.

Preferences, since they give the illusion of help, divert attention away from the actions that count. Many countries have learned that high tariffs, superficially attractive because they divert home demand to home products, are in fact highly damaging to the economy, and as a result Brazil, India, Turkey, and other nations have liberalized their trade regimes and reduced their tariffs in recent years.

But a policy of trade liberalization can only succeed if the markets of the rich countries remain open to the manufactures of the poor. While tariff preferences are of tertiary importance, assured market access is of prime importance. The poor countries would get a very bad bargain indeed if in exchange for tariff preferences they gave up some of those rights under the GATT that tend to impede the deliberalization of trade, as they would if the rich countries, on their part, having granted preferences, then invoked escape clause action more readily than hitherto because of local pressures.

Moreover, although the sentiment was no doubt well intended, the rich may have done a great disservice to the poor by giving up the principle of reciprocity so that the poor can enjoy the benefits of tariff reductions in the rich countries without having to "give up" anything in return.* If the argument above is correct, to improve their performance many poor countries must reduce their tariffs sharply. But the difficulties of reducing high tariffs are well known and deep seated. For vested domestic interests get established behind them and quite understandably resist changes in policies on which they have based investment plans, however inappropriate those policies may be for the economy. The principle of reciprocity is designed to hold out the promise of export gains to certain sectors of the economy and thereby to establish a counterweight to those who will be hurt by increased imports. But if these export gains can apparently be had anyway (only apparently, because, as we have seen above, high duties hurt export competitiveness even in the absence of foreign tariffs), there is little pressure, except from the economic planners, to adopt appropriate policies. Ironically, dictatorial countries may now have a much better chance of changing trade policies than democratic ones, and we may therefore find that over the medium term the former show a much better economic performance than the latter. Reciprocity attempts to build pluralistic support for tariff reduction. Since effective reciprocity would be virtually impossible to reestablish in the light of recent history, the rich countries should continue to use the fundamentally less palatable alternative of bribing poor countries with foreign aid to adopt sensible trade policies, or, to put it more negatively, of making aid conditional on certain policy changes.

The other important thing the rich countries can do is to facilitate the restructuring of their own output, which assured market access for the manufactured products from poor

*This overstates what actually occurred, since under the Most Favored Nation principle most poor countries benefited from tariff reductions, anyway—at least if they were adherents to GATT; what was really eliminated was the need for the larger poor countries to reduce their own tariffs in exchange for tariff reductions on products of greatest importance to them.

countries will inevitably entail, by moving away from those products that they can export competitively and instead concentrating on those products—capital goods and more sophisticated manufactures—for which they have a demand that is limited only by their capacity to earn foreign exchange. This means, in particular, that a larger *portion* of our growing consumer demand for light manufactures, such as children's clothing, simple fabrics, standard shoes, unsophisticated sports equipment, and so forth, should be satisfied from those poor countries that are competitive. At the same time a larger share of the growth of the American labor force and its capital stock should be devoted to more capital intensive and technologically advanced lines of production.

In the rich countries the impact of technological change and of changes in government demand on the structure of output have been far greater than the impact of imports, even with the recent rapid growth in imports of manufactures from the poor countries. One need only mention the sharp drop in government aerospace spending in 1968-69. But the charge of "cheap foreign labor" offers all too easy a scapegoat for those who are forced to change jobs as a result of shifts in demand away from their products. So we need active market adjustment policies for both families and firms, and above all the preservation of an environment of full employment and growth in which adjustment to change is relatively less painful.

That is the real partnership, barely touched upon by the Pearson Report, between rich and poor: sensible trade policies by the poor countries and assured market access, combined with active market adjustment policies, by the rich.

MULTINATIONAL CORPORATIONS: WHY BE SCARED OF THEM?

by John Diebold

Let me begin with three assumptions:

1. During the next two decades there will be a large transfer of manufacturing industry from the three rich industrial areas of the world (North America, northwest Europe, Japan) to the poorer areas to the south. It will include manufactures of both finished goods and components for export back to the richer countries. Between now and 1993 the rich third of the world will increasingly find both economic and social reasons to move into the postmanufacturing age and to shift manufacturing to the less developed countries (LDCs).

2. The multinational corporation (MNC) will be the mechanism initially most favored for this southward transfer of manufacturing. Often the MNC will be a wholly owned American (or European or Japanese) subsidiary. There are some advantages as well as disadvantages for LDCs in this. The best strategy for a developing country should be to put itself into a position where it can choose. My guess is that if a developing country has a thriving domestic business sector, it is likely that the multinational corporations will seek it out. It will then be up to the developing country to choose the terms to allow them. The development policy that will *not* succeed will be one that stops the growth of a domestic business ethos and that then erects barriers against the participation of foreign firms—which, as a result of these factors, will not want to come in anyway.

3. In some cases, host governments will inhibit economic development, either by mistake or because they do not want it. In many developing countries, the class struggle today is really between the "new men of government" and the "new men of business" (both domestic and foreign). These "new men of government" may win the struggle in some countries, either because they have the military on their side, or because the support of the masses can be won by a mixture of economic apathy and emotional romanticism (fostered by nationalism, anticolonialism, anti-Americanism, anticapi-

"Multinational Corporations: Why Be Scared of Them?" was published originally in *Foreign Policy*, Number 12, Fall 1973.

talism, and so on). But while this scenario is convincing as a sketch of what will happen in many of today's poorer countries some of the time, it is not convincing as a sketch of what will happen in all of them all of the time. At least some of today's poorer countries are likely to climb eagerly onto the development bandwagon, and there will then be an incentive to follow them. Those leading the climb will be the "new men of business" in the developing countries. Sometimes (as in Mexico and Japan) the policy they carry through will be one that restricts the import of technology through the particular medium of MNCs; sometimes (as in Brazil and Singapore) they will be self-confidently liberal in importing technology through MNCs. My belief is that both policies will sometimes work.

Gathering Pace

Business generated by multinational enterprises outside their home countries already amounts to about $350 billion worth of goods and services a year (three-fifths of it by U.S. companies). This is one-eighth of the gross product of the non-Communist world. The proportion is increasing rapidly, because the production of MNCs seems to be expanding at about 10 percent a year. On a crude extrapolation of recent trends, one could expect MNCs to be responsible for one-fourth of the production of the non-Communist world by the early 1980s.

If the host countries continue to receive multinationals, there is a strong probability that this last figure will prove to be an underestimate. Trends suggest that the growth of multinational business activity is likely to be even faster in the near future than in the immediate past, partly because (a) American companies have mastered the techniques of multinationalism, but largely because (b) Western Europe and Japan are very likely in the period 1973-93 to follow America's 1950-70 trend and to start "exporting companies and know-how, much more than goods, to the outside world."

The essence of the first argument is that there is a certain technique in "going multinational," namely, acquiring a degree of expertise in foreign tax laws, employment customs, written or unwritten business regulations, and social and political habits. That technique was pioneered in the 1950s and 1960s by the giants and is to some extent now almost available in packaged form (especially for U.S.

companies) and is made easier by the presence abroad of U.S. chambers of commerce, U.S. banks, and the like. Smaller U.S. firms may now take advantage of this development in countries where U.S. multinational corporations are already well established.

The key statistic for the second argument is that, at present, overseas production by European and Japanese companies is less than the annual value of their exports. This was true of America until the 1950s, but now production by U.S. companies abroad exceeds U.S. exports by five to one. The U.S. multinationals' production abroad has therefore become, quite suddenly, the most important form of American involvement in the world economy. During the next twenty years it is likely that the same will become true of the EEC countries and Japan and that their investment and export of know-how—like that of the United States—will go especially to the LDCs.

Until the last few years Japan's industry has been based on high-wage big firms and on low-wage small firms from which the big firms have bought their components. The "lifetime employment" system in Japan meant that the small firms held on to their cheap labor. The big Japanese firms thus broke down their production processes into systems where component work could be subcontracted to small firms, which made these components in ways that were efficient but did not require the use of much highly skilled or well-educated craft labor. Now, however, young Japanese will not go into low-wage small firms, and wages are leveling up. The Japanese, who unlike the northern Europeans certainly do not intend to allow mass immigration of unskilled foreign workers, intend to set up these "small firm" industries in some profusion in other parts of Asia with cheaper labor. They have already begun to do so. North American and West European industrialists might do well to study (and imitate) some of the ways in which the Japanese thereby subdivide their production.

Developing countries should also study the Japanese experience. Big Japanese firms are used to dealing with large numbers of small Japanese subcontractors, which regard themselves as independent firms. Some relationships between big Japanese firms and small Japanese subcontractors are not in the subcontractors' interests (for example, credit terms, monopoly dealings, and so on), but others provide an excellent framework within which small independent firms can grow. Governments of developing countries would be well advised to study the terms under which they would like locally owned firms in their own countries to develop along this potentially profitable road. These governments should suggest the sorts of subcontract arrangements into which local firms should and should not enter. And they should then encourage maximum competition to get the contracts that seem desirable. This effort might sometimes be aided by changes in local law (including the law of bankruptcy and debt collection), local credit facilities, local import and export regulations, and so on.

Should They Want Multinationals?

The recommendations above assume that developing countries should want multinational corporations in their lands. There are stong arguments to the contrary.

The arguments of the critics need to be taken as seriously as the arguments of the proponents. But it will be convenient to discuss the latter first, concentrating on those italicized in Table 1 (see pp. 140-41). The arguments in italics are those that I take most seriously on either side.

The main advantages of multinational companies to the developing countries are said to be economic rationality, efficiency, and the growing importance of the companies as exporters. I believe that this last point is going to become the crucial one for Latin America. Experience has shown that it is wise to try from the beginning to direct industrial development in Latin America in ways whereby the new industries have incentives to keep down inflation. Export oriented industries have such incentives, because cost increases prevent the selling of more exports. By contrast, development on the basis of attempted import substitution is much more likely to breed inflation.

Unfortunately, attempted import substitution was the main-spring behind most development programs in LDCs during the 1950s and 1960s, and it helped foster inflation rates of 50 percent a year and more. The switch to inflation-countering, export-oriented production came largely with multinationals. To quote Raymond Vernon's study, *Sovereignty at Bay:*

Table 1
The Debate over the Multinational Corporation (MNC)

Its Proponents Say

1. By focusing on *economic rationality*, the MNC represents the interests of all against the parochial interests of separate nations. It is the most effective available counter to rampant nationalism. Its only political weapon is that it can remove its benefits from developing countries that are politically unreliable or confiscatorily antibusiness: and this is an incentive toward responsibility that is in the poor countries' own interests.

2. The MNC is the best available mechanism for training people in countries for modern managerial skills.

3. No more effective instrument has been found for the diffusion of technology.

4. The MNC is the most promising instrument for the transfer of capital to the developing world, and its role will be crucial in overcoming the income gap.

5. The MNC's integrated and rationalized operations in many lands make it *incomparably efficient*. It has proved to be the only really effective instrument for economic development.

6. The MNC enhances competition and breaks local monopolies. To the consumer, it provides a better product at a lower cost. To the host country it can provide a *new export industry for tomorrow.*

7. Management of the MNC is becoming increasingly flexible, sensitive to local customs, and genuinely international in fact and in spirit.

8. The MNC is an agent of change that is altering value systems, social attitudes, and behavior patterns in ways that will ultimately reduce barriers to communications between peoples and establish the basis for a stable world order.

Its Critics Say

1. The MNC removes a significant part of the national economy from responsible political control, without escaping improper political influence, including influence from the governments of the MNC's home countries. The MNC is an invasion of sovereignty and frustrates national economic policies. It fragments industries, causing proliferation without hope of consolidation.

2. *It does not train people in entrepreneurial skills*, which is what a developing country most needs.

3. The transfer of technology is often minimized because: (a) research and development is generally carried out by the parent company; (b) the training of nationals of the host country for research and development posts is often neglected; (c) the technology itself is often closely held.

4. The cost of the capital brought by the MNC is far higher than the host government would be charged as a direct borrower in capital markets. The MNC invests relatively little of its own capital and buys up foreign enterprises with local capital. The profits of the MNC are exorbitantly high and too low a proportion of them are reinvested.

5. The rationalization of production is sometimes a *tax dodge*. The MNC distorts development programs by channeling its reported profits to countries where taxation is lowest, by manipulating charges for services and transactions to disguise real earnings.

6. Its sheer size and scope represents unfair competition to local enterprises. It tends to preempt the fast growing, advanced technology industries where profits are highest, ignoring older, more competitive fields.

7. The interest of the parent company must remain dominant, and the MNC cannot ever become genuinely international. Often, the MNC has resisted genuine internationalization by declining (a) to put foreigners into management and (b) to make shares of its affiliates available to nationals of the host country.

8. Far from breaking down barriers between peoples, the MNC aggravates tensions and stimulates nationalism. Moreover, there is every indication that *these tendencies will intensify in years ahead*.

The capacity to use the less developed countries as areas of production for export appears to have been intimately related to the multinational character of the exporters. Without multinational links, the subsidiaries probably would not have increased their exports on anything like the same scale. Illustrative of that tie is the fact that although U.S.-controlled manufacturing subsidies accounted for 41 percent of Latin America's manufactured goods exports in 1966, they were responsible for less than 10 percent of Latin America's gross manufacturing value added in that year. Even more to the point was the type of goods being exported. These were the products of industries in which barriers to entry were relatively high and in which successful marketing required a relatively advanced degree of sophistication and control. As a result, the marketing process itself generally required the services of affiliates as well as the supervision of the parent.

Critics will point out that often the subsidiary does not export to its country of origin, in order to avoid competing with the parent company and causing trouble with the labor force at home. But my guess is that this will be progressively mitigated by three factors: (a) consumer tastes are becoming more and more international; (b) there is a tremendous growth of new products; (c) the educational and training revolution will make the training of labor in the LDCs a much quicker, more scientific process.

On the second point, the biggest expansion in developing countries' manufacturing for export during the period 1972-92 may well take place in new products.

The reason why new products are especially successful exports for LDCs is partly that the know-how for producing them tends to be codified in a form easily transmitted to inexperienced labor forces. But it is chiefly because these new products are developed so quickly that production begins abroad almost before U.S. labor unions and business lobbies back home are sufficiently organized to realize that such industries exist!

A greatly expanding proportion of world manufacturing production during the period 1972-92 will consist of entirely new products. When the products are not entirely new, manufacturers will pretend that they are.

My third point above is that we are on the edge of a breakthrough in the whole concept of our learning and information processes. Business will probably adapt well to the new educational technology—better, indeed, than many schools and universities—because its focus is more on results than on defending institutional methods.

The training and information revolution is likely to include a huge expansion in computer-based education. In step with this codification of the learning process, multinational computerized data banks will become available that will aid decision makers in choosing where to locate production facilities all around the world, with an eye on the trainability of labor as well as on other advantages. The head offices of MNCs will use computers to handle logistic functions (such as purchasing raw materials, services, tools, components, and equipment), to plan and control the marketability of different countries' products in third countries, to handle all credit transactions (by the 1980s most foreign exchange transactions will be carried out by multinational computer systems that link together, on line, both large and small international banks), and to codify worldwide research.

We are also moving into a world in which the price of telecommunications will no longer depend on distance. Once enough satellites are put into space, and equipment is installed, the marginal cost of making a picture telephone call to China should be no more than the cost of telephoning the office next door.

Norman Macrae of *The Economist* has suggested where these trends might lead for business organization by the beginning of the twenty-first century, when three-fifths of today's population should still be alive:

As a prototype for the most successful sorts of firm in 30 or 40 years time, it may be most sensible to visualize small groups of organizers or systems designers, all living in their own comfortable homes in pleasant parts of the world and communicating with others in the group (and with systems designers) by picture phone: arranging for the telecommunication of the latest, best computerised learning programme on how to make a better mousetrap (or, more probably, how to make the next-successor-but-five to integrated circuits) rooftop to rooftop to about 2,000 quickly trainable, even if only newly literate, workers assembled before their two-way-teaching-in computer terminals by some just tolerably efficient organising subcontractor (also taught by long-distance telecommunicated computer lessons) in West Africa or Pakistan.

The logical and eventual development of this possibility would be the end of nationality and national governments as we know them. Less and less would people live out their lives where they were born; more and more would they live where they choose. Those people working in systems-designing and knowledge-producing jobs would merely have to live "hooked into" what would become easily transportable two-way terminals to the big computer networks. Those people working in goods-producing and goods-transporting jobs would have to take on-site jobs for their working years; but probably the working year for these people would become much shorter.

However, this is looking fairly far forward toward what some people will not regard as a world utopia.

Objections to Multinationals

I suggest that the three most valid objections to MNCs in developing countries, as italicized in Table 1, are: (a) they do not encourage local inhabitants in entrepreneurial (as distinct from operative and executive) skills; (b) they often fail to carry as large a tax burden as they might; and (c) MNCs can aggravate tensions and stimulate nationalism, and there is every indication that these tendencies will intensify in years ahead.

On the first point, I suspect that there is an easy rule of thumb. If a country can tap real entrepreneurial abilities among its own people, as in Japan and Mexico, then there probably will be a sufficient inflow of licensing agreements, proposals of joint ventures, and so on, to bring about the transfer of technology on terms acceptable to local people, without letting the MNCs dictate their own terms. But I suspect that the remaining LDCs will, by the end of this century, include a sad number that have kept out MNCs on the grounds that they think they have sufficient local entrepreneurial talent, but have found no support in the world market for their view.

On the second point, I suspect that many of even the biggest MNCs may soon run into a conflict. Intracompany transfers are used to make it appear that profits do not arise in high tax countries, but rather mainly in low tax ones. It is not sensible to say that poor countries should respond to this situation by giving generous tax concessions to MNCs, because this would be a beggar-my-neighbor policy; and some are very poor beggars already. I would be in favor of poor countries banding together to give competing tax concessions to MNCs (although they should be sensible and not make the standard tax rates exorbitant either); they should also employ some commission or international referee to report when intracompany transfers to dodge taxes have occurred.

It is the last point—the aggravation of tensions and national-ism—that is the most difficult. In confronting it, we do not handle easy and computable things like market research re-ports and tax assessments but rather difficult things like emotions.

Probably the best idea for tactful operation by multinationals has come from Professor Howard Perlmutter, who classified them as ethnocentric, polycentric, or geocentric. He sees these terms not as permanently descriptive of particular companies but rather quite often as phases through which a single company may pass. He points out that to be genuinely international is a state of mind and that many MNCs are extremely ethnocentric. Perlmutter tabulates the characteris-tics of MNCs as shown in Table 2 (p. 146).

Clearly, it seems desirable to move toward the right in this spectrum. The trouble is that though this diluted solution always sounds easy to advocate, it will generally be very dif-ficult to carry out.

Nationalism and the Future

C. P. Kindleberger has argued that "the nation state is just about through as an economic unit." This view is naturally not welcome in Africa and Asia at just the moment when countries there have emerged from the colonial link and become independent nation states for the first time. The leading men in those countries have reached the top by sometimes dangerous political endeavor, and they understandably do not like to be told that the eminence they have attained is pretty pointless anyway. This is one of the reasons for an angry socialist ideology in some of these countries and in some parts of Latin America. It is one reason why the governments of some developing countries, after deciding that the "time is ripe" to set up some domestic industry (often on very unscientific evidence), then try to raise capital and other resources domestically and set up an indigenous plant—perhaps resorting, on a contract basis, to some "buying in" of technology and management ideas from abroad. The danger is that they may purchase the wrong type of production know-how and management.

Nevertheless, this feeling of nationalism has to be lived with. My conclusions and recommendations therefore begin with some suggestions for developing countries and conclude with those for MNCs.

Table 2
Three Types of Headquarter Orientation toward Subsidiaries in an International Enterprise

Organization Design	Ethnocentric	Polycentric	Geocentric
Complexity of organization	Complex in home country, simple in subsidiaries	Varied and independent	Increasingly complex and interdependent
Authority; decision making	High in headquarters	Relatively low in headquarters	Aim for collaborative approach between headquarters and subsidiaries
Evaluation and control	Home standards applied for persons and performance	Determined locally	Find standards that are universal and local
Rewards and punishments; incentives	High in headquarters, low in subsidiaries	Wide variation; can be high or low rewards for subsidiary performance	International and local executives rewarded for reaching local and worldwide objectives
Communication; information flow	High volume to subsidiaries: orders, commands, advice	Little to and from headquarters; little between subsidiaries	Both ways and between subsidiaries; heads of subsidiaries part of management team
Identification	Nationality of owner	Nationality of host country	Truly international company, but identifying with national interests
Perpetuation (recruiting, staffing, development)	Recruit and develop people of home country for key positions everywhere in the world	Develop people of local nationality for key positions in their own country	Develop best men everywhere in the world for key positions everywhere in the world

Source: *Columbia Journal of World Business* (January-February, 1969), p. 12.

The two most important determinants of events in this field will be: (1) what governments of the LDCs try to do and (2) how businessmen react. I believe that LDC governments can improve their position—to get more out of the MNCs, if you will—in a way with which businessmen can come to terms. That at least is the promise. It is to that end that I have tried to formulate my recommendations.

Recommendations for Developing Countries

These are recommendations for the governments of developing Latin American countries. Many American businessmen will disagree with them, but I think that they are realistic.

1. Gear policy to the assumption that much export oriented manufacturing production will be switched in the period 1973-93 to the LDCs, especially to countries where the domestic tone of government is not antibusiness (with the attitude to local business often being more important than that to MNCs).

2. Examine and spur the increasing possibilities for small independent firms to become subcontractors to big foreign manufacturers (with a special eye on the great opportunities and particular problems involved in being subcontractors to big Japanese industry). Test whether this "subcontracting revolution" can be aided by changes in local import/export regulations, credit arrangements, business law, and government handling of foreign contracts.

Recognize, though, that simply to require local procurement runs the great risk of encouraging high-cost production among subcontractors. Ways should be found to insure that local procurement requirements do not become a burden on the whole enterprise's ability to export competitively.

3. Do everything possible to import education and training by telecommunicated, computer assisted, and visual-aid assisted means. It may be worthwhile to buy these programs competitively from multinational service corporations, to give performance contracts to profit-making as well as to non-profit-making bodies that provide pioneer educational experiments in particular areas, and certainly to buy courses broadcast via satellites from the great universities of the world. Moreover, I believe that nutrition is a field in which it ought to be possible to hire the services of a multinational service corporation. The MNC ought to be a specially useful

instrument in the struggle to overcome malnutrition, because it combines almost all the elements needed in the search for solutions: a capacity for large-scale research and development (R & D), access to the most advanced technologies, experience in, and knowledge of, other countries and cultures, and production and marketing know-how. To improve nutrition means primarily finding ways either to raise the protein content of food that is grown or to add to it in processing. Both entail dealing with age-old tastes and preferences. Improving nutrition may thus involve developing taste for a vegetable having a texture with which the individual is unfamiliar. Or it may involve persuading a woman to alter her cooking habits and the eating habits of her family. All this requires the MNC to have local partners of exceptional awareness and imagination. The developed countries, especially the United States, have not provided incentives for doing socially useful things. I believe that one of the great challenges before the developing world is to succeed in this, a field where the developed world has largely failed.

4. Recognize that investment and production decisions will increasingly be taken on the basis of information retrieved from giant multinational and computerized data banks. Take advantage of this, and gear your policies in a way that will not unnecessarily make all these data banks list you as a country in which it is a bad risk to invest.

5. Recognize that multinational operation, rather than joint ventures, may be better initially for export oriented industries (including some extractive industries) and large-scale advanced technology industries. But these MNCs should be required to put out more and more of their subsidiary functions for competitive local tender.

6. Recognize that joint ventures can be a very good way of importing technological know-how if the developing country has a large enough local business infrastructure to have several *competing* joint ventures in the industry concerned. But if your developing country cannot thus set up competing joint ventures, then it may sometimes be better either to allow an ordinary foreign MNC to enter on generous but non-monopolistic terms (because another foreign MNC might then come and compete with it) or else try to import foreign technology on *competitive* (that is, open to tender) fee-paying, or contractual terms.

7. Do not allow protection for the home market of more than, say, 30 percent of domestic value added.

8. Try to ensure that as many local industries as possible (especially those with multinational participation) become capable of exporting competitively. Even industries the main purpose of which is to substitute for imports should not receive very high protection once they are established.

9. Do not force—or even encourage—MNCs to pay wages above the local average, because this will cost you your main international competitive advantage. Try to impose proper taxes on the MNC instead, while allowing it the advantage of cheap local labor. Also, use the taxes to improve the nonwage standard of living of your people, as through the development of infrastructure.

10. Set up a joint arbitrating mechanism to decide whether the head office of the MNC in America or Europe is dodging taxes through the manipulation of charges for services and transactions on behalf of its local subsidiary. An arbitrating mechanism will shame the MNC out of trying the most obvious dodges that do exist; rigorous unilateral searching by your country's own tax inspectors, on the other hand, will sometimes be unfair, and often be expected to be.

Recommendations for American and European MNCs

Pending the development of clear and relatively stable policies toward MNCs by Latin American governments, American and European MNCs would be well advised not to overplay their hands. While these policies may or may not parallel the recommendations outlined above, they will eventually delineate—either formally or informally—the constraints and incentives under which the MNCs will be expected to operate.

American and European MNCs currently have no effective means of speaking with one voice, even if broad consensus were to be achieved. Therefore, it is incumbent upon MNCs to operate under a set of informal ground rules such that the constraints that the governments eventually do impose, and the concessions they grant, will be most favorable.

The ground rules I suggest are far fewer in number than my recommendations for the Latin American governments. They fall under the broad caveat of avoiding the impression that the host country is exploited, particularly economically.

More specifically, the American and European MNC operating in Latin America should hire out as much work as possible to local subcontractors, repair shops, service contractors, and the like, and it should acknowledge an obligation to give local nationals a sense of participation by training and employing nationals in top management, as well as by conducting some R & D locally.

The second of these informal ground rules involves neither seeking nor accepting special concessions unavailable to local businessmen. Nor should the MNC attempt to achieve domination by buying out local companies in traditional fields long favored by local investors.

Finally, in recognition of the fact that the host country benefits more from taxes that help infrastructure development than from wage inflation for favored labor forces, the MNC must refrain from avoiding taxes by manipulating charges for services and transactions on behalf of a particular affiliate so as to disguise real earnings. The higher productivity of the MNC can thus be of benefit both to the corporation and to the host government.

ALLOCATION OF
THE WORLD'S RESOURCES

WHO GETS WHAT ON THE SEABED?

by Evan Luard

Almost five years ago the United Nations began to discuss the issue of the seabed. Only a rather optimistic observer could conclude that a great deal of progress has yet been made toward the ultimate utopia to which all aspire: "an international regime" for seabed operation. But the major conflicts of interest and attitudes among the main powers and groups have become more clearly exposed. And plans are being made for a conference next year to draw up a treaty on a system of seabed exploitation.

Why has this question so far received so little publicity? It is possibly the most important issue that has ever come before the United Nations. It concerns, after all, the ownership and control of a substantial proportion of the earth's wealth. The seabed covers 70 percent of the earth's surface, and some believe it contains resources more valuable than those remaining on land. It is thus a major matter to know to whom they belong.

The resources are situated in an area that until recently had been regarded as no man's land: an international zone beyond all national jurisdiction. But even if that were still universally accepted, what does it mean?

Can anybody pick up what he can find on the sea floor, on the theory that finding is keeping (in legal terms, that the region is *res nullius*)? This would mean that only the most advanced nations, with an advanced technology, would be able to benefit.

Does it mean that coastal states should be able to extend their jurisdiction outward indefinitely and thus reserve exploitation of resources to themselves alone? This would mean that noncoastal states would be left out altogether, while the rest would benefit according to the length of their coastline.

Or does it mean that the resources should be regarded as international, belonging equally to all, to be exploited only on an internationally agreed-upon basis, perhaps under the

"Who Gets What on the Seabed?" was published originally in *Foreign Policy*, Number 9, Winter 1972-73.

direction of some international authority set up for the purpose? Though the most widely accepted view, this raises complicated questions about what system to use.

These are the basic issues. But there are a number of related questions that are almost equally important. Should national rights in the *waters* off the coasts, that is, fishing rights, be extended outward also, perhaps to the same distance as rights in the seabed? Would this, in turn, require the extension of all other rights on the surface as well? Does the control of pollution also require the extension of national jurisdiction, or some type of international control? What limitations, if any, are necessary on military uses of the seabed? If the limits of the territorial sea are extended, how should freedom of navigation be protected in straits and other coastal waters? And so on. It can scarcely be wondered, seeing the variety and complexity of the issues, that discussion has not yet progressed very far. The real question, given the size of the stakes and the sharply conflicting interests of different nations and groups of nations, is: will it be possible to reach agreement at all? And if it is not possible, what then?

The Resources

Let us first be clear about the areas with which we are concerned. Adjoining the coast is a strip where the land slopes down beneath the sea on a relatively shallow incline, until it reaches a point where it begins to slope more sharply. That point usually comes at a depth of 130 to 200 meters, though sometimes it is at 50 meters and occasionally as deep as 500 meters. In width this strip varies from a mile or two to 600 miles, according to the steepness of the slope. The area is known by geologists as the continental shelf (remember, this is the *geological* definition—we shall consider the legal definition later). Beyond it is another area, the continental slope, where the incline is much steeper. It is relatively narrow in width, often not more than 20 miles, and extends down to a depth of 2,000 to 2,500 meters. Beyond that again, where the incline becomes shallow once more, is the continental rise, sloping down to the abyssal plain, the bottom of the ocean, which averages around 4,000 meters in depth. But this plain is far from flat, for it contains seamounts and peaks reaching to the surface of the water and trenches going down at the deepest to around 11,000 meters. The shelf, the slope,

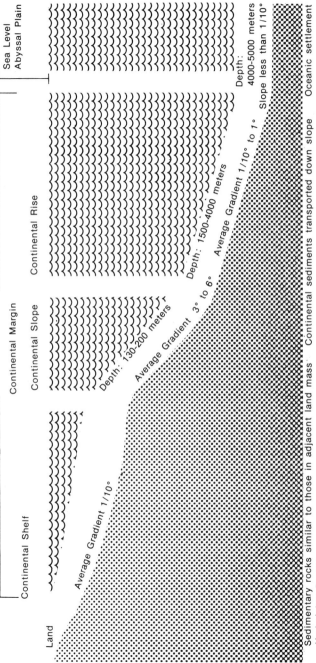

Land

Continental Shelf

Continental Margin

Continental Slope

Continental Rise

Sea Level
Abyssal Plain

Average Gradient 1/10°

Depth: 130-200 meters

Average Gradient 3° to 6°

Depth: 1500-4000 meters

Average Gradient 1/10° to 1°

Depth:
4000-5000 meters
Slope less than 1/10°

Underlying Basalt

Sedimentary rocks similar to those in adjacent land mass   Continental sediments transported down slope   Oceanic settlement

and the rise together are known as the continental margin. It is within this margin that most of the organic materials of the oceans—for example, oil and gas—are likely to be found.

What are the resources thought to exist in this area? The seabed is now known to contain a variety of materials, all of which may become economically important over the next few years. Some are at present fairly marginal. Phosphorite, a form of phosphate that can be used as fertilizer, is already recovered in some shelf areas. Deposits of tin and other minerals near the surface of the seabed have already been exploited by dredging off the coasts of Thailand and Malaysia. Diamonds are now being recovered off the coast of southwest Africa. The seabed contains magnesium and potassium, sand and gravel (which are at present the resources most widely exploited), and salt. And there are the newly discovered "hot brines," sediments that are enormously rich in a number of minerals, found where fissures in the seabed have allowed them to seep out from the earth's interior.

There are, however, two groups of resources that are of far greater significance than any of these. The first are the hydrocarbons—oil and gas—which are now being exploited at ever increasing depths. At present, most *production* takes place at depths below 100 meters, that is, well within national waters. But already *exploration* is common in waters that are 400 meters or more in depth. And by 1975 production, too, will be occurring at depths of over 200 meters.

As the depth of production increases, costs rise sharply. But there are a number of reasons why seabed production of oil, even at these depths, becomes increasingly attractive. First, a very large proportion of oil costs at present are those of transportation: seabed production, by eliminating most of these, may make up for the increased operating costs. Second, another large hunk of land production costs is represented by payments to producer governments, and these payments have risen sharply in the last few years; production in a country's own continental shelf eliminates them. Third, there are important balance-of-payments savings for the consumer country if it can produce oil in its own shelf area. Finally, there are obvious strategic gains for a nation that can minimize its dependence on external sources of oil. For all these reasons, an increasing number of oil companies are now extending production into deeper water. In so doing they will shortly be reaching out well beyond the basic limits of national jurisdiction laid down in the 1958 Convention on the Continental Shelf.

These trends are even more important in relation to gas. There is no real danger, despite the cries of the more strident environmentalists, that land sources of oil will be rapidly exhausted. But in the case of natural gas resource exhaustion is a genuine possibility, at least in certain areas. The United States at present consumes more than half the world's natural gas, which is drawn mainly from domestic sources. But U.S. deposits will be almost exhausted within a decade or so. There will undoubtedly be a big switch to undersea supplies.

Another seabed resource may be of still greater significance: the so-called manganese nodules. These are small potato-sized lumps of metal, irregular in shape, brownish or black in color, which are scattered about large parts of the seabed, especially in the deeper areas, in the Pacific, Indian, and Atlantic oceans. Though they are largely composed of relatively unimportant minerals such as iron and silicon, the nodules also contain considerable proportions of more valuable metals—especially manganese, but also copper, nickel, and cobalt. They are scattered in such profusion that, once satisfactory processes are devised for dredging them up, and for separating out the different minerals, they could be as important a source of supply as are mines on land. Dredging apparatus that has already been designed and demonstrated, both by Japanese and American companies, is capable of bringing up nodules from 3,000 and 4,000 meters, in volumes sufficient, it is claimed, to make production profitable. Similarly, it is claimed that processes for separation have been devised that would make possible the extraction of more valuable minerals at a competitive cost. One U.S. company, Deep Sea Ventures, believes that it will be in a position to begin regular production by 1975. Japanese companies are making equally optimistic predictions. If such production were to begin, it could soon account for a considerable proportion of the total supply of these metals. It could possibly, even allowing for increases in consumption, eventually displace land sources. If so, it could have a disastrous impact on the economies of those countries, mainly developing nations, that are dependent on the production of these minerals.

Those are the resources. To whom do they belong?

Traditional international law is not really very helpful. Until recently, few countries were interested in asserting rights in seabed areas. It is only in the last twenty years or so, therefore, that international law has begun to consider the matter at all.

Rights in the seabed were long thought to be synonymous with those on the surface of the sea, extending to three, six, or twelve miles from the shore, according to whatever were the claims maintained by the coastal state. From the last century onward, the coastal state was also accorded certain rights in the subsoil beyond its coast, for example, if it wanted to sink tunnels or to lay cables, so long as freedom of navigation was not affected. Only at the end of World War II were more sweeping claims in the seabed made.

In 1945 President Truman asserted, on behalf of the United States, claims to exploration and exploitation rights (but not sovereignty) within the "continental shelf." This term was not exactly defined, but was assumed to correspond with the geological shelf. There was little opposition to this move at the time. And, indeed, many other coastal states followed suit.

But since the geological shelf was an extremely imprecise term, it began to be important to formulate a more exact definition of the limits of national rights. Accordingly, from 1950 on, the International Law Commission began to consider the terms of a convention that would give a legal definition to the continental shelf. What finally emerged was the Convention on the Continental Shelf, which was then adopted at the Conference on the Law of the Sea in 1958. The definition was unfortunately highly ambiguous. The area was to be "adjacent to the coast," whatever that meant, and within the 200-meter depth limit. But it went on to qualify this in a way that left it open-ended: "or beyond that, to where the depth of the superjacent water permits of exploitation." In other words, a country could claim the continental shelf up to any depth, it seemed, so long as exploitation was possible there.

This qualification seems to have been intended to cover the cases where there is a deposit of oil that lies partly within and partly beyond the 200-meter line. It confirmed the rights of the coastal state in such a situation and prevented a company from a technologically advanced state's suddenly appearing to suck such a reservoir dry from the outer side. But if "adjacency" was loosely interpreted, it could allow the coastal state to extend its shelf indefinitely until it reached the midpoint of the ocean, or to go even beyond that (so long as it could exploit) to the point on the opposite side, where the next coastal state was able to do the same thing. Or so at least some maintained. One effect was that small islands, such as St. Helena, would be able to claim vast areas of the sea floor, if only they could find a company to operate on their behalf.

Advances in undersea technology in the last few years have made havoc of this definition. If nodule dredges come into operation that are capable of operating in waters of 3,000 or 4,000 meters depth, any coastal state might be able to claim, on the basis of the 1958 definition, large parts of the ocean bed lying off its coasts, on the basis that they could, if necessary, be exploited. The whole seabed, and all its vast resources, could thus conceivably be parceled out *to the complete exclusion of the noncoastal states.*

This was only one, though perhaps the most important, of a number of issues concerning boundaries. Another concerns the surface of the water. Over the last twenty years a number of states, especially in Latin America, have asserted claims to fishing rights, other jurisdiction, and in some cases sovereignty, to a distance of 200 miles. China has now joined this group. They argue, with some plausibility, that, since the United States and other countries made unilateral claims to neighboring resources on the sea floor some twenty-five years ago, why should they not do the same in relation to sea resources today? Some of them have few shelf or seabed resources, but have particularly valuable fishing grounds off their coasts.

Other problems concern the limits of jurisdiction for the purposes of pollution control (Canada has recently claimed a 100-mile limit), rights of navigation through straits, rights of navigation for warships in territorial waters and straits, rights of archipelago countries to draw boundaries around the outermost parts of their islands, the right to claim shelf areas based on small islands (Britain has recently asserted claims of sovereignty over Rockall, a tiny speck of rock in the Atlantic, in order to be able to claim the extensive shelf areas that slope from it, while Japan, China, and Taiwan are in conflict over some uninhabited islands in the China Sea for the same reason), and so on. These and a few other questions (the right to archaeological treasures in the seabed is a picturesque example) are now under discussion in the Seabed Committee.

In short, there is no lack of complicated and contentious legal issues. But the most basic problem of all concerns the regime for seabed exploitation.

The Debate

During the 1960s there was increasing concern over various isolated aspects of the seabed issue. Pollution, fish conservation, and other problems began to be discussed in various UN bodies. Unofficial organizations, in the United States and elsewhere, began to debate the wider problems. But it was not until Malta raised the problem as a whole in the General Assembly of 1967 that many governments, especially those of developing countries, became conscious of its importance.

In that year the United Nations set up an Ad Hoc Committee on the seabed, which surveyed the problem in general terms, commissioned secretariat studies, and finally recommended the establishment of a permanent Seabed Committee. Today, with 91 members, it comprises over two-thirds of the UN membership. This scarcely makes for efficient conduct of business, but it reflects the degree of interest that is felt on the issue.

Fundamental differences, in views and interests, have been revealed during the discussions of the committee. The poor countries generally want a strong system of international control, with high royalty payments to the authority, and maximum redistribution to the world community. The rich countries have laid stress on the need to secure adequate "incentives" for exploration and production and have favored a looser system with the minimum of bureaucratic control and maximum freedom for operators. The Soviet Union and its allies, consistently hostile to all extensions of international authority, have taken perhaps the most narrowly nationalistic attitude of all.

But there is another division of interest that is even more basic than that between rich and poor: that between the coastal and the noncoastal states. The coastal states inevitably favor wide boundaries, to ensure that as large a proportion as possible of the most valuable seabed resources (situated in the continental margin) is reserved for themselves. Noncoastal states (including states with very short coastlines) naturally demand the opposite: they want maximum redistribution from the maximum area. Some have proposed a seabed boundary of forty miles from the coast.

Despite these divisions there are some points that have been fairly widely agreed upon. All States accept that there *is* an international area beyond the limit (whatever it is) that coastal states may reasonably claim: in other words, that the coastal states cannot simply grab the whole seabed. All accept that an international seabed authority should be established with overall authority over this area (though, not surprisingly, there is sharp dispute about the powers it should have and the voting system it should use). Most agree that within the area there should be a system of licensing of seabed zones by the authority, either to states or to companies. It is generally accepted that these licenses would be granted for limited periods, subject to the payment of royalties, and would be conditional on an undertaking to exploit the area during that time at a certain level of production or rate of investment. Everybody agrees that there should be strict obligations to observe pollution and safety standards, and to preserve freedom of navigation in areas where exploitation is taking place. And there is widespread acceptance that there should be an international inspection system.

But this leaves a large number of major points in dispute. The varying views on a structure have been reflected in the proposals put forward by each nation and group, including the draft treaties which began to appear last year in considerable profusion. The most fully international system was proposed by the Latin American group, which wanted an operation by an international enterprise in the international area. Tanzania proposed that decisions be made by a two-thirds majority in the authority, with each nation having one vote, with the distribution of royalties to all states in inverse proportion to UN contributions. Britain and France each proposed highly nationalistic systems, with a division of the seabed by blocks to states, and with governments taking most of the responsibility in the areas awarded to them. The Soviet Union and Poland supported an authority with highly restricted powers, and decisions within it by consensus, subject to veto (but the proposals of these two were not identical; Mongolia, Czechoslovakia, and Hungary, landlocked states, have also taken a somewhat independent line).

The most interesting and original plans are those of the United States and Malta. Each of these provides for a kind of intermediate zone between the national continental shelf and the international zone proper. In this zone the coastal state would retain considerable powers, including that of choosing the operators, but would make payments to the seabed authority for operations. This is a system highly favorable to coastal states (as each of these is). But if the outer limit of the intermediate zone was not too wide (and the United States has indicated its willingness to negotiate this), it could in fact have some advantages. Some international revenues (though the proportion going to the international system should be higher than the United States has so far proposed) would be secured for all operations outside the 200-meter line (the narrowest possible limit) and would become available for redistribution.

In 1970, after two years of negotiation, the Assembly approved (with only thirteen abstentions, including the Communists) a Declaration of Principles concerning the seabed, which was intended to serve as a guideline for future exploitation and as the basis for a treaty. Though some of the principles were vague and ambiguous, others were specific and significant. The resources of the seabed were for the first time explicitly recognized as the "common heritage of mankind," a recognition that will perhaps preclude attempts at national appropriation, either by the extension of coastal state jurisdiction or on the basis of discovery. It was stipulated that exploitation should be for the benefit of all mankind, especially developing countries, thus implying the need for a system of royalty payments for international redistribution. But the most important provision was that exploitation would only be undertaken in accordance with an agreed-upon "international regime"; and governments would ensure that persons and companies under their jurisdiction complied with that regime. This seemed to rule out unilateral measures, either by governments or by companies, to stake out claims in the seabed before a treaty had been agreed upon. A few Western governments reserved their rights on this point; it might, therefore, still be possible for governments deliberately to obstruct agreement on a regime and to claim that, as a result, they had been released from this undertaking. But the Declaration of Principles represents at present a relatively firm commitment by the governments of the rich countries not to permit the companies now being formed for seabed exploitation to operate in the deeper areas (where most of the nodules are) until an international system has been negotiated. It will be instructive to see how vigorously this commitment will be implemented by the governments concerned in the coming years.

The second decision made in 1970 was to call a full-scale international conference, "in 1973 if possible," on the law of the sea and the international regime. This is a vast agenda, including all the most controversial questions of sea law, which have remained undecided for years, from the width of the territorial sea to the huge and complex question of a seabed regime. Much of the committee's time since then has been spent on preparing for the conference, though it has only just managed to reach agreement on the list of subjects to be discussed, let alone begun discussing the terms of the articles and conventions themselves. It is thus difficult to believe that a constructive conference on these issues could take place by next year. For such a conference to succeed, all except the most basic issues would have to be largely tied up in advance, and that stage is a very long way off. It is likely that there may be a series of conferences in coming years. In this case it might be possible to have a preparatory conference in 1973 which could reach agreement on the procedures to be followed.

The Key Issues

Whenever the conference takes place, a clash is certain to occur. What will be the main points in dispute?

On some issues, the beginnings of a compromise can be discerned. On the breadth of the territorial sea, there has been a strong move in the last few years (outside Latin America) toward a general acceptance of twelve miles. The rich nations will probably have to accept the idea of some kind of "economic zone" or "preference zone" in which the coastal state would have exclusive or preferential rights for fishing, and perhaps for seabed resources as well. There is an increasing disposition to define the continental shelf, that is, the limit of coastal jurisdiction over seabed resources, in terms of distance rather than depth; and it is theoretically possible and politically attractive (especially to many developing countries) to provide the same limit for seabed rights as for fishing. Such a limit might be set at fifty miles from the coast. Rights of free navigation within that area would have to be preserved and defined.

This would be the simplest, and perhaps the best, type of solution on limits. It would represent a reasonable compromise between the minimalists, at present holding out for a three-mile territorial sea and freedom of fishing beyond, and the maximalists, which claim limits of two hundred miles for all purposes. And it would be a fair assessment of the interest that coastal states can legitimately claim.

More difficult problems surround the nature of the international regime. First, the authority clearly cannot be established on the basis of majority voting and one nation, one vote (if only because the big powers would not enter at all on this basis); but neither should any nation or small group of them (as under the U.S. proposals) exercise a veto. The simplest solution is to have a council of perhaps thirty nations, elected on the basis of geographic representation, and including adequate representation for noncoastal states, and to require, say, a four-fifths majority for any decision. This would maximize consensus without allowing vetoes or weighting votes.

Harder still are the questions relating to the scale of royalties and the system of redistribution. There is a lot to be said for the intermediate zone system suggested by the United States and Malta. This zone might stretch from fifty to one hundred miles from the coast; in it, the coastal state would retain some degree of control, but would pay a considerable part of the royalties to the international authority. The effect is to reduce the sharp division between the national and the international area. This lessens conflicts on boundaries by asking coastal states to *share* resources rather than to forego them altogether.

There are two questions that will be of vital importance. One of these concerns the system of licensing. It is now widely assumed that there will be direct licensing to governments, which will in turn license companies. This reflects the fact that it is governments that are deciding the question. But it is, in fact, the worst possible system. It would provide a multiplicity of separate regulations and jurisdictions in a peculiar patchwork all over the seabed. It would make effective pollution control difficult to enforce. It would maximize disputes over the boundaries of seabed blocs. Above all, it would maximize the power of the big companies. They would be in the position of selling their skills to 135 different governments, most of them totally without technological capability, thus competing desperately with each other to secure the companies' services. If, on the other hand, licenses went directly from the authority to the companies, the negotiating position would be reversed; the companies would then be competing with each other to acquire concessions from the authority. This latter method is therefore the way that would maximize revenues for the international system and for the international community generally. It would be a pity, and a tragic irony, if the nationalist pretensions of developing governments to acquire their own little pocket-handkerchiefs of seabed had the effect of putting them at the mercy of the big corporations which they say they most fear.

The second vital question concerns the outer limit of national control. Here there is an absolute conflict of interest between the coastal and noncoastal states. There is a real danger that the coastal states, perhaps encouraged by the Latin American example, may increasingly jump on the 200-mile bandwagon to grab the largest possible proportion of the resources for themselves. This would largely exclude the noncoastal states from sharing in the benefits, at least in oil and gas, for the foreseeable future. It will thus be an interesting test whether some of the bigger developing countries, such as Brazil, Argentina, and Chile, are willing to show in their policies the same concern for small and poor neighbors that they demand the rich countries show them. Landlocked countries already have serious economic problems of their own. They are mainly very poor: of the twenty-five "least developed" countries recently defined by the United Nations, about half are landlocked. If they are to gain any benefit from resources that cannot reasonably be regarded as the property of any one state, it is essential that the limit not be too wide. The 50-mile limit suggested here is roughly the average distance of the 200-meter depth line from the coast all over the world and would thus seem a reasonable compromise.

The system that would bring the greatest benefit to developing countries in general would therefore be one that provides for a narrow boundary and for licensing direct to companies. This is also the system that would represent the most significant step forward in the present international system. The opportunity is provided here to establish for the first time a form of international control of common resources. This could secure rational utilization, the preservation of the international environment, and redistribution to poorer countries. In a sense, if the rich countries were prepared to be farsighted and generous, an embryonic form of international socialism would come into operation.

It would be unrealistic, however, to hope that any government decision is likely to be much influenced by idealistic concern for the international community. It is one of the tragedies that here, as in other cases, decisions that are of vital concern to the world as a whole will be reached only by national governments, concerned only with national interests, conceived in the narrowest terms. But even national decision makers may be conscious of the need to set up a system that will prove stable and secure. Such a system can exist only if it has obtained the goodwill of most governments of the world. Consensus, therefore, remains important. It is a mistake to think that all the cards are in the hands of the rich governments: it is doubtful, for instance, if any company will be enthusiastic about undertaking production if it is likely to find itself challenged in its rights by a large section of the international community—and perhaps by navies acting on their behalf?

The rich countries, as well as the poor, will have to give as well as take if a viable seabed system is to come into operation.

NEW DEAL OR
RAW DEAL IN RAW MATERIALS
by Theodore H. Moran

Strong feelings of economic nationalism have been giving many countries that produce raw materials both the occasion and the courage to kick the foreign investor out. Huge multinational corporations are losing their mines, wells, or plantations to nationalists in the underdeveloped countries and seem almost powerless to prevent it. The companies involved —in copper, iron, or petroleum, in rubber, bananas, tea, or timber—often got their toehold in the heyday of old-fashioned imperialism. And so it comes naturally to many observers to look on approvingly, if not with secret glee, at the turnabout: if United Fruit is pushed off the plantations in Central America, if Union Minière is nationalized in the Congo, or Anaconda and Kennecott are nationalized in Chile—hurrah!

Customarily, the first question then must be: can these nationalistic countries, reaching at last for a kind of economic "independence" in their raw materials industries, manage to maintain an efficient production process? Could General Ovando or his successors resist the temptation to reward supporters in the Bolivian army by filling the former Gulf Oil offices with members of their families? If the foreigners in the mines of the Roan Selection Trust desert Zambia, can President Kaunda find enough Zambian technicians to replace them? Will President Velasco have better luck than American Smelting and Refining or the International Petroleum Corporation have had in controlling political strikes in Peru's major unions? Maintaining efficient production and keeping costs low would clearly seem to be concerns of first importance for the new economic nationalists. They may have to devote all of their attention to this. If those countries that are struggling in their own terms for a kind of independence cannot keep their efficiency at the production stage, then they may indeed be killing that famous goose that laid the extraordinary eggs.

"New Deal or Raw Deal in Raw Materials" was published originally in *Foreign Policy*, Number 5, Winter 1971-72.

But the relationship between economic nationalism and the multinational corporations is more complex than the traditional fears or hurrahs would suggest. Even if economic nationalists can manage to surmount the problems of maintaining efficiency at the production stage, they may still find that they have not gained their independence—rather they are more "dependent" than ever. Perhaps they have too easily accepted the conventional Marxist argument that large industrial societies need the raw materials of the Third World and will collapse without them. This has led the nationalists to assume that by controlling the sources of raw materials, they would be in a position of consummate strength. More properly, the argument should be that the large industrial countries need secure sources of raw materials so badly that they will pay the price of neutralizing economic nationalists who threaten to upset the old and dependable system.

The internal dynamics of the multinational firms that have lost out to, or been threatened by, economic nationalism are already beginning this process of neutralizing the nationalists' position. Most of the international enterprises in the natural resource business are complex, vertically integrated corporations. They control all the stages of their industry from production, through refining and processing, to fabrication and distribution to the various consumers (they now sell either to their own subsidiaries or to established customers by means of long-term contracts in semicontrolled world markets). And they have not merely been standing still and weeping over their losses to the current wave of economic nationalism. With neither malice nor conspiracy, they have been acting to the extent of their powers to protect themselves.

The large multinational corporations are by no means all-powerful. But they still have the ability, in many cases, to shift the greatest benefits of various industries away from the production stage over which they are losing control to other stages over which they exercise more influence, and to shift the greatest burdens and costs of the industry onto the nationalistic "independents." In the decade of the 1970s we may well see the large industrial countries and their international corporations paradoxically appear to win from this movement of economic nationalism, and the primary producers of the Third World will lose.

What determines the relative strength of the economic nationalist vis-a-vis the multinational corporation when the former displaces the latter at the production stage of a raw materials industry? What are the powers of multinational corporations to shift profits to another stage of their operations outside the range of the economic nationalist, or what are the powers of economic nationalists to exploit their position as strong and equal members of an international oligopoly?

The present article will analyze precisely this question: is it reasonable to expect a kind of "independence" for many countries the primary products of which have until now been controlled by foreigners, or is it more likely that economic nationalists will find themselves facing new forms of "dependence," perhaps worse than anything they have experienced in the past?

1. Vertical Integration: A Success Story

No two industries in the natural resources field are identical. But the success of most primary product oligopolies—from tropical agriculture through ferrous and nonferrous metals to oil and petrochemicals—has come from their uninterrupted vertical integration. In the past, multinational companies controlled, and could count as their own, all the stages from the mines or wells or plantations, through processing and fabricating, to the distribution and sales to final consumers in the large industrial countries. The profits (or "surplus") generated by such a system—whether accruing to private stockholders or providing funds for public welfare and national development—have come, and will continue to come, from the restriction of competition and the maintenance of vertical integration.

Many of the large and powerful multinational corporations that have traditionally handled the international flow of raw materials began at the production stage with control over bananas or tin, copper or oil. They gradually worked themselves toward vertical integration—expanding to include refining and processing stages, and then fabricating plants. Finally, they moved to control, make "orderly," the marketing and distribution channels to consumers in the major industrial countries. Frequently the process was reversed: companies that refined or fabricated or consumed moved backward to secure their own sources of supply. Many of the new entrants to the natural resource oligopolies at the production stage have come from among the final users of the product that have integrated backward, often with the support of their governments. From whichever direction, the movement was toward a totally integrated corporation. The Anaconda Company, formerly the largest of all natural resource firms outside of petroleum, is a good illustration of both processes: in copper, nickel, and molybdenum, the company has been moving forward from mines through processing; in aluminum, the company has moved from fabricating back into securing its own sources of bauxite in the Caribbean. Anaconda's slogan, "From Mine to Consumer," would fit closely the operations of many other multinational corporations.

To understand the limits within which economic nationalists can maneuver in exercising their hard-won "autonomy" at the production stage, it is necessary to examine the rationale for vertical integration. The justification for vertical integration might better be described as a kind of risk avoidance than as a straightforward profit maximization. Whenever the producers or consumers of raw materials were faced with the threat of being at the mercy of oligopolists at some stage they did not themselves control, they acted to insure themselves against that risk.* In times of slack demand, producers do not want to face a few strong buyers at the processing or consumer stage. In times of heavy demand, processors or consumers want to be assured of steady, dependable sources of supply—sources at least providing them with the same relative supply as is had by their competitors—and they, too, do not want to be at the mercy of a monopolistic producer or group of producers.

Sometimes the easiest way to insure against the risk of suddenly facing a monopoly is to buy into the next stage upstream or downstream of one's operations. The result is vertical integration through formal ties of ownership. At other times informal patterns of vertical integration can be established through "loyal buyer-seller ties" at producers' prices, through long-term contracts, and through joint financing. Inelasticities of supply and demand shift bargaining power

*This process can be represented in profit-maximization terms: the company estimates the expected reduction in profit that might result from the oligopolistic threat and measures that reduction against the expense of removing the threat.

abruptly from buyer to seller and back again. To hedge against this risk, even producers and consumers that have no ties of ownership between them prefer to trade in established patterns and are willing to pay a premium or accept a discount, at various stages in the business cycle, in order to preserve the informal system of vertical integration. John Tilton,* for example, has found that most sales in aluminum, bauxite, copper, lead, manganese, tin, and zinc are based on stronger and more dependable ties than merely price considerations.

This examination of the rationale for vertical integration in natural resource industries has two crucial implications for determining the position of the economic nationalist who takes over the production stage in his country. If the stage he has taken over is sufficiently competitive that he can never be a monopolist, then there is no incentive for a processor or consumer to maintain ties with him rather than buying from alternative suppliers; if the stage he has taken over is sufficiently noncompetitive that he can always behave like a monopolist, then there is equally no incentive for a processor or consumer to maintain ties with him rather than integrating backward and developing alternative supplies.

Between these two extremes lies the promise of success for the economic nationalist. At the two extremes lies the danger to the economic nationalist—and the promise of new forms of "dependence."

2. Profit Where Profit Is Due

It is possible, then, to begin to generalize about what determines the relative strength of the economic nationalist vis-à-vis the vertically integrated multinational corporations with ties that are being broken at the production stage. What are the powers of the multinational corporations to shift profits to another stage of their operations outside the range of the economic nationalist, or to shift most of the burdens and risks of the international industry onto the new "independent" producers?

* John E. Tilton, "The Choice of Trading Partners: An Analysis of International Trade in Aluminum, Bauxite, Copper, Lead, Manganese, Tin, and Zinc," Ph.D. thesis, Yale, 1966; a shorter version with the same title was published in *Yale Economic Essays*, VI (Fall 1966).

Table 1
Banana Acreage in Central America:
United Fruit

	Guatemala	Honduras	Costa Rica	Panama
1963	20,749	20,971	27,737	31,000
1966	7,350	25,618	21,046	26,322

Source: Henry Arthur, James Houck, George Beckford, *Tropical Agribusiness Structures and Adjustments—Bananas* (Boston: Harvard Business School, 1968), p. 53.

The attempt to make broad statements about many different industries is always hazardous. But the principle involved in all cases is initially simple: the relative strengths of the economic nationalists or the multinational corporations in the international industry depend upon who controls the stage where the greatest barriers to entry are located. Once this question is answered, it is necessary to go on and examine whether, in those cases where the economic nationalists do control the crucial stage in the industry, they can successfully exploit their position of strength.

In industries where there are no great barriers to the entry of competition at the production stage—such as bananas, sugar, or coffee, for example—the nationalizations of farms or plantations will not give the economic nationalist a very great position of strength. Until the mid-1950s the United Fruit Company was totally integrated vertically from plantations in Central America through transportation, importation, and distribution of bananas to wholesale ripeners in the United States. In response to nationalistic pressures, United Fruit began to sell back many of its plantations in Guatemala and Panama to domestic farmers or to the government (see Table 1). It then supplemented its remaining plantations with purchases from independent producers in the open market at competitive prices. In 1963 United Fruit needed to purchase 23 percent of its requirements on the open market; in 1966 the company did not happen to need any open market purchases to supplement its own output. In short, most of the burden of fluctuations in supply and demand was passed entirely onto the share of the market represented by competitive independents. The parent company, meanwhile, kept control of the crucial stages of organizing transportation and distribution of this perishable commodity.

With other industries, the point of oligopoly control lies neither at the production stage nor at the marketing and final distribution stage, but rather at the refining or processing stage. In the production of aluminum, for example, the techniques and scale of capital involved in refining the ore are the important factors in determining the barriers to the entry of competition. In reducing bauxite to alumina to aluminum, the amounts of capital necessary to build huge sources of electrical power—complete with dams or coal fields and railroads—as well as to construct the newer processes of smelting and refining, narrow the possibilities of "autonomy" for Jamaica or Guinea. The bargaining position of these countries vis-à-vis large vertically integrated corporations such as Alcoa or Pechiney is not strong, even though their raw ore bases are relatively rich. These same factors partially explain Bolivia's problems in nationalizing the tin industry from the Hochschild or Patiño interests after the 1952 "revolution." The complicated Bolivian ores still had to be smelted at plants in England or Texas City, Texas, controlled by the former owners, who were now busy developing new competitive sources in Thailand, Malaysia, and Indonesia.

Thus, the relative power of multinational corporations and economic nationalists depends upon where the greatest barriers to entry lie in the vertical chain from mine or plantation to processor and distributor. One can predict, then, how multinational corporations will react when faced by the growing wave of economic nationalism. The corporations will try to shift the bulk of the profits generated within the system to a stage over which they still have firm control, and they will try to shift the burden of the uncertainties and risk in the industry onto the new "independents." Nationalists who have been tied into a corporate system stretching into the large industrial markets may take over the production stage only to find themselves members of an increasingly competitive and highly volatile impersonal market.

Faced with such a prospect, the economic nationalist may well find that his best strategy is to remain a part of the integrated corporate system, while playing a careful game of tax brinksmanship to recover as large a share of the system's profits for his government as he can. He is aided in this respect by United States tax law which encourages corporations, especially in Latin America, to realize as much of their profits as possible within the jurisdiction of the underdeveloped countries.*

3. Copper and Oil: Negotiating From Strength

Tropical agriculture, tin, and aluminum have the crucial stage that establishes the oligopoly power of the industry outside the reach of the economic nationalist. What about raw materials industries where the greatest barriers to entry exist at the production stage?

Those countries that control the stage where the crucial barriers to entry are found—as in the production of copper or oil—should be in a position of great strength. And the initial evidence indicates that indeed they are. Tax rates have, in general, risen in nationalistic countries that produce oil and copper; thus, the local competence and bargaining position of the governments of Iran and Libya, Chile and Zambia have increased (see Table 2). In the copper industry, during the Vietnam war the major copper exporting countries—Chile, Peru, Zambia, and the Congo (the CIPEC** countries)— shifted their pricing away from various corporate producers' prices to a soaring open market price and enjoyed an old-fashioned bonanza. They then imposed an excess profits tax on the producing corporations in order to retain the overwhelming bulk of the profits in the integrated system for themselves. In short, they successfully presented the companies and the consumers with concerted monopoly power at the production stage and won out.

More recently, the major oil exporting countries—from Venezuela through Iran (the OPEC† countries)—have taken advan-

---

*The deferral feature of the Foreign Tax Credit in effect provides subsidiaries of U.S. businesses with an interest-free loan amounting to the U.S. tax liability of unremitted profits. In less developed countries, the absence of a "grossing up" requirement on the Foreign Tax Credit means that taxes paid to a host government relieve a company of much more of its tax liability than taxes paid to the U.S. government. Finally, special provisions for Western Hemisphere trading corporations reduce the U.S. tax liability of companies operating in Latin America by 14 percent.
**Intergovernmental Council of Copper Exporting Countries.
†Organization of Petroleum Exporting Countries.

Table 2
Host Country Share of Pre-Tax Profits
of Foreign Investors in Raw Materials Enterprises

	Venezuela (Oil)	Chile (Copper)
1930	*	16%
1940	58%†	28%
1950	51%	58%
1955	52%	69%
1960	68%	65%
1965	66%	69%‡

*Not available. Probably less than 30 percent.
†1943.
‡1964.

Source: Raymond Vernon, "Foreign Enterprises and Developing Nations in the Raw Materials Industries," *The American Economic Review*, Vol. LXI, no. 2, May 1970, p. 125, compiled from R. F. Mikesell, ed., *Foreign Investment in the Petroleum and Mineral Industries: Case Studies of Investor-Host Country Relations* (Baltimore: Resources for the Future, Inc., The Johns Hopkins Press, 1971).

tage of European fuel shortages, the closing of the Suez Canal, and climbing tanker rates to threaten European consumers with a cutoff of supplies. The result of the Tehran agreements of 1971, granting higher taxes to the producing countries, will be to increase revenues from petroleum by the fantastic sum of $11 billion to an eventual $23 billion per year.

But the political dynamics of nationalism have pushed some of the copper producing countries (Zambia, Chile, the Congo) not just to drive a harder bargain from a position of strength vis-à-vis the companies and the industrial consumers, but to nationalize the foreign corporations and take control of their own destiny. The same process seems to be starting with Algeria and Venezuela in the oil industry. And the trend will certainly accelerate well before the Iranian Consortium oil concession ends in 1979. Will the countries that control the stage of a vertically integrated industry where the barriers to entry are highest be successful in maintaining their position of strength?

The answer depends upon the ability of their state agencies and national governments to play the delicate game of the international oligopolist.

4. Playing by the Rules

To join and preserve an oligopoly, one must play according to its rules. The rules of the international copper and oil industries are to prevent dilution by new entrants, especially on the part of processors or consumers integrating backwards, and to extract oligopoly profits while avoiding making the customers (or their capitalist or socialist governments) feel that they are facing an intolerable situation of monopoly power at a stage that they do not control. Whether economic nationalists such as Libya or Peru, Iran or Chile come to occupy a strong position within the international oligopoly depends upon how scrupulously they learn the rules of the industry and build their own formal or informal ties of vertical integration into the large (socialist and capitalist) industrial markets. To do this they must establish themselves as dependable sources of supply that do not use every bit of monopoly power at every phase of the industrial business cycle. The alternatives are to destroy the oligopoly and lose its lucrative benefits or be excluded from the oligopoly and have the bulk of its risks and uncertainties shifted onto them.

As we have already seen, established customers are a very valuable asset to a producer of oil or copper; a steady source of supply is a very valuable asset to the customer. Only in classical economic theory were goods pictured as being bought, sold, or exchanged in a market place. In reality, the multinational corporations in the oil or copper industries invest a great deal of time and effort into creating dependable sales positions. Producers are willing to charge less for secure outlets. Their customers are willing to pay more for relatively secure sources of supply. It is not enough for buyers and sellers to try to meet casually in the commodity exchanges. In times of high prices and extreme shortages, anybody can sell copper or oil. To survive the vicissitudes of the business cycle, however, and to insure a steady and dependable growth of sales require formal or informal ties of vertical integration into the markets of the large industrial consumers. An integrated system obviously has real costs, since, as Tilton observed, the participants do not buy and sell as they would if they were acting only according to price. But such extra cost has historically been worth the price to the members of the oligopolies and to their governments, objectively or subjectively, in terms of avoiding risk.

In an industry that values vertical integration, a nationalistic producer must offer his buyers the same appeal as a private corporate producer and at a cost that does not induce the buyer to become a producer himself. The oligopoly member exerting every strength he has at every moment of time will become the supplier of last resort. Even if he is successful in inducing some other members to follow his lead, then substitution, the development of alternative sources, the backward integration of consumers to new ore bodies or new oil fields will all work to dilute the oligopoly. In short, the nationalistic producer, like the corporate producer, must skillfully and successfully play the oligopolists' game, where everybody loses if one member tries to make a sudden move to increase his own advantage, but everybody wins if all can act together.

But the possibility of playing the delicate oligopolists' game is particularly difficult—perhaps even impossible—for those countries where the politics of nationalism have already carried them to the point of closing in on or taking over the oil or copper industries. Governments in power keep office, and opponents try to take office, by showing that they can squeeze more out of the prominent national export industry than has been done before. In the short run, such claims are often correct. A government in power would have trouble explaining why it frequently accepted producers' prices in copper lower than that in the free market, or why it did not use every bit of market power in the oil industry whenever it had the chance. And parties out of power, or economic groups eager for foreign exchange and added revenues, would find it easy to exploit this issue in national politics. In short, the politics of nationalism push the government to the point of confronting the consumer with the full force of monopoly power at every stage of the industrial cycle.

In the copper industry, Zambia, Chile, Peru, and the Congo left the corporate producers' price during the Vietnam war, when that price was low, and tried (unsuccessfully) to raise their price to the level of the corporate producers' price when it was high. In such a situation, it is clear why the nationalists slowly become suppliers of last resort—they offer fabricators and consumers no incentive to establish ties with them. Even the open market is preferable to a producer that always confronts his buyers with the full strength of his position. Consumers try to buy from the integrated system of corporate producers as fast as the companies can expand output, and they are constantly tempted to integrate backward to the production stage themselves. As the international copper oligopoly becomes more diluted, more and more of the "regular" sales or long-term arrangements will be covered between the large corporate producers and their major fabricators or industrial consumers, while the nationalists' share will be treated as a spill-over market—subject to great fluctuations in volume and price. Onto the nationalistic independents will be shifted the burden of risk and instability for the international industry as a whole.

In the oil industry there is a great deal more leeway for the nationalistic producers (from Venezuela or Algeria to Saudi Arabia and Iraq) to raise the share of the profits that accrues to them without challenging the structure of the entire industry. At the same time, the final price of fuel oil (for the consumer) could be raised quite a bit before there is a widespread possibility of substitution by coal or nuclear power. Powerful interests associated with European coal, natural gas, and nuclear power had a strong influence in the acceptance of higher fuel oil prices at Tehran in 1971, overshadowing the welfare of European consumers as a whole. But the Tehran accords showed the reality of what has previously been only a nightmare—the strategic vulnerability of industrial countries that face the risk of suddenly being at the mercy of monopolistic producers.

It is difficult to predict when the interests of an industrial government and the interests of its largest multinational corporations will coincide, when a government may intervene to protect an Anaconda or a United Fruit. But it is much less difficult to hypothesize that industrial governments, like industrial consumers, do not like to be faced with the risk of monopoly power upstream from their central operations. It is likely that the policies of the industrial countries will increasingly encourage or subsidize the restructuring of international industries by multinational corporations to suit their (joint) needs. The desire to avoid facing a monopolist has, of

course, been the rationale for stockpiling, first during war-
time and then on a continuing basis, by the United States and
the United Kingdom. Given their experience with the copper
and oil industries, other European countries have been seriously considering the possibility of stockpiles (including petroleum) to increase their bargaining power vis-à-vis these
nationalistic producers, and they have been considering the
possibility of subsidizing their domestic corporations (as the
Japanese already do) to develop alternative sources in "secure" areas from Canada to Australia and Indonesia. At the
same time, socialist or Communist state trading agencies
outdo their capitalist counterparts in desiring to avoid risk, to
insure the dependability of suppliers. In any but the shortest
run and for the materials least important to an industrial
economy, both capitalist and socialist governments will act
to neutralize the risk of facing a monopolist.

The result could be the worst of all possible worlds for the
economic nationalists: a dilution of the international oligopolies together with the relegation of the nationalists to the
position of a spill-over market onto which has been shifted
the bulk of fluctuations and risk for the entire industry.

5. Learning to Live with Economic Nationalism

Any rational oligopoly strategy—whether under state or private corporate control—consists of profiting from barriers to
entry by keeping prices high, of collecting an economic rent
from final consumers through control over scarce resources
or scarce techniques of production. In a vertically integrated
oligopolistic industry, the policy implications for the
economic nationalist depend upon where the crucial barriers
to entry are located.

Where the barriers to entry in a vertically integrated industry
lie outside the control of a nationalistic government, taking
over the production stage may only destroy the benefits of
the corporate oligopoly for the country. A better strategy is to
negotiate over the taxation of corporate profits to the extent
possible for the corporations to stay and increase their
production.

Where barriers to entry lie within the control of the nationalistic government, the interests of the country are best served
by maintaining its place within the international oligopoly
(alone or in joint venture with the original corporation) and by

playing carefully according to the rules. The extent to which this is in fact possible, given the dynamics of the politics of nationalism, remains to be seen.

The foreign minister of Chile under President Allende, Almeyda, addressed the United Nations on behalf of many countries when he claimed that the large industrial societies do not understand economic nationalism or the drive for independence that is now taking place in the underdeveloped regions. But the future in the age of the low profile could prove to hold not Hickenlooper retribution but economic irony: the economic nationalists may well come to suffer from the fact that the industrial nations do learn to live with economic nationalism—in fact, learn to live with it too well.

Without determined effort on the nationalists' part, the future will hold new forms of dependence and domination. They are the ones who must now learn to live with their own economic nationalism and national pride. Their future depends upon whether they can develop the institutions and the capabilities necessary to lead a strong, interdependent economic existence.

IS THE OIL SHORTAGE REAL?
OIL COMPANIES AS OPEC TAX
COLLECTORS

by M. A. Adelman

The multinational oil companies have become, in the words of the board chairman of British Petroleum (BP), the "tax collecting agency" of the producing nations. In 1972 these companies operated the greatest monopoly in history and transferred about $15 billion from the consuming countries to their principals. If the arrangement continues, a conservative estimate for 1980 collection is over $55 billion per year. Much of that wealth will be available to disrupt the world monetary system and promote armed conflict. Oil supply is now much more insecure. Monopoly, the power to overcharge, is the power to withhold supply. Among nations, an embargo is an act of war, and the threat of an oil embargo ushered in the Organization of Petroleum Exporting Countries (OPEC).

The oil companies are now the agents of a foreign power. They will be blamed for impairing the sovereignty of the consuming countries, and quite unjustly. They only did the will of the OPEC nations and of the consuming countries themselves, notably the United States. The consumers' "strange and self- abuse" is the key to how the events of 1970-71 turned a slowly retreating into a rapidly advancing monopoly.

The most important player in the game is the American State Department. This agency is deplorably poorly informed in mineral resource economics, the oil industry, the history of oil crises, and the participation therein of the Arabs with whom it is obsessed; in fact, State cannot even give an accurate account of its own recent doings.

Prediction is unavoidable but risky. In 1963 I thought that, abstracting from inflation, a price of $1 per barrel at the Persian Gulf was not unlikely fairly soon. In terms of 1963 dollars it did go to 92 cents by early 1970. As predicted, supply remained excessive, and the companies could not control the market. But on the political side, the prediction went all wrong in 1970-71. Although I had warned that the producing countries might threaten a cutoff of supply, and urged insurance against it, I was much mistaken to call it an unlikely

"Is the Oil Shortage Real? Oil Companies as OPEC Tax Collectors" was published originally in *Foreign Policy*, Number 9, Winter 1972-73.

event. Nor did I expect the consuming countries, especially the United States, to cooperate so zealously.* I may be equally wrong to expect that consuming countries will continue this way for most or all of the 1970s.

The unanimous opinion issuing from companies and governments in the capitalist, Communist, and Third Worlds is that the price reversal of 1970 and 1971 resulted from a surge in demand, or change from surplus to scarcity, from a buyers' to a sellers' market. The story has no resemblance to the facts. The 1970 increase in consumption over 1969 was somewhat below the 1960-70 average in all areas. The increase in 1971 over 1970, in Western Europe and Japan, was about half the decade average. In the first quarter of 1972, Western European consumption was only 1.5 percent above the previous year. By mid-1972, excess producing capacity, a rarity in world oil (that is, outside North America), was almost universal and had led to drastic government action, especially in Venezuela and Iraq. The industry was "suffering from having provided the facilities for an increase in trade which did not materialize." A drastic unforeseen slowdown in growth and unused capacity would make prices fall, not rise, in any competitive market.

Some powerful force has overridden demand and supply. This force did not enter before the middle of 1970, at the earliest. Up to that time the trend of prices had been downward, and long-term contracts had been at lower prices than short-term contracts, indicating that the industry expected still lower prices in the future, even as far as ten years ahead.**

If demand exceeds supply at current prices, sellers and buyers acting individually make new bargains at higher

---

*My publications summarized are: "Les Prix Pétroliers à Long Terme," *Revue de l'Institut Français du Pétrole,* December 1963; (trans.) "Oil Prices in the Long Run," *Journal of Business of the University of Chicago,* April 1964. Price evolution: See Ch. 6, Appendix, of *The World Petroleum Market,* Resources for the Future, 1972. Supply cutoff: U.S. Senate, Subcommittee on Antitrust and Monopoly of the Committee on the Judiciary, *Government Intervention in the Price Mechanism,* 91st Cong., 1st sess., 1969.

**Growth rates and price trends: *The World Petroleum Market,* Ch. 8; *BP Statistical Review of the World Petroleum Industry; Petroleum Press Service,* June 1972, p. 222. Quotation from "Presentation to a Meeting of Financial Analysts in Tokyo on Friday, May 12, 1972," by F. S. McFadzean, managing director of Shell.

prices. When supply exceeds demand yet prices are raised, the conclaves, joint actions, and "justifications" are strong evidence of collusion, not scarcity.

More precisely: in a competitive market, a surge in demand or shrinkage in supply raises price because it puts a strain on the productive apparatus. To produce additional output requires higher costs; unless compensated by higher prices, the additional output will not be supplied.

If there were increasing long-run scarcity at the Persian Gulf, discoveries falling behind consumption, the reservoirs would be exploited more intensively to offset decline, and to maintain and expand production. More capital and more labor would be required per additional barrel of producing capacity. In fact, between 1960 and 1970 (the last year available), the investment needed per unit of new crude oil capacity fell by over 50 percent, despite a rising general price level. Labor requirements (which are both for construction and operation) have fallen even more drastically. Supply has not only not tightened, it has been getting easier.*

The world "energy crisis" or "energy shortage" is a fiction.** But belief in the fiction is a fact. It makes people accept higher oil prices as if they were imposed by nature, when they are really fixed by collusion. And sellers of all fuels, whatever their conflicts, can stand in harmony on the platform of high oil prices.

---

* *The World Petroleum Market*, Ch. 2 and Ch. 7. For later data, see my paper, "Long Run Cost Trends" in John J. Schanz, ed., *Balancing Supply and Demand* (1972).

**The United States "energy crisis" is a confusion of two problems. First, environmental costs are slowing down electric power growth and threatening blackouts. The worse the slowdown, the less the drain on fuel supply. Second, there has been gradual exhaustion of lower-cost oil and gas resources in the Lower Forty-eight States. Natural gas deserves special mention, for the world has been deeply impressed by American business executives and cabinet members rocketing about the world like unguided missiles in search of gas supplies, particularly coming hat in hand to beg gas of the Soviet Union. One folly has led to another. Prices of American natural gas have been held at a level well below what would clear the market, generating a huge excess demand, all channeled overseas. Import prices have soared and will probably rise further if domestic price-fixing is not abolished. Profits to the overseas producing nations who own the gas will be lush. American companies have tried to arrange deals and obtain a part of the gains; American government officials have helped the stampede. The gas shortage could be abolished by the simple expedient of abandoning price ceilings. Gas might still be imported, but at lower prices, in smaller amounts. The strain on coal and oil resources would actually be less, since higher domestic prices would increase domestic supply of natural gas.

Table 1
Persian Gulf Production and Reserves
Zero Discoveries Model, 1971-85

1971			
Production		6	BBY
Reserves		367	BB
Production/Reserves		1.6	%
Reserves plus 50 percent		550	BB
1971-85			
Average Growth per year	8	11	%
1985			
Production	17	25	BBY
Cumulative 1972-85	143	178	BB
Remaining	407	372	BB
Production/Reserves	4.0	6.7	%

BB = billion barrels
BBY = billion barrels per year; a billion = one thousand million.

Source: 1971 production and reserves, from *Oil & Gas Journal*, December 31, 1971.

Twenty years ago, the Paley Commission made the classic statement of the problem: "Exhaustion is not waking up to find the cupboard is bare but the need to devote constantly increasing efforts to acquiring each pound of materials from natural resources which are dwindling both in quality and quantity. . . . The essence of the materials problem is costs."

It is worth assuming arbitrarily that supply will tighten in the future. The worst that can happen is zero new discoveries. Table 1 shows Persian Gulf production and reserves in the zero-discoveries model, recognizing that reserves in fields known in 1971 can be expanded by development and discoveries of new pools in the old fields. The assumption of 50 percent expansion is highly conservative in the light of American experience, considering also that probably most Persian Gulf reserves (like most production) are in fields discovered in the last twenty years.

In 1950 Persian Gulf reserves were estimated at 42 billion barrels, mostly in eight large fields still producing today at ever higher rates with no peaking out. In 1951-71 inclusive 47 billion barrels were extracted. At the end of 1971 reserves were 367 billions, mostly in twenty-six large fields, including

the original eight. On the basis of production, one may estimate that nearly half the reserves are in fields operating in
1950, nearly a fourth in fields discovered in 1950-59, between
a fourth and a third in 1960-69 discoveries, which have the
greatest expansion potential (reserve data from *BP Statistical
Review of the World Oil Industry* and *Oil & Gas Journal*).

Production growth in 1971-85 is estimated first according to a
recent BP forecast of 7.7 percent, which takes account of
rising U.S. imports, to come mostly from the Persian Gulf.
Doubtless also it registers, as does a Shell forecast, the ces-
sation of growth in European imports as North Sea oil and
gas takes over.* Indeed, Persian Gulf shipments to Europe
will probably be lower in 1980 than in 1972—rising and then
falling in the interim. But to be on the safe side, we also estimate 1972-85 production by extrapolating the long-time
growth rate.

The cumulated production 1972-85 is subtracted from expanded end-of-1971 reserves. The higher the production-reserve ratio, the higher is cost, all else being equal. The zero-
discoveries model is drastic to the point of absurdity. Moreover, it sets to zero the reserves of African and Persian Gulf
natural gas, which at current prices are worth producing, and
which equate to an additional 90 billion barrels oil equivalent.
Even so, the 1985 production-reserve percent is much lower
than is planned for similar, that is, high capacity, reservoirs
in the North Sea or Alaska, which are usually in the range of 7
to 11 percent.

Depletion of reserves at the Persian Gulf is only about 1.5
percent a year. It is uneconomic to turn over an inventory so
slowly. But Persian Gulf operators have not been free to expand output and displace higher cost production from other
areas because this would wreck the world price structure.
Therefore, it is meaningless to average production-reserve
ratios for the whole world, as is too often done. A barrel of
reserves found and developed elsewhere in the world is from
five to seven times as important in terms of productive ca-

---

*Assume that American imports from the Persian Gulf rise at a constant per-
centage rate from 310 TBD (thousand barrels daily) in 1971 to 10 MBD (million barrels daily) in 1980 and to 15 MBD in 1985. Then cumulative imports
are 7.5 billion barrels through 1980 and 23.4 billion through 1985; respec-
tively, 2 percent and 6 percent of end-of-1971 Persian Gulf reserves. In the
next fifteen years many times more than these amounts will be developed
into new reserves, even if there are zero discoveries of new fields.
McFadzean, op. cit., Chart 11 on Western Europe.

pacity as a barrel at the Persian Gulf. In other words, one could displace production from the entire Persian Gulf with reserves from one-fifth to one-seventh as large. And this is perhaps the only constructive aspect of the current drive for self-sufficiency in oil. This zero-discoveries model yields a much higher production-reserves percent, hence a substantial increase in investment requirements and current operating costs per barrel. Today at the Persian Gulf, capital and operating costs are each about 5 cents per barrel; under our extreme assumptions, they are roughly double. The difference between 10 and 20 cents measures the value of discovering new fields: it takes the strain off the old.

No Basis for Fears

The zero-discoveries model only estimates the worst that could happen; it is not a prediction of what will happen. When the procedure was applied in 1965, current and projected costs were higher than they are now, since many new discoveries have freshened the mix, not to speak of improvements in technology.

There is no more basis for fears of acute oil scarcity in the next fifteen years than there was fifteen years ago—and the fears were strong in 1957. The myth that rising imports (of the United States) will "turn the market around" is only the latest version of the myth that rising imports (of Europe and Japan) would "dry out the surplus in 1957-70."*

More generally: supply and demand are registered in incremental cost, which is and long will be a negligible fraction of the current crude oil price of about $1.90 per barrel. Hence, *supply and demand are irrelevant to the current and expected price of crude oil.* All that matters is whether the monopoly will flourish or fade.

In Europe and Japan there was a mild and temporary shortage of refining capacity in early 1970. At the same time, a tanker shortage put rates at the highest level since shortly after the closing of the Suez Canal and raised product prices.

In May 1970 the trans-Arabian pipeline was blocked by Syria which sought to obtain higher payments for the transit rights, while the Libyan government began to impose pro-

*M. A. Adelman, *The Present and Future State of the World Oil Industry* (lectures, Japanese translation) (Petroleum Association of Japan, 1965), pp. 11-33, and *The World Petroleum Market*, Ch. 2; also National Petroleum Council *U.S. Energy Outlook*, Vol. 2 (1971), pp. 41-53.

duction cutbacks on most of the companies operating there, to force them to agree to higher taxes. Although the direct effect of the cutback and closure was small, the effect on tanker rates was spectacular, and product prices and profits shot up.

The companies producing in Libya speedily agreed to a tax increase. The Persian Gulf producing countries then demanded and received the same increase, whereupon Libya demanded a further increase and the Persian Gulf countries followed suit. Finally, agreements were signed at Tehran in February 1971, increasing tax and royalty payments at the Persian Gulf as of June 1971 by about 47 cents per barrel, and rising to about 66 cents in 1975. North African and Nigerian increases were larger. In Venezuela the previous 1966 agreement was disregarded and higher taxes were simply legislated. These taxes are in form income taxes, in fact excise taxes, in cents per barrel. Like any other excise tax they are treated as a cost and become a floor to price. No oil company can commit for less than the sum of tax-plus-cost per barrel.*

Government-Company Harmony

The multinational companies producing oil were amenable to these tax increases because as was openly said on the morrow of Tehran, they used the occasion to increase their margins and return on investment in both crude and products. In Great Britain the object was stated: to cover the tax increase "and leave some over." And the February 1971 tax increase was matched by a product price increase perhaps half again as great. The best summary of the results was by a well-known financial analyst, Kenneth E. Hill, who called them "truly an unexpected boon for the worldwide industry."

Mr. Hill rightly emphasized product price increases, but arm's length crude prices also increased by more than the tax increases. When the producing countries made fresh demands later in 1971, an American investment advisory service (United Business Services) remarked that tax increases were

---

*Tax is calculated as follows: output multiplied by posted prices equals fictional "receipts." Production costs are subtracted, and, however calculated, they are very small. The difference is the fictional "profit," which goes usually 55 percent to the nation. Thus the tax per barrel is completely independent of actual receipts, and only very slightly affected by costs, hence almost completely independent of profits. Therefore, it is an almost pure excise tax.

actually favorable to óil company profits. And 1971 was easily the best year for company profits since 1963, although there was a profit slide off later in the year, as competition in products—though not yet in crude—again reasserted itself.

The price pattern is set for the 1970s. From time to time, either in pursuance or in violation of the Tehran-Tripoli "agreements," the tax is increased, whereupon prices increase as much or more, but then tend to erode as the companies compete very slowly at the crude level and less slowly at the products level. Thus, prices increase in steps; yet at any given moment there is usually a buyer's market, that is, more is available than is demanded at the price, which is under downward pressure.

The companies' margin will therefore wax and wane, but they benefit by the new order. They cannot, even if they would, mediate between producing and consuming nations. As individual competitors, they are vulnerable to producing-nation threats to hit them one at a time. As a group, they can profit by a higher tax through raising prices in concert, for the higher tax is that clear signal to which they respond without communication. The Secretary General of OPEC, Dr. Nadim Pachachi, said truly that there is no basic conflict between companies and producing nations. The then head of Shell, Sir David Barran, spoke of a "marriage" of companies and producing governments. Most precise of all was Sir Eric Drake, the chairman of BP, who called the companies a "tax collecting agency," for both producing and consuming country governments. There is, however, a difference in kind between serving a government in its own country to collect revenue from its own citizens and serving a government to collect revenue from other countries.

Leading Role of the United States

Without active support from the United States, OPEC might never have achieved much. When the first Libyan cutbacks were decreed, in May 1970, the United States could have easily convened the oil companies to work out an insurance scheme whereby any single company forced to shut down would have crude oil supplied by the others at tax-plus-cost from another source. (The stable was possibly locked a year after the horse was stolen.) Had that been done, all companies might have been shut down, and the Libyan government would have lost all production income. It would have been helpful, but not necessary, to freeze its deposits abroad. The OPEC nations were unprepared for conflict. Their unity would have been severely tested and probably destroyed. The revenue losses of Libya would have been gains to all other producing nations, and all would have realized the danger of trying to pressure the consuming countries. Any Libyan division or brigade commander could consider how he and friends might gain several billions of dollars a year, and other billions deposited abroad, by issuing the right marching orders.

Failure to oppose does not necessarily imply that the United States favored the result. But there was unambiguous action shortly thereafter. A month after the November agreements with Libya, a special OPEC meeting in Caracas first resolved on "concrete and simultaneous action," but this had not been explained or translated into a threat of cutoff even as late as January 13, nor by January 16, when the companies submitted their proposals for higher and escalating taxes.*

Then came the turning point: the United States convened a meeting in Paris of the OECD (Organization for Economic Cooperation and Development) nations (which account for most oil consumption) on January 20. There is no public record of the meeting, but—as will become clear below—there is no doubt that the American representatives and the oil companies assured the other governments that if they offered no resistance to higher oil prices, they could at least count on five years' secure supply at stable or only slightly rising prices.

The OECD meeting could have kept silent, thereby keeping the OPEC nations guessing and moderating their demands for fear of counteraction. Or they might have told the press they were sure the OPEC nations were too mature and statesmanlike to do anything drastic, because after all the OECD nations had some drastic options open to them too . . . but why inflame opinion by talking about those things? Instead, an OECD spokesman praised the companies' offer and declined to estimate its cost to the consuming countries. He stated that the meeting had not discussed "contingency arrangements for coping with an oil

*Neither *The New York Times* nor *The Wall Street Journal* in their stories on the subject (January 14, 17, 19, 1971) had any reference to any retaliation or concerted action on the proposal.

shortage." This was an advance capitulation. The OPEC nations now had a signal to go full speed ahead because there would be no resistance.

Before January 20 an open threat by the OPEC nations would not have been credible, in view of the previous failure of even mild attempts at production regulation in 1965 and 1966. But after the capitulation, threats were credible and were made often. (This is clear from a careful reading of the press in January and February 1971.) They culminated in a resolution passed on February 7 by nine OPEC members, including Venezuela but not Indonesia, providing for an embargo after two weeks if their demands were not met. The Iranian Finance Minister, chief of the producing nations' team, said: "There is no question of negotiations or resuming negotiations. It's just the acceptance of our terms." The companies were resigned to this, but wanted assurances that what they accepted would not be changed for five years.

The United States had been active in the meantime. Our under secretary of state arrived in Tehran January 17, publicly stating his government's interest in "stable and predictable" prices, which in context meant higher prices. He told the shah of Iran the damage that would be done to Europe and Japan if oil supplies were cut off. Perhaps this is why the shah soon thereafter made the first threat of a cutoff of supply. It is hard to imagine a more effective incitement to extreme action than to hear that this will do one's opponents great damage.

Resistance to the OPEC demands would have shattered the nascent cartel. As late as January 24 the shah told the press: "If the oil producing countries suffer even the slightest defeat, it would be the death-knell for OPEC, and from then on the countries would no longer have the courage to get together."

When the Tehran agreement was announced, another State Department special press conference hailed it, referring many times to "stability" and "durability." They "expected the previously turbulent international oil situation to calm down following the new agreements." They must really have believed this! Otherwise, they would not have claimed credit for Mr. Irwin or for Secretary Rogers or have induced President Nixon's office to announce that he, too, was pleased.

They must have said this in Paris in January and again at an OECD meeting in May. We now live with the consequences.

State Department representative James Akins told a senate committee in February 1972: "The approach we made in the Persian Gulf [was] primarily because of the threat to cut off oil production. . . . We informed the countries that we were disturbed by their threats, and these were withdrawn very shortly after our trip." The public record outlined above shows that the threats of embargo began after the under secretary's arrival, culminated in OPEC Resolution XXII.131 on February 7, *and were never withdrawn*.

Scraps of Paper

The oil companies knew better than to take the "agreements" seriously; they had been there before. To be sure, one could cite many a statement by an oil executive about the "valuable assurances of stability," but this was ritual. The London *Economist*, always in close touch with the industry, expected any agreements to last only a few months, given the "persistent bad faith." The best summary was made by *Petroleum Intelligence Weekly*: "If such agreements were worth anything the present crisis wouldn't exist."

This was borne out in August 1971. Devaluation of the dollar, the occasion for new demands, was, of course, an incident in the worldwide price inflation to which the Tehran and Tripoli agreements had adjusted by providing for periodic escalation. Moreover, Persian Gulf revenues were mostly not payable in dollars. The new element in the situation was not the increased dollar cost of imports to the producing countries, but the fact that prices in dollars increased, especially in Germany and Japan. This was another windfall gain to the companies, just as in early 1970. Again the producing countries were able to take most of that gain in the consuming countries because the multinational companies were the producers of oil as well as sellers of refined products.

The "oil companies had hailed the agreements as guaranteeing a semblance of stability in oil prices . . . they would seek to pass on the impact of any new cost [tax] increases." The new demands, said the chairman of Jersey Standard (Esso, now Exxon), were a violation of the Tehran agreements, but "the industry will solve these problems just as our differences with them were reconciled earlier this year and before," that is, higher taxes and higher prices. This was precisely correct both as to substance and as to ritual. The OPEC governments made their demands. The companies made an offer. The governments refused it and broke off the talks. The companies made a better offer, taxes were raised again, and crude oil prices with them.

Even before this deal, the producing nations had already made an additional demand, for so-called "participation." The companies said they were distressed that the agreements "have not led to the long peace . . . that they had anticipated." They would resist the demands as a violation of the agreements. Whereupon the governments "announced that they would take part in a 'combined action' if they didn't receive 'satisfaction,'" and the companies agreed to negotiate. In March, the Aramco companies, which account for nearly all output in Saudi Arabia, conceded participation "in principle."

"Participation," recently negotiated by companies and various Arabian governments, is a misnomer. "Pseudo-participation" would be more apt. "Participation" does not mean that the government actually produces or sells oil or transfers it downstream for refining and sale. As we shall see later, selling oil is what Saudi Arabia wisely aims to avoid. "Participation" is simply an ingenious way of further increasing the tax per barrel without touching either posted prices or nominal tax rates, thus apparently respecting the Tehran agreements. Once the tax increase is decided, everything can be cut to fit. The same oil is still sold or transferred by the same companies. On the terms discussed early in 1972, "participation" would mean about 9 cents more tax per barrel.* Those who believe that this assures supply, stable prices, and a solution to the balance-of-payments problem will believe anything.

There has been unparalleled turbulence since the State Department special conference. Venezuela dispensed with the

*The concession company and host government need to determine four items: (a) the government owes the concessionaire a certain sum per year to cover the amortized cost of the equity share; (b) the government loses the taxes it formerly received on the share it now "owns"; (c) the concessionaire owes the government the "price" of the oil that the government owns and that it now "sells" to the company; (d) the concessionaire owes the government its pro-rata share of the year's profits of the operating company. The subject of the negotiation is by what amount (c + d) shall exceed (a + b). The 9 cent estimate is from *Petroleum Press Service*, April 1972, p. 118.

elaborate sophistry of "agreements" and legislated: an additional tax increase in 1971 and again in early 1972 with another expected in early 1973; nationalization of natural gas; the requirements that companies deposit increasing sums of money lest they permit properties to run down before the national takeover in 1984; and the extension of this "reversion" to all facilities rather than only to producing facilities.

Confronted with declining production because output was cheaper in the Persian Gulf, Venezuela set minimum production rates, with fines for insufficient output.

In Libya, the government followed the Persian Gulf countries in demanding and getting an increase on the same pretext of monetary adjustment, and also in demanding participation, whether "participation" or the real thing is not yet clear. In December 1971, when Iran seized two islands near the mouth of the Gulf, Libya seized the properties of British Petroleum in "retaliation"; any stick is good enough to beat a dog.

The Algerian government took two-thirds of the output of the French companies, which were "compensated" with what little remained after deducting newly calculated taxes.

In Iraq, the operating Iraq Petroleum Company (IPC) cut back output sharply during 1972 for the same reason as existed everywhere else in the Mediterranean (where the main field delivers via pipeline)—costs plus taxes were lower at the Persian Gulf, where capacity was being quickly and cheaply expanded. Iraq demanded that production be restored, and that IPC make a long-term commitment to expand output by 10 percent per year. The IPC counteroffer not being acceptable, Iraq made headlines by seizing the Kirkuk field June 1, then offered forthwith to sell at "reduced and competitive prices" for spot delivery or long-term contracts. This threat was aimed at the most sensitive point of the world oil industry: the permanent potential oversupply which in Iraq (and other countries) had already been made actual. Price cutting is intolerable in a cartel; to avoid it, a flurry of complex negotiations began. A loan was soon made by other Arab OPEC members. "Behind the Arab nations' action . . . lies an offer by Iraq to sell its newly nationalized oil at a cut rate, which would have driven down the revenues received by the other countries for their oil." This may also explain the gentleman-like behavior of the expropriated IPC, which did not attempt to blacklist Iraq oil to be sold in non-Communist markets.

Onward and Upward with Taxes and Prices

The genie is out of the bottle. The OPEC nations have had a great success with the threat of embargo and will not put the weapon away. The turbulence will continue as taxes and prices are raised again and again. The producing nations are sure of oil company cooperation and consuming country nonresistance. This is a necessary condition. There are two purely economic reasons why the situation cannot be stable.

1. The crude oil price can go much higher before it reaches the monopoly equilibrium or point of greatest profit.

The average price in Europe of a barrel of oil products in 1969-70 was about $13 per barrel. It is higher today. If the new tax rates were doubled, say, from $1.50 to $3 per barrel at the Persian Gulf, a straight pass-through into product prices would be an increase of only 10 to 14 percent. It is doubtful that such an increase would have any noticeable effect on oil consumption. Moreover, about half of the European price consists of taxes levied by the various consuming country governments. The producing nations have long insisted that in justice they *ought* to receive some or most of this amount. Be that as it may, most or all of this tax *can* be transferred from consuming to producing nations, with help from consuming country governments, which dislike unpopularity through higher fuel prices. The Italian government collaborated early in 1971.[*]

The current price of oil, however far above the competitive level, is still much less than alternatives. The producing nations are not a whit displeased by big expensive projects to produce oil or gas from coal or shale or tar sands, because such efforts are a constant reminder of what a bargain crude is, even at higher prices. Particularly outside the United States, nuclear power sets a high ceiling, coal a much higher ceiling. The price of British coal has long and well served sellers of fuel oil in Britain, who priced at or slightly below coal equivalent. Small wonder that the head of Shell appealed in October 1971 for maintenance of a British coal industry.

There has, therefore, been much discussion, mostly oral, of the goal for the Persian Gulf nations being the U.S. price; or

[*]Dr. M. S. Al-Mahdi, chief of the Economic Department of OPEC, in a paper partly summarized in *Middle East Economic Survey*, July 14, 1972, p. 11, estimates the 1970 Western Europe average consumer price as $13.14, of which 57.3 percent was tax. See also: *Directions des Carburants: 1969*. Italian collaboration: *Petroleum Intelligence Weekly*, May 24, 1971.

$5 per barrel, and so on. These are attainable goals, and we must, therefore, expect attempts to reach them.

2. The producing nations cannot fix prices without using the multinational companies. All price-fixing cartels must *either* control output *or* detect and prevent individual price reductions, which would erode the price down toward the competitive level. The OPEC tax system accomplishes this simply and efficiently. Every important OPEC nation publishes its taxes per barrel; they are a public record, impossible to falsify much. Outright suppression would be a confession of cheating. Once the taxes are set by concerted company-government action, the price floor of taxes-plus-cost is safe, and the floor can be jacked up from time to time, as in early 1971, or early 1972, or by "participation."

It is essential for the cartel that the oil companies continue as *crude oil marketers*, paying the excise tax before selling the crude or refining to sell it as products.

Were the producing nations the sellers of crude, paying the companies in cash or oil for their services, the cartel would crumble. The floor to price would then be not the tax-plus-cost, but only bare cost. The producing nations would need to set and obey production quotas. Otherwise, they would inevitably chisel and bring prices down by selling incremental amounts at discount prices. Each seller nation would be forced to chisel to retain markets, because it could no longer be assured of the collaboration of all the other sellers. Every cartel has in time been destroyed by one, then some members chiseling and cheating; without the instrument of the multinational companies and the cooperation of the consuming countries, OPEC would be an ordinary cartel. And national companies have always been, and still are, price cutters.*

Chiseling will accelerate if national companies go "downstream" into refining and marketing. One can transfer oil to downstream subsidiaries or partners at high f.o.b. prices, but with fictitious low tanker rates or generous delivery credits. The producing nation can put up most of the money or take a minority participation, or lend at less than market interest rates. One can arrange buy-back deals, barter deals, and exchanges of crude in one part of the world for availability

---

Petroleum Press Service, February 1972, pp. 53 and 64, notes that Algeria and Libya have shaved prices to move product.

elsewhere. The world oil cartel in the 1930s was eroded by this kind of piecemeal competition, and the same result can be expected for the new cartel of the 1970s if the individual producing nations become the sellers of oil.

The Saudi Arabian petroleum minister, Sheik Yamani, who designed "participation," warned in 1968 against nationalizing the oil companies and making them "buyers and brokers" of crude oil. This would, he argued truly, lead to "collapse" of oil prices and benefit only the consuming countries. The experts retained by OPEC also warned in 1971 that "participation" must not interfere with marketing of the oil through the companies. More recently, in 1971, Sheik Yamani warned that "participation" had to provide the right kind of "marketing operations." In 1972 he added: "We are concerned that prices in world markets do not fall down."

OPEC has come not to expel, but to exploit. And if the excess crude oil supply were not permanent, Sheik Yamani would have no cause for the "concern" he rightly feels.

We may therefore conclude: the producing countries can raise prices and revenues further by jacking up the excise tax floor, in concert. Conversely, if and when the consuming countries want to be rid of the cartel, they can take their companies out of crude oil marketing. To avoid taxation, they can decommission the tax collecting agents who are their own creation.

So far, the consuming countries have gone in precisely the opposite direction. As they develop high cost substitutes, and strive to get their respective companies, public or "private," into crude oil production and marketing, they will rivet the tax collection agency more firmly on their necks. It is time to ask why they do this, and whether the policy may change.

One can only guess at the unstated reasons why the United States has put OPEC in the driver's seat. First, American companies have a large producing interest in the world market. In 1971, American companies produced about 6.5 billion barrels outside the United States. For every cent of increase in prices above that in tax, there is an additional $65 million in profit.* Second, the higher energy costs will now be imposed on competitors in world markets—and in petrochemicals, higher raw material costs as well. Third, the United

*See *The World Petroleum Market,* Ch. 8, note 32, for the calculation.

States has a large domestic oil producing industry. The less the difference between domestic and world prices, the less the tension between producing and consuming regions.

Fourth, the United States desired to appease the producing nations, buying popularity with someone else's money and trying to mitigate the tension caused by the Arab-Israeli strife, which, however, is irrelevant to oil. If the Arab-Israeli dispute were settled tomorrow, the producing nations would not slow down for one minute their drive for ever higher prices and taxes. The acknowledged leader of the Persian Gulf nations in early 1971 was Iran, which has in one important respect—the Trans-Israel Pipe Line—actually cooperated with Israel more than has the United States, which in 1957 and 1968 discouraged the pipeline.*

The State Department View

In a recent speech—to the West Texas Oil and Gas Association—the director of the State Department Office of Fuels and Energy, James Akins, professed he could not sleep for worry over the possibility of a "supply crisis" caused by even one Arab nation's stopping oil production. Such a "crisis" is a fantasy. Five Arab countries produce an aggregate of one MBD; they would never be missed. In 1951, Iran, producing nearly 40 percent of Persian Gulf output, shut down; yet 1951 Persian Gulf output actually rose. No Arab or non-Arab country is nearly that important today. In the winter of 1966-67, Iraq—about 10 percent then, as now—shut down, and there was not even a ripple on the stream.

If any proof were needed that an Arab boycott will hurt only the Arabs and soon collapse, the 1967 experience should suffice. *The Wall Street Journal,* for example, said that the former Secretary-General of OPEC, Francisco R. Parra:

can't conceive of any political situation arising in the Middle East that would lead to confiscation of investments held by the oil companies. Should another Arab-Israeli war break out, Mr. Parra doesn't expect any repetition of the unsuccessful attempt by the Arab nations to embargo oil shipments to some Western nations. "I don't believe oil can effectively be used as a political weapon by withholding supplies from market—there just can't be an effective selective embargo," he asserted.

The Oil Import Task Force report, signed by the secretary of state and not contested on this point by the minority, ex-

* *The Wall Street Journal,* February 20, 1957 (the State Department thought a pipeline through Iraq would be preferable) and *Platt's Oilgram News Service,* April 22, 1968.

plained why partial shutdowns or boycotts could not be sustained, concluding: "Thus to have a problem one must postulate something approaching a total denial to all markets of all or most Arab oil." It might help if State explained why it no longer agrees.

Along with warnings about "the Arabs," the State Department has taken to warnings of oil scarcity. Thus, Under Secretary Irwin warned the OECD in May 1972 of a worldwide "shortage" of 20 MBD by 1980 because of rising consumption. Mr. Irwin's speech was widely noted and commented on. Three weeks later, Iraq moved at Kirkuk, confident of eventual success because of the "growing energy requirements of the industrialized countries" and growing U.S. imports.

Mr. Akins had already outdone Mr. Irwin in a speech to the Independent Petroleum Association of America (IPAA), warning that "by 1976 our position could be nothing short of desperate" and that Persian Gulf reserves would decline after 1980. The basis of these fears is a well-kept secret which the economist cannot penetrate. But the prediction of a Persian Gulf price of $5 by 1980 must be taken seriously. There was not even a perfunctory disclaimer of expressing only personal opinions in the speech, or in another one to the National Coal Association. He is voicing government policy. In another speech, he spoke of the "widespread recognition . . . that it is not in the Arabs' interests to allow the companies to continue expansion of production at will, and that the producing countries, most notably Saudi Arabia, must [sic] follow Libya's and Kuwait's leads in imposing production limitations."

It seems odd to have an American official telling "the Arabs" they should restrict output. Kuwait has found the argument persuasive and has limited output. But this is the only clear example. Libyan oil is overpriced, that is, overtaxed, and better bargains are available elsewhere. In fact, the expulsion of British Petroleum in December was seen as a "windfall" to the industry because of excessive supply. According to Platt's Oilgram News Service, "Companies have been anxious to reduce production in Libya but 'no company has the courage to do it and now Libya is making BP do it 100 percent,' one observer said." No other Arab country has restricted, and "few . . . are likely to follow Kuwait's lead," despite the State Department's telling them they "must."

Saudi Arabia is engaged in a record expansion of capacity. So is Iran; its finance minister directly rejected the argument in March 1972. For the whole Middle East, 1972 drilling was expected in February to exceed 1971 by a massive 74 percent.

Akins also makes the baffling statement (in the IPAA speech) that "the sellers' market" arrived in June 1967. Yet prices continued to slide for three years more, and Mr. Akins himself notes that neither buyers nor sellers knew the "sellers market" had come. He never explains it. Almost surely he refers to the Suez Canal closure, which by raising transport costs should somewhat *weaken* the demand for crude oil. But the effect of the Suez closure is negligible either way. Reopening of the canal would equate to a 9 percent addition to the world tanker fleet, which has been growing at nearly 13 percent per year: loss of the canal is a loss of eight and one-half months' growth. Indeed, the presence or absence of the Suez Canal is less than the error of estimate of the tankers available at any given time.*

The same State Department source feared a world shortage because "the Arabs" [sic] would find it difficult or impossible to raise the "enormous sums of capital" needed for new production. In 1970 (the most recent year available), total production expenditures in the "Middle East," that is, the Persian Gulf *plus* some substantial expenditures in Turkey, Israel, and Syria, *plus* some payments to governments, amounted to $300 million. In 1972, the revenues of the Persian Gulf nations will amount to about $9 billion. (See Table 2 below.) The expenditures are less than two weeks' revenues. The Kirkuk field just confiscated in Iraq requires less than $4 million annually to maintain the rate of output—revenues from one day's capacity output.

If the producing nations had to spend $300 million in order to obtain $600 million in revenue, a 100 percent return, they would spend that money; the alternative would be to receive nothing at all. And the $300 million net revenue would be about 3 percent of the tribute they obtain today by using the multinational companies. In other words, to talk about their "needs" and "plans" is totally irrelevant to how much they can get before they can spend.

Perhaps the OPEC countries (including the non-Arabs, which do not exist for State but do produce 45 percent of OPEC oil)

*G. I. Jenkins, "Company Uncertainty and Decision Making," *Petroleum Review*, June 1972, p. 213.

may be convinced that they should restrict output in concert because oil in the ground will appreciate faster than money in the bank. Perhaps, too, there will be discussion in the United States about why our government is so poorly informed on oil economics, why it repeats "Arabs-oil . . . oil-Arabs" as though slogans proved something logic could not, whether the national interest is well served by sponsoring, supporting, and urging on the cartel, and whether our interests may change when, as is generally expected, our imports are substantially larger.

The Changing American Interest

First, security has been greatly impaired for all importing countries by the cohesion of the OPEC nations, which made an embargo feasible.

Second, the balance-of-payments impact will soon turn unfavorable to us, as it is to all other importers.[*]

The fact will slowly be recognized that nearly all of the oil deficit could be abolished by getting American companies out of crude oil marketing, to produce on contract for the producing countries, who could then compete the price way down. The companies' profits (and contribution to the balance of payments) would not be much less, and in the long run they might be greater, as the experience in Venezuela proves: the companies producing there are at, or over, the loss line.

Larger American imports will, if anything, tend to put the world price down. The process was seen on a small scale after 1966, when quotas on (heavy) residual fuel imports were lifted. Imports increased considerably, and the price *decreased.* Moreover, concern over air pollution was growing rapidly, and alarm was felt over possible loss of markets for residual fuel oil. Hence, the Venezuelan government made agreements with Esso and Shell, granting them lower taxes on production of low-sulfur fuel oil. This bit of history was too rapidly forgotten.[**]

---

[*]Secretary of Commerce Peterson, in *The New York Times,* June 20, 1972, p. 51, estimates the American balance-of-payments deficit on oil account as $26 billion a year in 1980 if imports are 4.38 billion barrels. This implies $5.94 per barrel delivered, hence probably about the same $5 per barrel f.o.b. at which State aims.

[**]*The World Petroleum Market,* Ch. 7.

The declining price of fuel oil in the face of greater demand would be inexplicable in a competitive market, but it is to be expected when the price is far above cost. It is exactly what happened in Europe to embarrass coal. The hope of greater profits on increased sales, and the knowledge that large buyers have now an incentive to roam the market and look for every chance of a better deal, means that one must reduce the price before one's rivals tie up the good customers. As American quotas are relaxed, refiners who have a crude deficit will become exactly the kind of large-scale buyer whom Sheik Yamani rightly fears.

The prospect of world prices rising because of large-scale American imports has alarmed Europe and Asia, and the United States government has gladly fanned those fears. But they have no basis in theory or experience.

Let the reader excuse our saying again what needs to be said often: larger consumption only raises price in a competitive market, by raising marginal cost. In so awesomely non-competitive a market, cost is not relevant because price is ten to twenty times cost. Supply and demand have nothing to do with the world price of oil: only the strength of the cartel matters.

Other Consuming Countries

Consuming governments are staying in the same groove that served them badly between 1957 and 1970, and worse afterward. Prices had risen in the 1950s because the oil companies were able to act in concert without overt collusion: they responded to a signal from the United States. Prices then jumped for a time when the Suez Canal was cut. The reaction was fear of shortage. One heard in 1957 what one hears now: "True, reserves are ample, but in 15 years, say by 1972, they will mostly be gone! We must guard against the shortage, obtain concessions of our own, protect domestic energy industries against future scarcity, and so on." Thereby the consuming countries committed themselves to high oil prices.

The consuming countries were even more ready to fear these imaginary demons because they had invested heavily in coal. The decline in fuel oil prices after 1957 was greeted with disbelief and resentment. Prices of oil assumed in government energy plans and forecasts were always much higher than actual market. In 1962 (and 1964) the EEC (European Economic Community) energy experts made a long-term forecast of heavy fuel oil at $18 per metric ton, when it was about $13. They were bitterly denounced for so low a forecast. Yet even now, in mid-1972, fuel oil in Western Europe is only $14.50, that is, in 1962 prices, $10.75 per ton. Seldom has so costly a mistake been so long and stubbornly maintained. Nationalized industries—and others that could be influenced or pressured—were and still are reserved to coal. Worse yet, the artificial European coal prices became a cost standard for building nuclear power plants; in Great Britain they are wildly uneconomic.

The costly insistence on self-sufficiency was mostly uninformed fear of the multinational oil companies. The more the companies lost control of the market and competed down the price of fuel oil, losing profits thereby, the more resentment at their "ruthless economic warfare." As late as 1972 a British economist still writes of the oil company "design" to drive out coal. Fear of the multinational firms leads consuming countries not only to protect coal but to seek "their own" oil through government owned or sponsored companies. Thereby the consuming country government acquires a vested interest in high oil prices. Low oil prices, or the possibility thereof, become not an opportunity but a scandal, to be ignored as far as possible.

The fear of shortage in the 1970s, as in the 1950s, leads to attempts to obtain oil concessions. It may make sense to run risks in new areas where governments will keep taxes low. There is much oil that is profitable to find and develop at today's prices, even at costs twenty-five times that in the Persian Gulf. A non-Japanese can hardly object when Japan proposes to spend some $3 billion in the near future to find and develop new oil resources. If spent in new areas, it will certainly add to the wealth of the world, and—perhaps—not be a loss to Japan. But there is nothing gained in seeking new concessions in the old areas or in buying into old concessions. Such a policy does not add any resources. The price paid for concession shares will discount the profits, which may not continue long. Perhaps worst of all, in committing itself to take oil from "its" concessions, the consuming country loses all independence in buying and is worse exploited than it could ever be by the multinational companies.

The French Experience

The policy of seeking "independence" has been carried
farthest in France. In 1962 agreements were reached with
newly independent Algeria, inaugurating a "new type" of relationship, free from the burden of colonialism, and so forth.
(One hears similar language today in Japan.) In early 1971 M.
Fontaine described in *Le Monde* the dreary succession of
broken promises, seizures, spoliation, and the like. Yet no
more than the French government could he or his newspaper
bring itself to discard the policy; there were supposed political advantages, such as lessening Soviet influence in the
western Mediterranean. The logical result was the two-thirds
confiscation in 1972 of what they had fondly thought to be
"their own" oil.

The head of ERAP, the wholly state-owned French company
(as distinguished from Compagnie Française des Pétroles,
only 35 percent state owned), summed up ten years' experience and loss of the Algerian oil as "une opération blanche."
Had the funds been invested at a steady rate and drawn a
7 percent return, private or social (hospitals, schools,
highways, and so on), it would have been worth one-third
more in 1972. But that is only a small part of the real social
cost. There has been substantial French aid to the Algerian
economy, and French oil prices have been among the highest
in Europe. But the French insist on rose-colored glasses. A
break-even operation is viewed as economic. High oil prices
and aid to Algeria, loading French industry with heavy costs
and taxes that reduce its export capability, are viewed as a
help to the balance of payments.

Four months after Algeria was written off, France was ap-
proached by Iraq, which had seized the Kirkuk field from Iraq
Petroleum Company. Experience had taught Iraq who was an
easy mark. In 1961 it had seized the whole IPC concession
outside of fields actually producing; but although the
expropriated area included the great undeveloped North
Rumaila field, nobody leased it. Then in 1967, after the Six-
Day War, France obtained a large concession in Iraq for
ERAP, "ratified with great pomp in Baghdad (and hailed
throughout the Middle East) as a great victory over Anglo-
American imperialism." The usually sober *Le Monde* was
thrilled. Someone was needed "who would not flinch" when
IPC "showed their teeth," someone "capable of braving the

anger of the members of IPC." Because of France, the "Anglo-Americans [lose] any chance of expansion into the hitherto-unexplored parts of the country." They have been outmaneuvered; they cannot block France from "a place in the untouched zones of Iraq without provoking a grave political crisis." This is their just reward because "on the morrow of the last war they would not let France into the game in this region."

Having used North Rumaila as bait to take in the French, Iraq dangled it before others, then decided to develop the field itself, with Russian assistance. There was great annoyance in France, where doubt was expressed that Iraq was capable of developing the field. But in April 1972 shipments began in the presence of Mr. Kosygin, who exclaimed, "Arab oil to the Arabs!" By early 1971 ERAP had found three fields worth developing, whereupon Iraq demanded higher payments than those called for in the contract. ERAP was willing to give more, but not as much as demanded, and negotiations dragged on. Predictably, the French blamed the deadlock on the machinations of IPC, which was said to be trying to block French intrusion into what *Le Monde* called "the private hunting preserve of the Anglo-Saxons."

In June 1972, when Iraq seized the Kirkuk field and threatened price cutting, it "preserved French interests in Iraq." Surely, it told newsmen, the French ought to be no more scrupulous in Iraq than were the Americans who had offered to do business with Algeria after the confiscation of French interests there. France, said *Le Monde*, feared a rejection of the Iraq offer "would harm its prestige in the Near East and would be taken as a break with Gaullist policy in the region," while acceptance would allow France to "serve as a bridge between the West and the left wing regimes of the Arab world, a role whereby she, alone, can hope to counterbalance the growing Soviet influence." (Does the Gaullist policy help in oil matters, or does France accept higher oil costs in order to keep the policy going? One wishes for something intelligible.) A few days later came a Soviet-Iraq agreement on economic cooperation. This was no break in policy; the Baghdad regime had lifted its ban on Communist political activity and accepted two Communists in the government. But, of course, the greater the Soviet influence, the greater the need to counterbalance it, hence the more concessions would be made to the Baghdad regime in oil affairs.

When the strong man of the Iraqi cabinet, Vice Premier Saddam Hussein, visited Paris in June, he had a resounding success. The agreement with France gave CFP (the French partner in IPC) "une position privilégiée," which comes to this: CFP is obliged to lift its full share of Iraq oil for ten years under the same conditions as before the nationalization—exactly that long-term commitment that it rejected as too expensive when it was a partner in IPC. Small wonder that CFP did not want this "position privilégiée." "The reason is simple—the price is too high. . . ."

France also acquired the "right" to buy additional crude—which Iraq had just offered to all the world at reduced prices. But France will buy not at reduced but at "commercial prices," that is, higher than what is charged to any knowledgeable arm's length buyer who has alternatives. Finally, France will extend about $80 million of long-term credits to Iraq. This, and future credits and grants, is an unacknowledged addition to the price of the oil.

Thus, the French have again been had, most royally, and by their own strenuous effort.

How are we to understand this rigid determination that France have "its own" oil, whereby France is humiliated and cheated?

Two elements of an explanation are worth suggesting, because they are not peculiar to France. One is the romantic political aura surrounding oil, which lets all manner of nonsense sound plausible. "Whatever touches on oil is at once adorned with romance. No other raw material stirs the imagination like this one, nor the taste for flowery language," wrote Edgar Faure in 1938. Another key is to be found in such phrases as "oil-hungry France" or "France assured of oil needs," and so forth. Similarly, in discussing Japan, Professor Brzezinski speaks repeatedly of "access to raw materials"* as being so self-evident and serious a problem that it need not be explained. Yet we cannot point to one example of lack of access. To pay for "access," by higher prices or otherwise, makes no sense, no matter how one views the future:

1. The price of crude oil, set by a world monopoly, is many times what is enough to make it worthwhile to expand out-

*Zbigniew Brzezinski, The Fragile Blossom: Crisis and Change in Japan (New York: Harper and Row, 1972), pp. 46-47, 71. In justice to Professor Brzezinski, one should note that he slides quickly from "access" to "price," which is the only real problem.

put. Therefore, even if price declines, and especially if it rises, there will always be more crude oil available than can be sold, as there is now and has always been.

2. Assume the contrary: that oil is becoming increasingly scarce, and that the price will reach $5 or whatever. At this price, the market is cleared, and just as with a monopolized market, anyone who can pay the price gets all he wants.

3. There is a real fear, exploited but not created by the U.S. government, that massive American oil and gas imports will somehow preclude buyers from other countries, especially if the producing nations take the advice to limit output. Let us assume they do so. Then lower-cost, more profitable companies will outbid their rivals for the limited supply. Japanese iron and steel companies, for example, are obviously much lower cost than their American rivals. The dwindling of the American export surplus seems to show a higher cost level; if so, high oil prices will harm this country more than others.

4. One often-expressed fear is that the American multinational companies will divert supplies to American customers in preference to non-American. But if there is some constraint such that both groups cannot be fully supplied, then the price must rise. To imagine American companies deliberately holding down the price, in order to precipitate a shortage, in order to be able to discriminate, is fantasy. They would not wish to do it, and their masters, the producing nations, would not allow it.

5. The OPEC nations may wish to deny oil to some particular country. But if some or even most of them do so, the capacity of others will be available, and at most there will be a reshuffling of customers. Yet let us now assume that all OPEC nations unite to boycott one country. They must also prevent diversion of supplies of crude oil and products from other consuming countries to the victim. Yet nobody has suggested why the OPEC nations should join in this profitless persecution. Moreover, the supply of non-OPEC oil is large relative to a single consuming country's needs.

6. Even if "access" is a real problem, it is useless to try to obtain access through a company owned by the consuming nation, since real power is in the producing nation.

The obsession with a false problem of "access to oil" wastes time and distracts attention from the real problem of security of supply. The old or new multinational companies can do nothing good or bad for security because they have no control of supply, no power to cut off anybody or to protect them from cutoff. Nobody owns oil at the wellhead or underground reserves any more except the governments that have the physical force above ground.

A Look Ahead

Oil supply is threatened by one and only one danger: a concerted shutdown by the OPEC nations. No single nation can do any harm. The rhetorical question "Would you like to see Saudi Arabia supply one-third of the oil?" is only marginally relevant. The fewer the sellers and the larger their market shares, the easier for them to collaborate and act as one. The central question is their union or disunion. If a single large seller breaks away, or if a few minor ones do, the cartel breaks down in a stampede for the exit. The cartel is only needed, only exists, to thwart the basic condition of massive potential excess capacity—ability to expand output at costs below prices—and prevent it from becoming actual.

Hence, lower prices and secure supply are the two sides of the same coin: absence of monopoly, or impotence of disunion.

The monopoly may still have its finest hours before it, and prices should rise well into the decade. The fewer the sellers the better, and there will presently be fewer Persian Gulf states. Most of them have too few men, and stuffing them full of money makes them worth occupying. A decade ago, Iraq claimed Kuwait and was only stopped by the threat of force (the British presence, now gone). Iraq will be even more ready to occupy Kuwait if Iran occupies the Kirkuk area, site of the great oil field just expropriated. The local population are not Arabs but Kurds, Indo-European in language and Sunnite Moslem in religion, like the Iranians. If they behaved themselves, the Iranian army might be hailed as liberators from the chronic bloody struggle with the Baghdad regime. A new pipeline to the Mediterranean could go through Iran and Turkey.

The important consuming countries show no sign of understanding their plight; in mid-1972 "European nations are believed to be concerned that another stalemate [on "participation"] could impair vitally needed oil supplies. . . .

The companies are under considerable pressure to reach an agreement."*

Also, the large consumer countries have export interests that will benefit by the higher oil prices because of oil nations' greater purchasing power. Export industries often have disproportionate political power, even if the real economic benefit to the nation, higher incomes to labor and capital than from the next best alternatives, is piddling compared to the outflow on oil.

Europe is rapidly becoming an important oil producer. Some European countries will become small net importers, some will be large net oil sellers. The head of Norsk Hydro oil operations recently noted Norway's "economic interest in high prices." He recognized that the OPEC gains "were forced through by threats of a boycott." Instead of maundering about "political stability," he defined it: "first and foremost a political system under which agreements and terms of licenses are respected even if the circumstances may have changed. . . [and under which] everyone feels secure that supply will be maintained in all circumstances." It is an indirect but devastating comment on American policy.

The less developed nations will suffer the most, with no offsets. For example, India today consumes about 150 million barrels per year and is expected to use about 345 billion in 1980. The burden of monopoly pricing is direct (paying higher prices for imports) and indirect (being forced to find and produce higher cost domestic oil). It amounts in total to about $225 million ($1.50 x 150 million) per year, and it is increasing rapidly. Yet at the 1972 United Nations Conference on Trade and Development (UNCTAD) meeting there was no breath of criticism of the oil producing nations. Solidarity prevailed: things were felt to be going well "on the oil front," and, said *Le Monde,* the same ought to happen on other fronts.

This favorable public attitude also holds in the developed countries. A private monopoly that extracted $1.5 billion per year from consumers would be denounced and probably destroyed; were it American, some executives would be in jail. An intergovernmental monopoly ten times as big is viewed as a bit of redress by the Third World.

*A. P. dispatch in *International Herald Tribune,* August 19-20, 1972.

Now one may approve this double standard, or deplore it, or laugh to keep from crying, but it is a truth with consequences: no important resistance seems likely in the near term. In time, attitudes may change.

1. The fictitious "world energy crisis" will gradually fade, as it did after 1957, and the slow growth of understanding of oil prices will resume. This influence is minor but not negligible.

2. In 1972 the transfer from consuming to OPEC nations will be about $15 billion. (See Table 2). If the tax doubles (and the price is therefore about $3.35) and if output increases by 8 percent per year, then the 1980 transfer will be over $56 billion per year. This is a very conservative forecast as compared with those of the departments of State or Commerce, as cited earlier.

3. Some of the billions will be spent in ways some consuming countries find irksome or dangerous. The large amounts paid to Libya have already cost the NATO nations additional payments to Malta, for which Mr. Mintoff could not have bargained without Libyan help.

4. Payments to the producing nations will total about $242 billion over the nine years 1972-80. If these nations spend, say, three-fourths on goods and services from abroad and save 25 percent by buying foreign assets, the additions to their holdings will be about $61 billion. The oil companies see themselves as the decently paid investment managers for this fund; as Schumpeter said, "This is the way the bourgeois mind works, always will work, even in sight of the hangman's rope."

There will be monetary disorders when large holders speculate against a particular currency. Unlike in the oil market, where the producing countries must act in concert or accomplish nothing, even a single nation with big enough foreign balances can do substantial damage to the world monetary system or try to bring down a government it dislikes.

5. Security of supply has been severely impaired by the Paris capitulation and the great success of the threat of embargo. Hints of "concerted action" since then have been too numerous to list. Even more upsetting than the threats are the assurances. For they imply power to stop the flow.

Table 2
Approximate OPEC Revenues, 1972

Area	Estimated 1972 output (billion brls)*	Per-barrel revenues**	Total revenues ($ billions)
Persian Gulf	6.50	$1.42	$9.2
Libya, Algeria	1.20	2.14	2.6
Nigeria	0.63	1.85	1.2
Venezuela	1.10	1.61	1.8
Indonesia	0.37	1.50	0.5
			$15.3

*Output assumed at same rate as first quarter 1972.

**Petroleum Intelligence Weekly: Persian Gulf, February 14, 1972; Libya, Algeria, May 15, 1972; Nigeria, May 3, 1971, and July 3, 1972; Venezuela, December 27, 1971; Indonesia, rough guess.

Security of supply—limited but genuine—can be had by stockpiling, combined with detailed plans for severe rationing supplemented by high excise taxes, to reduce oil consumption and thereby increase the effective size of the stockpile. The expense will be heavy (but had the consuming countries done this years ago, they would have made large savings).

The larger the reserves piled up by the OPEC nations, the greater their power to withhold oil. Hence, the higher the price, and the greater the insecurity, the easier for the OPEC nations to make it still more expensive and insecure. The consuming countries can have cheapness and security only by a clean break with the past: get the multinational oil companies out of crude oil marketing; let them remain as producers under contract and as buyers of crude to transport, refine, and sell as products. The real owners, the producing nations, must then assume the role of sellers, and they should be assisted in competing the price of crude oil down. The Yamani prescription will be as sound then as in 1968, or 1971, or 1972.

It is a simple and elegant maneuver to destroy the cartel by removing an essential part—the multinational company as crude oil marketers fixing the price on a firm excise tax floor. But this would only minimize conflict and confrontation; it is too late to avoid them. The producing countries, like many raw troops, have been welded by success into a real force, and the huge sums they receive and accumulate will be both the incentive and the means to fight, by embargo, monetary disruption, or even local wars. There will be nonnegligible damage. To have put the power and motive into the producers' hands was light-minded folly by the American government.

Moreover, clean breaks with past policy are rare. The honest confession of error is less likely than is anger at the cartel's local agents, the multinational companies, and attempts to restrict and penalize them. Yet this misconception is exactly what has led to past mistakes. Bypassing the companies to make direct deals with producing nations can be helpful only when the objective is clearly seen: to mobilize national buying power, encourage domestic oil buyers to avoid established channels, and help compete prices down. More often, such deals sacrifice all buying independence in a vain attempt to get a good "connection," or placate a production nation, and only raise costs.

The greatest difficulty in following the Yamani formula is the need for the leading consuming countries to act together. For example, the United States tax law might recognize, either by statute or judicial decision, that the "income" taxes paid to OPEC nations were really excise taxes, hence not deductible from U.S. income tax. Higher taxes coupled with the unceasing demands of the OPEC countries might well push one or more of these companies past patience or profit, and they would withdraw to become a contractor or buyer, helping to undermine the cartel.

Yet today other large consuming countries would fall over themselves trying to get one of their countries into the empty slot and would promise anything to the producing nation. Hence, it would be literally worse than useless for the United States to take the first steps without firm assurances from at least France, Germany, Italy, and Japan that they would not try to replace the American company. These countries are still obsessed with vain notions of getting "access" or "security" through their own companies, and the suggestion that they refrain from taking their "just share," ending their long-resented "exclusion" from "the game," seems an obvious attempt to help the American companies keep their predominance. It is an old sad story. If one looks for the "real motives," he will never hear what is being said.

The multinational companies will probably survive the crisis. Yet there is a real danger that they will be forced out of crude oil production. This would be a grievous waste of resources and could precipitate a genuine shortage of crude oil.

What happens to oil in the 1970s depends altogether on the consuming countries. If they are as slow to learn as they have been, then the projection of $55 billion annual tribute paid the OPEC nations by 1980 may be surpassed. But they may also learn that transferring those billions is not only dangerous but *unnecessary*. Their energy economics would need to be updated at least to 1952, when the Paley Commission explained that shortage means only cost; they might then see that the "world energy shortage" is a myth, that crude oil continues in oversupply, as the Venezuelans, the Iraqis, and the Saudi Arabs have recognized. And the consuming nations' strategic thinking would need to be updated at least to 1914, when Winston Chruchill, who was then a young fox, not an old lion, explained to the House of Commons that access to oil is only a special case of monopoly; the power to withhold is the power to overcharge.*

*See J. E. Hartshorn, *Oil Companies and Governments* (1967 ed.), pp. 255-260.

AN ATLANTIC-JAPANESE ENERGY POLICY
by Walter J. Levy

The prosperity and security of the whole free world depend on sufficient availability of energy on satisfactory economic terms.

During the next ten to twenty years, oil will provide the mainstay of the world's energy supplies. In practical terms, because of the size of known reserves and the lead time for finding and developing new oil and other energy resources, the world's growing needs will be supplied predominantly by huge increases of oil imports from the Middle East—mainly from the Persian Gulf area.

Directly connected with this, the consuming countries will face the following: the cost of oil imports will rise tremendously with extraordinarily difficult implications for the balance of payments of many consuming countries; foreign exchange accumulations and the international use of such funds in the case of some of the major oil producing countries, such as Saudi Arabia and Abu Dhabi, could cause serious problems; a complete change is developing in the relationships between the oil producing, importing, and home countries of international oil companies and the national oil companies of producing and importing countries.

The formulation of a realistic energy policy for the oil importing countries cannot be limited to the Atlantic nations but must include Japan. It should also encompass other developed nations and should take account of oil importing developing countries in Latin America, Africa, and Asia.

But the primary responsibility for the formulation of policy and organization inevitably belongs to the Atlantic group plus Japan—and their need for action is urgent.

Basic Data on Energy Supply and Finance

If present U.S. policies and trends are left to take their course, oil shipments from abroad will advance from about 4.7 million barrels per day in 1972 to over 11 million barrels per day in 1980, while the oil imports of Europe and Japan combined are estimated to advance during the same period from 18 to 30 million barrels daily.

"An Atlantic-Japanese Energy Policy" was published originally in *Foreign Policy*, Number 11, Summer 1973.

The preponderant part of all these imports will have to come from the Middle East. Their output will rise from 18 million barrels daily in 1972 to an estimated 35 to 40 million barrels daily by 1980. The United States will, for the first time, compete with Europe and Japan for major oil supplies from the Middle East. The Middle East's share in total U.S. oil imports will, by 1980, amount to about 50 to 55 percent and in those of Western Europe and Japan to about 75 to 80 percent. There is little doubt that Middle East oil reserves are sufficient to cover these requirements, but without very large new discoveries this situation might change during the 1980s.

The USSR will most likely remain self-sufficient in its energy requirements, and it may also continue to export oil and natural gas.

Two more sets of data are most relevant for the formulation and urgent implementation of energy policy. The total value of U.S. net imports of energy materials, mostly oil, may, according to U.S. Department of Commerce data, easily reach $18 billion to $24 billion annually by 1980, those of Europe $23 billion to $31 billion, and those of Japan $12 billion to $16 billion—as compared with $2.3 billion, $8.5 billion, and $3.1 billion, respectively, in 1970. The revenues likely to accrue to Middle East producing countries can tentatively be estimated at about $40 billion annually by 1980—as against $9 billion in 1972—with Saudi Arabia alone accounting for as much as perhaps half of the 1980 total. In some of the countries, such as Saudi Arabia and Abu Dhabi, a large part of these funds could not possibly be absorbed internally.

The United States simply cannot afford an ever increasing overdependence for its oil supplies on a handful of foreign, largely unstable, countries. Otherwise, its security—and that of its allies—as well as its prosperity and its freedom of action in foreign policy formulation will be in jeopardy. But the United States does have a realistic and economically manageable alternative—accelerated development of its large domestic resource potential for conventional and synthetic hydrocarbons and nuclear energy.

Even though such alternatives may now look expensive, the cost of foreign oil imports is likely to escalate and eventually approach the cost of alternative sources of supply that could be developed in the United States.

If all realistic actions to increase its domestic energy supplies were to be taken with utmost urgency, U.S. dependence on total energy imports by the early 1980s might be limited to perhaps around 20 percent—instead of somewhat over 30 percent if present trends were permitted to take their course—and probably would not exceed the "danger" level. But, as of now, continuing dependence of Europe, Japan, and the United States on Middle East oil appears to be inevitable.

Power Structure Changes of International Oil

In the immediate postwar period, the international oil companies effectively supplied the bulk of the ever increasing energy requirements of the free world. From 1946 to about the late 1950s, the companies—on the basis of their rich Middle East oil concessions and at least indirectly because of the immense power of the United States—were able to dispose of their oil reasonably freely and on favorable commercial terms.

Moreover, the United States itself was on balance independent of foreign oil imports and possessed a sizable reserve productive capacity from which our allies benefited substantially during the Iranian crisis and, with some short delays, during the first Suez crisis.

By 1960, when the Organization of the Petroleum Exporting Countries (OPEC) was established, the relative power position of the United States was beginning to decline as Europe, Japan, and the USSR acquired new strength. It was also the time when the developing countries began to play a more important role in world affairs. OPEC's ever growing influence in international oil operations was beyond doubt at least in part the result of a certain inability and inflexibility of the international oil industry and their home governments to anticipate, assess, and adjust to the changes that had begun to erode their paramount position of political and economic influence in oil producing countries.

During the next twelve years, from 1960 to 1972, OPEC and its members succeeded, to begin with, in achieving minor increases in the government take of oil producing countries, and, since the early 1970s, in enforcing a quantum jump in the royalty and tax payments levied on production, capped in 1972 by the so-called participation agreement. Assuming present arrangements are implemented, for the Arab producing countries in the Persian Gulf participation means an immediate 25 percent interest in existing concessions, leading to 51 percent control within nine years. National oil companies of the major Middle East producing countries will thus become the largest sellers of crude oil. Algeria, Libya, and Iraq have already taken over a very substantial part of the previously foreign-owned oil production, and the current Indonesian oil contracts also leave the Indonesian National Oil Company free to dispose of a substantial part of the oil discovered by foreign oil companies.

During the same period, the U.S. domestic oil outlook underwent drastic changes, and its reserve productive potential began to disappear. By 1972, with imports of close to 5 million barrels per day, we had become one of the largest importers of oil.

Power of the Major Oil Producing Countries

There is little doubt that the major oil producing countries, especially of the Middle East, have acquired an immense potential for power—as long as at least two of the more important producers are able to maintain a reasonably united front. Saudi Arabia alone will soon have a pivotal role in supply.

Their power will in due course derive not only from their effective control over immense oil resources, but also from their control over unprecedented financial resources which they will be able to extract from the oil purchasers. Moreover, large monetary reserves will give them the freedom to restrict their oil production for political or any other reasons.

The control that the producing countries will be able to exercise over their oil production and exports is not only based on their participation in the national oil producing companies, but also stems, perhaps even primarily, from the exercise of their sovereign power over companies operating in their countries. There is ample precedence for such use of power, with the reluctant acceptance of the oil companies and their home governments: the Kuwaiti and Libyan restrictions on production, the prohibition of exports to certain countries, including in certain circumstances even the parent countries of the oil companies, the Venezuelan oil legislation establishing practically complete control over oil operations, which were totally under foreign private ownership. This list could be extended to foreign oil activities in almost any of the major producing countries.

To all intents and purposes, fiscal arrangements and payments to the producing countries are subject to nearly unilateral determination by the producing countries, as reflected in the Tehran and Tripoli "dictates."

Peremptory demands for national ownership of tanker transportation, of reinvestments in oil exploration, of refining, petrochemical, and other related industries are bound to be made. The establishment of levels of production and of the size and direction of exports are also "recognized" methods of controls.

In this connection it is noteworthy that the development of the tremendous oil resources of the Middle East does not really reflect any extensive industrial involvement of the economies of the oil producing countries or any important contribution by their people. The oil producing industry operations in these countries are limited fundamentally to a small enclave.

Even though, under recent arrangements, a substantial part of the national companies' entitlements will be sold back to their foreign partners, it is only a matter of time before the national oil companies will dominate the market for nonintegrated third party sales of crude oil. They will become major suppliers to national oil companies in many of the importing countries of the world and will probably also deal directly with foreign refining and marketing affiliates of the international oil companies. In fact, effective competition in crude oil sales between the producing affiliates of the international oil companies and their partners, the national companies of the producing countries, may become very difficult if not impossible, as the producing countries' governments might not only establish the levels of production but also determine the tax-paid cost and the prices at which the greatly increasing quantities of crude to which their companies will become entitled will either be sold back to their foreign partners or to their own customers.

Coupled with the expansion of crude oil sales, the national oil companies of some of the major producing countries will obviously work out deals for joint refining and marketing in importing countries. Likewise, the producing countries, by taking over ownership or control of an ever expanding tanker fleet to carry their oil exports, will not only increase their revenues, but further enhance their power over the international oil trade.

With Saudi Arabia unable to absorb its vastly expanding oil revenues in its local economy, it is quite possible that by the early 1980s the surplus funds annually available to it may be on the order of $15 billion plus. The large and continuously growing inflow of foreign funds that would accrue to the treasuries of a few Middle East governments, and to a small number of their privileged citizens, will far exceed any accumulation of foreign exchange holdings in modern times. Realistically, such amounts could probably not be placed into long-term or short-term investments, year in, year out, without risking severe international repercussions and potentially extensive restrictions on the free flow of capital. It is most unlikely that the United States, or any other developed country, would permit continued massive foreign investments on a scale that could conceivably result in foreign takeovers of important companies and industries. Moreover, the reverse flow of dividends and interest would soon add an additional unmanageable balance-of-payments burden to the oil import bill of many countries. Nor could the short-term money markets handle such excessive and volatile funds without undermining the world's monetary arrangements.

The dilemma confronting us is acutely disturbing, as any proliferation of international restrictions on capital or short-term movements of funds would, in and by themselves, be most harmful to our financial markets and monetary system. In the affected Middle East oil and capital surplus countries, any restrictions on their investments abroad would probably be accompanied by restrictions on the output of oil. Obviously, if the income of oil producing countries were to be "sterilized," it would be more advantageous and completely rational for them to limit their oil exports. This would then further aggravate the world oil supply situation. However, controls over the level of oil production are unfortunately likely to be introduced anyhow, even without any hostile political or economic motivation of the producing countries, for reasons of conservation and wise resource management—at least in some of the major oil producing countries—and certainly as soon as their reserve-to-production ratio begins to decline significantly. A recent pronouncement by the Saudi Arabian minister of petroleum has clearly suggested such a course of action. Interestingly, his statement was coupled with the suggestion that in order to assure continued supplies, oil imports from his country be given a privileged position in the U.S. market.

Some of the major Middle East producing countries will thus become two-pronged power centers, both as suppliers of oil and as extraordinary accumulators of capital—with the latter further strengthening their ability to withhold oil from importing countries over a considerable period of time by drawing on their financial reserves for their budgetary and trade requirements. There is little doubt that this accumulation of oil and of money power—obtained like "manna from heaven," and, at least for the time being, not accompanied by any substantial contribution in political, managerial, or technical competence—would bring with it tremendous and lopsided shifts in the balance of power of a potentially explosive character.

Not the least of the dangers posed by this extreme concentration of oil power and "unearned" money power is the pervasive corruptive influence that this will nearly inevitably have on political, economic, and commercial actions in both the relatively primitive and unsophisticated societies of the producing countries and the advanced societies of the dependent industrialized nations.

Further complicating factors must be taken into account. Within the area itself there are many deep-seated conflicts such as those of Iran versus Iraq, Iraq versus Kuwait, Saudi Arabia versus Abu Dhabi, Libya versus the traditional Arab countries, and so on. Also, there is an underlying rivalry between Iran and the Arab States of the Persian Gulf for hegemony in the area, which may sooner or later erupt into an open power struggle implicating also the Communist and non-Communist allies or sponsors of the various Middle East countries. In addition there are the explosive implications of the Israeli-Arab issue.

All of these actual or potential confrontations fundamentally affect the oil companies. When the activities of the companies extend to several of these countries, they will most likely be drawn sooner or later into many local area conflicts. Moreover, the producing countries will hold companies responsible for their home government policies and expect them to support the producing countries' political, strategic, or economic interests. The companies will nearly inevitably be asked to match any arrangements that either their affiliates or any of the other international oil companies (or sometimes even any newcomer company) make with governments of most other Middle East oil countries. And with the underlying rivalry between the Arab countries and Iran, either faction would feel compelled to be able to claim that it has struck the most advantageous bargain with the oil companies. National pride and jealousy are bound to provoke a one-upmanship that would lead to endless escalations and no end of trouble. This is exactly what is happening as a result of the simultaneous negotiations on participation with the Arab nations, on one hand, and on a differently structured deal with Persia, on the other—and also in connection with developments in Iraq concerning the nationalization of the Iraq Petroleum Company. Accordingly, the outcome in Iran and Iraq, any potential repercussions on the participation agreements with the Arab countries, and especially whether or not and, if so, how long the companies will be able to keep any equity interest in their various oil producing arrangements are, as of the time of this writing, still undetermined.

Finally, it must not be forgotten that none of the national governments is really stable and that the societies involved are still largely backward; there are always serious doubts whether any existing arrangements would survive the end of any current regime.

Limitations on Oil Companies in Producing Countries

It is clear that participation is mainly a device through which the oil producing countries plan, by arrangements with the international oil companies, to obtain complete control over their countries' oil operations.

It represents a grand design by the producing countries to forge an alliance with the oil companies in which the producing countries, while pursuing their national objectives, would still be able to take advantage of the large distribution outlets, the investment capabilities, and the technical know-how of the oil companies. This is reflected perhaps most succinctly in the pronouncements of Mr. Yamani, the Saudi Arabian minister of petroleum. His whole approach is based on the assumption that the oil companies would one day turn out to be the natural allies of the producing countries. As he explains it, he wants participation because the weight of the national oil companies in producing countries should be combined with that of the oil companies so as to: (1) protect the concessions from nationalization by providing an enduring link between the oil companies and the producing countries, (2) gain control over the oil operations while maintaining the flow of foreign capital and expertise and obtaining marketing outlets for the output, (3) prevent competition between producing countries as sellers of crude in open market, which would lead to a drastic drop in prices and producing government revenues, (4) maintain thereby price stability, and through the implementation of participation even secure an immediate increase in world crude oil prices from which the producing countries would benefit, (5) achieve through this combination a position of influence in the oil markets, and (6) make it difficult for any producing country to insist on an "abnormal" increase in production. As the Kuwaiti finance and oil minister plainly put it, "What we called phased participation is in fact phased nationalization. This is precisely the situation and its implications."

It must be clear that even though the producing countries will start initially with a minority ownership, they will have a powerful voice on investment, production levels, size of exports and their destination. As a corporate partner representing at the same time the sovereign, they possess all the power they need to control and direct the companies on all phases of the operations in the producing country and probably even on many phases of their operations abroad, holding their local interest in oil production as hostage.

Perhaps sensing this, an American top executive of an international oil company in an early statement on participation demands said that the key role of the international oil companies, to satisfy the needs of both the producing and consuming countries, is "best performed when the commercial enterprise is freed from the pressures of conflicting ideologies and of the clashing political systems. These differences inevitably arise when governments of producing countries have a direct participation in running the oil industry or when government-to-government negotiations are substituted for the company bargaining with the host government." The commercial framework of operations "would be subverted if we were to adopt an alternative of serving either group of nations exclusively." A top executive of one of the largest European international oil companies stated that a position of 51 percent participation by the producing countries would be "almost intolerable," as the oil companies would have almost all the operating responsibility without any freedom of investment and without control of production levels.

Subsequently, another top executive referred more positively to the new participation agreement with some of the oil producing governments in the Middle East as an example of building "more stable future relationships," though he conceded, "I won't pretend this was an easy adjustment."

I am afraid that the earlier pessimistic evaluations and reactions of the oil companies' executives to the participation demand will prove to be the correct ones, notwithstanding the firm assurances by the present Saudi Arabian government that Middle East oil should and will be viewed solely commercially and not politically. This is certainly not the position of most other Middle East producing countries and cannot realistically be depended on. A cold-blooded assessment of the real power relationships of the international oil company with the various countries where it operates must lead to the conclusion that its oil production, on which the continued operations of its upstream and downstream facilities are completely dependent, is now or will soon be under the effective control of the producing countries. At the same time, the producing countries will probably deliberately arrange their and the companies' affairs so that the industry's single most important after-tax profit center will, as in the past, be located in the producing countries.

There is thus very little doubt about the change in the role of the oil companies from a bridge between producing and importing countries to what may, in fact, turn out to be that of junior partners of the producing countries. The oil companies will thus be unable to continue to act as an independent-intermediary commercial force in international oil relations; instead, the producing countries will tend to treat them as service companies under their control that will undertake admittedly essential worldwide logistic, technical, financial, production, and distribution operations.

What we are facing, therefore, is a shift of the major center of power over international oil from the home countries to the producing countries. Whether the companies like it or not, they will be compelled to protect their huge interests in the producing countries by adjusting and coordinating their policies and actions with the directives and policies of the producing countries, hoping that their operations in their home countries and the importing countries will not be seriously upset.

The role that the oil companies will be able to play in any of their future dealings with producing countries is thus inevitably severely circumscribed. They cannot be expected to take a strong and determined stand in such negotiations with the sovereign of the country on which their whole prosperity depends and with national companies that are their partners and will in due course acquire the controlling interest in their operations. Moreover, they will have to argue that as long as they are able to secure the availability of supplies for importing countries—even at steeply escalating costs—they also serve the interest of their customers by not risking a confrontation that could lead to interruption of supplies; and as long as the companies are able to recoup such costs from the consumer, they would also protect their own commercial viability. The companies, as private organizations and under the terms of reference applicable to commercial corporations, cannot possibly be expected to carry by themselves the burden of protecting not only their own interests but also those of their customers.

There are thus serious doubts whether the kind of negotiating problems we are facing now can be handled effectively solely through a common posture of the companies or by any other kind of intercompany arrangements. The approach followed in earlier negotiations, when most of the oil companies with foreign production negotiated as a group with OPEC producing countries on matters that vitally affect the tax-paid cost and oil supplies of almost every oil importing country of the free world, must thus be subjected to a most searching review. In particular, it would appear that a broad understanding on energy policy among the various importing and home governments involved is absolutely necessary to avoid misuse of bargaining power by the oil producing countries.

New Role of Importing Country Oil Companies
Based on their predominant investment position in all phases of the local oil industries, the international oil companies will continue to be a most important factor in the refining and distribution of oil in practically all of the countries of the free world. They will also represent the most diversified single

source of crude oil supplies, even though ever increasing quantities will be sold in the international oil trade by the national companies of producing countries. The international oil companies will also continue to make perhaps the most important contribution to diversified exploration, to technology, and to expanded investments.

A course by the United States that would, through the exploitation of its domestic energy resources, lower American dependence on Middle East oil and thereby reduce the competitive bidding-up and depletion of Middle East oil reserves would, however, be a constructive contribution to the oil position of the free world.

But beyond that, the United States has additional possibilities to put a "first mortgage" on some of the richest oil resources in the Middle East. Saudi Arabia controls by far the largest known reserves developed by American oil companies, and the Saudi Arabian government has already evinced its interest to conclude special deals with the United States for increasing oil deliveries. No doubt Iran would be keen to do likewise. However, acceptance by the United States of preferred treatment would be extremely disruptive to its relations with other countries.

The reactions of other importing countries to the Saudi offer is reflected in a statement of the French state-owned oil company Elf-Erap. In referring to the worries that such a policy would cause, it comments: "What an inducement to the raising of crude oil prices if the money paid by Europe and Japan should be invested through the producing state in the country of origin of these companies strengthening their power. Who would still be able to maintain that the companies which produce in Arabia are impartial intermediaries between these countries and the European consumer?"

Along the same line of reasoning Italy's national oil company ENI suggests that the Common Market conclude direct oil supply agreements, in return for cooperation in the producing countries' development plans, to prevent a supply monopoly of the major international oil companies, especially because American and European interests are not identical. Positions expressing similar reactions have been taken by several other major importing countries.

This prevailing fear is perhaps best summarized in a 1972 draft recommendation unanimously approved by the Western

European Union but apparently not endorsed by the Council of Ministers:

... much of the oil imported by Europe is shipped under the American flag. The Middle East oil question is therefore mainly a commercial matter for the United States.

For Western Europe, on the other hand, it is a vital matter and the interests of consumers do not tally with the interests of the international companies. Increased participation in the capital of petrol companies by the Arab States or even nationalization would not necessarily be a catastrophe for Europe.

A European oil policy should take account of these factors and in no case be linked with the international oil companies. This means Europe could reach agreement directly with oil-producing countries, help them to develop a national oil industry and purchase the oil thus produced. ... Europe has no interest in becoming involved in a vain conflict for defense of the oil companies; its interest is to collaborate closely with the Arab States.

But whatever their motivation, the national companies of importing countries will, in any case, greatly expand their foreign supply operations. While such diversification might provide a modicum of added supply security, any new such ventures would be subject to the same kind of political and economic risks as those of the international oil companies.

Also, investments by the producing countries downstream in importing countries are unlikely to take place or to be permitted on a really massive scale; but even if this should occur, these investments are unlikely to provide a much higher degree of oil supply security if the producing countries, for reasons of their own, should decide to withhold oil supplies. Their downstream investments would not constitute an effective hostage in the hands of the importing countries because the latter's continued dependence on oil supplies would be of much greater urgency than the threat of expropriation or the loss of current revenue from such investment.

Moreover, foreign crude secured by a national oil company of an importing country would most likely be given a preferred position in the home market. If so, its dependence on what would most likely be a rather limited number of sources of oil imports would make it even more vulnerable to interruption— and to unilaterally imposed cost increases. If the importing countries would follow a course of "go it alone" in a "*sauve qui peut*" spirit, each one of them would also become the target for potential political and economic blackmail such as some of them have already experienced. They would run the grave risk that their policies and actions would be subverted by considerations of securing or protecting their access to foreign oil; ultimately, such an approach will prove to be futile, and the price for the oil and the political or other terms under which it could be obtained might easily become untenable.

Obviously a continuous process of yielding valid rights, not through genuine bargaining but under threats by the producing countries and a general posture of subservience by the oil companies and the importing countries—as has occurred in recent international oil "negotiations"—must undermine not only the prestige of the importing nations and of the companies but equally the respect for any arrangements concluded with them. Only a coordinated approach to energy policy by the relevant importing countries could really prevent such harmful consequences.

The Interests of the Home Countries of the International Oil Companies

The change in power relationships affecting the operations of the international oil industry also has a far-reaching effect on the position of the companies in their home countries. The interests of the home countries in their international oil companies have in the past centered around their supply capabilities for their own country and its allies, their support of the power position of the home country that was implied in control over international oil resources, the contribution of the companies to the balance of payments, and their essential role in meeting ever increasing worldwide oil requirements.

The ability of the companies to provide secure supplies because of their investment in foreign oil is now no longer absolute and assured. Experience during the first Suez crisis in the case of the United Kingdom and France, and during the Six Day War in the case of the United States and the United Kingdom, has shown that even U.S., British, or French controlled foreign oil could be and was—even though for a short period only—embargoed on shipments to the home countries. While in earlier years the United States was only a marginal importer of Middle East oil, in contrast to the United Kingdom, in the future the United States will become one of the largest single importers of such oil. On the other hand, with the development of the North Sea resources, the United Kingdom—if it could under Common Market rules effectively reserve its domestic oil production for its own use—might be able to achieve a substantial lessening of its dependence on Middle East oil imports.

The same questions hold for the extent to which Anglo-American ownership provides supply assurance to our allies. As a matter of fact, some of our allies fear that American ownership of foreign oil might endanger their supply if there should be conflict between the United States and the producing countries.

In the past, control over the international oil companies could be and was used as a political instrument by their home countries in their relations with importing countries—as the United States apparently did during the first Suez crisis or, say, for oil trade with Cuba, and so on. This possibility, to use the control over foreign oil for political-strategic purposes of the home countries, is disappearing fast.

The contribution of the international oil industries to the balance of payments of their home countries is indeed substantial, but it is relatively more important for the United Kingdom than for the United States. In the future, with large increases in U.S. oil imports and the continued need for reinvestment abroad, the balance-of-payments concern of the United States with regard to international oil may be directed more to the huge and escalating foreign exchange costs of oil imports rather than to the benefits of profit transfers from international oil operations. In the United Kingdom, on the other hand, the development of the North Sea resources may relieve the oil trade bill sufficiently so as to maintain a predominant interest in the profit transfers from British international oil companies.

In sum, therefore, the fundamental interest of the United States is moving somewhat closer to that of an oil importing country. On the other hand, the United Kingdom might, for the reasons cited above perhaps, pay more attention to the profit pattern of its companies from international oil operations.

There are, however, important additional qualifying factors affecting the security position of the home countries, and especially the United States, with regard to their oil supplies—independent of their position as home countries of worldwide oil companies.

What is relevant now is not so much any influence that the international oil companies may or may not be able to wield in producing countries, but the interest that producing countries have in maintaining an effective relationship with the United States. After all, the United States is the most important political, economic, and military power of the free world, and, incidentally, also presents one of the largest and highest priced markets for imported oil. This, above all, explains Saudi Arabia's and also Iran's interest in trying to conclude special oil supply arrangements with the United States—not the investment of U.S. oil companies in their country, which, as far as Iran is concerned, would anyhow be a minority interest. Moreover, the United States offers the most important potential outlet for their capital investments and constitutes one of the largest sources for capital equipment, consumer goods, and military hardware.

Finally, the United States is the only power that can effectively assure protection against Communist—Soviet as well as Chinese—external and internal incursions. It is the one country that the traditional regimes of the two most important oil producing nations of the Persian Gulf—Iran and Saudi Arabia—believe they can depend on for the maintenance of their governments and for the security of the Persian Gulf area.

In the light of the U.S. possibilities for developing domestic potential in conventional and nonconventional hydrocarbon and energy resources, and its opportunity for establishing a special oil relationship with the two most important Middle East oil producers, there is little doubt that if it so desires, the United States could go it alone.

With the development of the North Sea oil fields, the United Kingdom will be less dependent on Middle East oil than any of its Common Market partners. Nevertheless, apparently the United Kingdom, in the Paris Summit Meeting of October 1972, was pressing for an early formulation of an energy policy for the Community that would guarantee certain and lasting supplies under satisfactory economic conditions.

This policy suggestion must be evaluated within the context of today's stark realities: that unilateral and diverse policies of the various European nations and of Japan cannot provide real supply security or contain the financial problems connected with the international oil trade, that the international oil companies no longer possess the bargaining strength, if left to themselves, to be effective negotiators with producing countries with regard to the availability and cost of oil, and that such a state of affairs would provide the most cogent reason for the importing countries to work together toward an energy policy.

But the ultimate interest of the most important producing countries in the Middle East that have not fallen under Russian domination is bound to remain the protection of their independence, and that can only be achieved by close and friendly relationships with the United States. The United States will thus continue to be the dominant factor in world oil, not because of the foreign oil interests of its companies, but primarily because of its standing in the world balance of power. An energy policy applying solely to the Community would, I believe, be only the first step toward a really effective policy.

The Need for an Atlantic-Japanese Energy Policy

Beyond doubt, U.S. relations with Europe and Japan are in disarray. There are many outstanding unresolved problems.

Perhaps instead of establishing a grand design that would encompass a resolution of all major contentions and areas of conflicts, it might be more fruitful to proceed pragmatically on an issue-by-issue basis and tackle first those problems where the chances of an Atlantic-Japanese policy, or at least of an agreed-upon coordinated approach, would seem to be most promising. (The European Common Market was preceded by the establishment of a much more limited joint effort, the European Coal and Steel Community.)

The problem of the future energy position of the Atlantic-Japanese complex of nations is one of the most important issues confronting each country individually and in a group. What is likely to induce the various countries to agree to cooperation and mutual adjustments is the existence of a severe outside threat to their security and prosperity, resulting from their dependence on oil supplies from a few foreign sources, coupled with the potential danger of a flood of foreign funds that could harm their own economies and the world's monetary system.

The weak and unstable foreign political societies where the world's oil and money power centers are located could, for reasons of their own or because stirred up by the potentially adversary policies of the Russians and even perhaps the Chinese People's Republic, create great difficulties for the various countries of the free world. The United States as well as the United Kingdom would—shortsightedly, to be sure—by themselves probably be able to resolve their energy problems, partly at the expense of other importing countries. But as mentioned before, it is to the United States, more than to any other nation of the free world, that pivotal producing countries look for their political and strategic security; and this advantage could redound to the benefit of all oil importing countries. Neither the Common Market nor Japan alone or in combination could provide a comparable total package of advantages for the well-being of the major Middle East oil producing countries.

If, therefore, the United States abstains from any attempt to try to obtain unilateral benefits, however short lived they might prove to be, and is willing to participate in an energy policy in a new Atlantic-Japanese partnership, it might thereby provide protection for its partners against potentially very serious oil supply emergencies. Obviously, the latter, too, must then forego the temptation of looking only at their immediate self-interest without regard to others—a policy that they could in any case not pursue successfully over any period of time. Only then would it be possible for the importing countries to pursue a rational policy for their energy imports and avoid bidding against each other or being played against each other with ever escalating political and economic demands being made upon them. Only then would it be possible for Atlantic-Japanese and especially U.S. power to become an effective countervailing factor in international oil.

The need for a joint or at least coordinated policy is urgent, because any delays in which conflicting approaches to producing countries are made by the individual members of the Atlantic-Japanese group of nations will accelerate not only the disintegration of the partnership but will further encourage arbitrary and dictatorial demands from the producing countries. Moreover, as some of the producing countries accumulate large surplus reserve funds, it might become much more difficult, if not impossible, for the importing countries to influence their policies.

It would appear, therefore, that Europe and Japan need something from the United States which it is in the interest of the United States to give, that is, its adherence to a coordinated Atlantic-Japanese energy policy, in, as the game theorists would call it, a positive sum game through which all sides would gain.

This does not imply that any of the partners should necessarily be inhibited from pursuing separate diplomatic and economic initiatives within the broad spectrum of developing Middle East relationships and the framework of an Atlantic-Japanese energy policy.

The OECD (Organization for Economic Cooperation and Development) Oil Committee has for many years served as the most significant international organization encompassing the Atlantic-Japanese group of nations. It provides a basis for the exchange of information and coordination and expert analyses on oil developments. Most important, it has established policies for emergency stockpiling and, within certain limits, for the emergency apportionment of oil supplies in the OECD European area; during oil emergencies it has, in fact, served as a clearing body to achieve an equitable division of available supplies among its members.

The Common Market is presently engaged in a slow and difficult effort to establish an energy policy for its members. But national policies of individual members could severely slow up the establishment of a Community policy as long as there is no overriding conviction on the part of its members that the Community countries in combination would decisively add to their individual bargaining strength.

In the light of the changed power relationships of today, an effective energy policy of a new Atlantic-Japanese partnership must inevitably go further than either the OECD or the Common Market have advanced so far. Obviously, however, such a policy would build on the valuable achievements of the OECD and the Common Market.

Fortunately, there is a substantial consensus, in the United States as well as in the Common Market and Japan, on the need for a coordinated or even joint approach to the energy problem. It is reflected in many official pronouncements during the last year or two.

The United States, in a 1972 statement before an OECD Council Meeting, officially expressed its readiness for such cooperation:

It is imperative for the world's major consumers of oil and other forms of energy to take joint and coordinated action, starting now, to increase the availability of all types of energy resources; to lessen, to the degree possible, an overdependence on oil from the Middle East, to coordinate the response of consuming countries to restrictions on the supply of Middle East petroleum, and to develop jointly and cooperatively a responsible program of action to meet the possibility of critical energy shortages by the end of this decade.

The OECD itself is again engaged in a study of the world energy situation, and this will hopefully lead to concrete recommendations for action by the member governments. The Common Market Commission considers it necessary to substitute or extend liaison in the energy field between the Community and other energy importing countries in order to provide a better exchange of information and produce common solutions.

Japan, through its Overall Energy Council, an advisory body to the minister of international trade and industry, recommended in 1971 that while it was necessary for Japan in order to assure stable oil supplies at low cost to behave independently of any foreign influence in all aspects of oil industry activities, it must also cooperate with other consuming countries:

To this end it is necessary for Japan to promote with them and their national oil companies exchange of information and mutual understanding and to explore possibilities for constructive cooperation on the part of oil consuming countries toward the formation of an organization in which debates are held among the countries with international oil companies and the oil-producing countries on the basic policy concerning the world oil situation.

As the Natural Resources Survey Mission, sponsored by the Japanese foreign office, put it in its report published in 1972, Japan must engage in active participation in international cooperation with advanced countries on oil matters and "must refrain from being passive as has been the case thus far. It must take full advantage of opportunities such as an OECD Oil Committee meeting where industrially advanced nations meet, through which Japan could clarify her oil policy on international cooperation before the OECD member countries."

Outline for an Atlantic-Japanese Energy Policy

The major goal of an energy policy for a new Atlantic-Japanese partnership must be to try to cope with the common problems of the security of oil supplies and the financial issues related to it. While nobody can guarantee that such a policy will lead to a completely satisfactory resolution of all the problems, it should at least be possible to contain them. Future bargaining in international oil would no longer be lopsided—that is, between the producing countries as a group and the oil companies (be they the internationals or the national companies of importing countries) with the latter "negotiating" under the threat of being treated as virtual captives of the producing countries—but would engage the extraordinary political, strategic, and economic power of the Atlantic-Japanese group of nations.

If such "countervailing power" to OPEC should really become a factor in international oil, which indeed it must, there is some reasonable hope that international oil and financial arrangements could be set up on a rational and manageable basis and that OPEC would no longer be able, as Mr. Yamani put it in October 1972, through its coordination and unity to "prove time and time again that it can enforce its demands."

Some fear has been expressed that such a grouping of oil importing countries might unnecessarily provoke a confrontation with the producing countries. But circumstances have significantly tipped the balance of power during the last few years. Through the establishment of OPEC an organization was created that formulates policy guidelines for major producing countries; by the threat of withholding supplies to companies that do not submit to its demands and by other means, it can provide enormous power and overwhelming bargaining leverage for each of the producing nations. Moreover, the Organization of Arab Petroleum Exporting Countries (OAPEC) has stated its intention to establish official relations with countries of the EEC, either collectively or individually. To this purpose, it announced in 1971 that it is setting up a committee to coordinate the relations of its member countries with the EEC countries.

The subject matters to be covered by the energy policy could be put in the following broad categories:

1. Develop a program for optimum diversification of supplies, based on a study and review of energy demand and supply, including tanker, pipeline, and refining availabilities.

2. Develop new energy sources, especially atomic energy and energy from unconventional sources, through a joint research program.

3. Create national and multinational incentive, investment, and guarantee programs for the development of new energy sources.

4. Establish broad terms of reference and parameters acceptable to the oil importing countries for oil supplies from producing countries; these should cover purchases, service contracts, concessions, and so on.

5. Set up a contingency system for stockpiling, rationing, and equitable sharing of imports between all members, to be put into effect in case of an overall or specific country emergency.

6. Set up a joint and coordinated research program that looks into all methods of conservation of energy, including research on battery-powered cars, nuclear-fueled shipping, savings in motor car transportation, and so on.

7. Review and coordinate programs of economic development and technical assistance for producing countries.

8. Review prices, costs, and the balance-of-payments effects of oil imports for member countries and for developing countries; set up a program for support and adjustment if necessary.

9. Review the government revenues of major oil producing countries and their impact on world trade, world capital flows, and short-term money markets; set up a program of financial cooperation—if necessary.

10. Review the dependency of Middle East producing countries on exports from the free world's oil importing countries: for industrial and agricultural goods, military equipment, technical know-how, shipping, and services. Assess in light of this the mutual interdependence and the means that might be available to cope with an oil or financial emergency.

The administration of the energy policy might be entrusted to a special new-level International Energy Council, composed of member states with a top-level permanent staff having generally recognized and incontestable professional and practical experience. The timing and method of its establishment, its organizational structure, the range of its executive and/or advisory powers, the procedures on voting, and the rules governing ratification and implementation of its decisions and its relationship with the various member countries and their oil companies would, of course, be determined in a process of give and take through international negotiations. It will, obviously, be very difficult indeed to achieve any such agreement; but it may well be the only remaining chance to attempt to safeguard the interests of the importing countries, the home countries, and those of their oil companies. Whatever the odds, it must certainly be tried, and there is no time to be lost.

The above proposal presents, of course, only one of several possible approaches to an Atlantic-Japanese energy policy and its implementation. In particular, a great deal of thought must be given to the problem of whether it would be feasible and advisable to restructure the present OECD Oil Committee or its High Level Committee so that the conclusion and implementation of an Atlantic-Japanese energy policy could be handled within the framework of the Committee. While this might require substantial changes in the powers and functions of the OECD Oil Committee, it might be more expeditious and easier to reach an agreement on a revision of an existing international organization concerned with the oil policy of importing countries than to start from scratch and establish a completely new international body.

The competence and functions of the International Energy Council, however it were to be set up, as well as those of the member countries and those of the oil companies, must, of course, be clearly delineated. The policy framework established by the Council would set the limits within which the countries as well as the oil companies would handle their affairs, taking into account their changing responsibilities and capabilities.

At the same time it would try to provide an effective basis for protecting the supply security of the oil importing countries through encouraging the development of added supplies, diversification, investment incentives, research, assuring sufficient tanker and refining availability, and so on. Through stockpiling, coordination of rationing policy, and especially through an emergency import-sharing agreement among all members, an oil embargo by producing countries against selected countries would become much more difficult, if not practically impossible; in such circumstances the producing countries would have to be prepared to cut their oil supplies to all member countries—with unpredictable, dangerous consequences.

The conclusion of an effective arrangement for emergency import sharing between the Atlantic nations and Japan would presuppose that each member country, including, of course, the United States and Japan, would be prepared to share with its partners its own import availabilities in an equitable manner on the basis of agreed-upon principles. The establishment of substantial stockpiles of oil by the various importing countries, again including the United States and Japan, would provide them in case of emergency with time for possible supply-demand adjustments, for efforts to resolve equitably any underlying conflicts with the producing countries, or, if everything else fails, for initiating whatever measures are required to protect their security. Arrangements on sharing of import availabilities and stockpiling applicable to all nations of the new Atlantic-Japanese partnership may well prove to be the touchstone and provide the foundation for a broadly conceived energy policy such as that outlined above; they may well be considered as the essential initial step on which it should be possible to achieve more easily an early international agreement.

Likewise, a joint or coordinated policy on dealing with supply, trade, and financial problems related to oil would have the best chance to lead to rational and manageable solutions of the very difficult issues that are bound to arise. The producing countries could no longer, so to speak, pick out consuming countries one by one; OPEC itself has, in its own resolutions, introduced similar measures of solidarity among the producing countries.

Moreover, the companies in their negotiations on prices and payments to producing governments, which will come up for revision by 1976 at the latest—and which OPEC's secretary general has already described as the next major issue—

would no longer be exposed to unilateral dictates as in the past. Their negotiating stance would be based on broad terms of reference, such as might be recommended or formulated by an International Energy Council, similar to the practice OPEC is applying in suggesting the basic position for producing countries. There need no longer be the hectic and somewhat improvised discussions and confrontation between oil companies and producing countries, as experienced between 1970 and 1972 in the Tripoli-Tehran and participation arrangements, which were brought about by ultimatums of the producing countries rather than through genuine negotiations.

Under current conditions, as pointed out earlier, there would be very little if any bargaining leverage left with the oil companies if, in their negotiations with the producing countries, they were to depend solely on their own strength. Only a firm backing by all major oil importing countries could provide the necessary countervailing power that would permit the oil companies to establish a credible negotiating stance. The companies, acting within their terms of reference and within the framework of a coordinated energy policy, could thus count on a backing that should enable them to handle international oil negotiations and their implementation.

In this connection, an additional factor in the assessment of the respective bargaining leverage by either side would undoubtedly be the awareness that there is a limit to which the oil companies, together with the importing countries, could be held hostage by a threat to their access to reserves in producing countries; in certain circumstances it might be preferable to abandon the role of hostage and to turn away from the reserves and reappear as competitive buyers of crude from the producing countries. Since the captive concession-holding companies would no longer be at their behest, one might expect that OPEC unity would erode and that producing countries would eventually compete with each other for export sales to the companies, which would derive purchasing power from past investment in and current control over transport, refining, and marketing facilities—the power to dispose.

The importing countries, through extending economic and technical cooperation to the developing producing countries, should contribute to the advance in their standard of living, the diversification of their economic activities, and the expansion of their general import and export trade. Hopefully, the producing countries will in due course become such an integral part of the world economy that they would be much less tempted to take radical measures that might sever these links. If the dependence of the producing countries on continued oil revenues, flow of trade, and friendly political and economic relations with the free world is such that they could not risk more than a very short interruption, then and only then will the producing countries act with circumspection and probably be sufficiently discouraged from attempting to impose an oil embargo.

In particular, the producing countries would be constrained to exercise great caution not to confront importing countries or their companies—if firmly backed by all major importing countries—with unreasonable demands if the turmoil resulting from a confrontation is likely to undermine the regimes of the oil producing countries, or if they would have reason to fear that their actions might provoke dangerous international repercussions affecting their integrity and security.

Moreover, the producing countries are fully aware that if their relations with the major importing countries should deteriorate gravely, they may have to rely on Russian support, which not only could not provide anything comparable to the benefits they are enjoying from dealing with the free world, but would confront them with grave political and other risks.

Obviously, too, the more essential oil supplies from the Middle East become, the more attractive a target it would offer for Russian subversion and control. For the Communist world, the concentration of oil and money power in a few small countries in the Persian Gulf, at their back door, presents an enviable opportunity to attempt to undermine the political and economic strength of the free world by "peaceful means" through the encouragement of all the nationalistic and centrifugal tendencies that already exist in the area. However, any serious threat to Middle East oil supplies could, in such circumstances, easily lead to a confrontation between the major powers. Only friendly relations with the free world, including the United States, can hold the Russians at bay. A united or coordinated Atlantic-Japanese posture with regard to oil provides the most persuasive safeguard for the security, prosperity, and integrity of the importing as well as producing countries.

What I am suggesting, therefore, in proposing the establishment of an Atlantic-Japanese energy policy, is not designed to lead to escalation of international oil problems, as a prelude to a confrontation with OPEC, but is, I believe, *the only way to avoid confrontation.* Also, while taking account of the changed role and power of the oil companies, it will strengthen them in their relations with producing countries, rather than leave them and the importing countries at their mercy.

This approach presents the most effective means to make obvious to all concerned that the Atlantic-Japanese group of nations could not and would not sit by passively if the flow of international oil and the world's monetary arrangements were to be jeopardized by arbitrary conditions or unacceptable political and economic pressures. The mere awareness that there are practical limits to the exercise of "oil or money power" by the producing countries may well prove to be the most effective deterrent to its misuse.

There is an urgent need for coordinated planning and action by the government of the United States together with its Atlantic partners and Japan. Inevitably, a newly established Atlantic-Japanese energy policy and measures designed to achieve optimum energy security for the free world would lead to a much greater involvement of governments in what had previously been considered to be industry affairs, with all that this may imply. But there are no realistic alternatives, and the time for action is now, if not yesterday.

SEABEDS MAKE STRANGE POLITICS
by Ann L. Hollick

The United States is obviously the world's foremost maritime power, but its two long coastlines and its Hawaiian and Alaskan archipelagos also give it substantial coastal interests. U.S. ocean policy is, therefore, characterized by much conflict between coastal and maritime interests and represents a series of tenuous compromises. Since the first announcements in 1970 of U.S. policies on seabed resource exploitation and other law of the sea issues, the policy compromises have evolved steadily away from ones favoring military-strategic interest to ones favoring coastal economic interests. This evolution has been due in part to international pressure and in part to an increase in policy influence of domestic interest groups with coastal concerns.

The ocean policy process involves a blend of domestic and foreign policy considerations. As domestic interests have become more involved in the policy process, the foreign policy latitude of both the State Department and White House has diminished. Few issues of foreign policy impinge on such a complex array of national and commercial interests in the United States and abroad and involve such a complex interaction of interests and prespectives within the U.S. government. At the heart of the ocean issues is the allocation and use of ocean space.

While the Nixon-Kissinger NSC system has ensured that contentious ocean policy questions come to the White House for resolution, other factors have allowed lower-level bureaucrats to retain substantial policy control. The process leading up to a White House decision, and even the decision itself, is largely determined by the skill of contending bureaucrats in formulating and presenting options for presidential consideration. Then, of course, the implementation of policy, once a presidential decision is reached, allows the bureaucrat substantial freedom from White House supervision. This is especially true of ocean policy, where the subject is relatively technical and its urgency is not self-evident. This not only

"Seabeds Make Strange Politics" was published originally in *Foreign Policy*, Number 9, Winter 1972-73

results in a rather closed group of interacting policy experts but also tends to insulate these decision makers from ongoing White House review.

As announced in August 1970, U.S. policy with respect to the exploitation of seabed minerals favored a narrow zone of national jurisdiction and the establishment of an international seabed regime beyond. Exclusive coastal state control over the mineral resources of the continental shelf would extend only to the 200-meter isobath. Beyond that, in an intermediate zone reaching to the outer edge of the continental margin, the coastal state would act as a "trustee" for the international seabed authority. In the deep seabed the authority would license the exploitation of minerals, and a substantial portion of the revenues generated in the international area (including the intermediate zone) would be distributed to developing nations.

In the last two years, U.S. policy has shifted away from insistence that national jurisdiction be limited to the 200-meter isobath; increasingly, the United States is responding to strong international and domestic pressures in favor of a broader national resource or economic zone. The government now simply delineates the provisions that must apply in undefined coastal zones of national resource jurisdiction. In such areas, the United States insists on international agreement to certain standards and provisions for compulsory dispute settlement to protect other uses of the area and to safeguard the integrity of investments.

On the second set of major ocean policy issues—territorial seas, straits, and fisheries—the U.S. government has also moved toward greater concessions for coastal interests. In August 1971 the U.S. government indicated that it was prepared to agree to a twelve-mile territorial sea provided that international agreement was reached on freedom of transit through and over international straits that would otherwise be closed by this extension of the territorial sea. At the same time, the United States was prepared to accept limited preferential rights for coastal nations over the fishery resources off their shores. While the U.S. position on straits and the territorial sea has remained virtually unchanged since this announcement, the U.S. fishing position has evolved toward acceptance of coastal state management of coastal and anadromous species* of fish.

*Such as salmon, which spawn in fresh water.

Seabeds: The Policy Participants

Only four domestic interests have had a significant influence on or involvement in policy formulation—the petroleum industry, the military, the hard minerals industry, and the marine science community. The most powerful private interest in the seabed debate has been the petroleum industry. Equally powerful, and in most instances in opposition to petroleum, has been the Defense Department. While the military and the scientist are interested in mobility on the oceans, the petroleum and hard minerals industries share a new interest in the exploitation of fixed mineral resources. The clash between these new and old ocean uses has been the central element in the formulation of U.S. seabed policy. Seabed policy has two major aspects: (1) the delimitation of national jurisdiction over seabed minerals and (2) the nature of the seabed regime to be established beyond national jurisdiction. Each of the four interests is concerned with different aspects of seabed policy. While the petroleum industry is primarily interested in determining the location of the boundary of national jurisdiction, the hard minerals industry is concerned with the seabed regime to be established beyond that boundary. The military and the marine scientist are concerned with both of these questions insofar as they might affect their mobility on the oceans. Conflict has therefore arisen over both the national boundary and the international regime—between Defense and the petroleum industry in the former case and between Defense and the hard minerals industry in the latter. The clash over the boundary issue began earlier than that over the regime and has been much more virulent, due in no small measure to the relative power parity of Defense and petroleum interests.

The policy dispute over the boundary began with the 1968 discovery that seabed petroleum deposits are generally limited to the continental margin. On the basis of these findings, major segments of the U.S. petroleum industry moved quickly to stake out a policy position on the location of the continental shelf boundary. Strongly supported by the National Petroleum Council and the Department of the Interior, the petroleum industry argued that it was vital to the nation's security to ensure independent sources of petroleum by affirming national control of all the energy resources of the continental margin. The alternative, they said, would be a dangerous dependence on foreign petroleum.

The industry urged the U.S. government to assert unilaterally sovereign rights over offshore seabed resources to the outer edge of the continental margin. This, they argued, would in no way impair high seas freedoms in the area. Underlying the industry's policy recommendation was the traditional belief, shared by both the domestic and overseas branches of the petroleum industry, that in gaining access to resources off the U.S. coasts as well as off those of other nations it was safer and more profitable for American firms to deal bilaterally with coastal nations rather than with an unfamiliar international regime, possibly weighted against U.S. interests.

As the petroleum industry began to advance this position within the government, the Defense Department position on the boundary moved in the opposite direction. The military observed that the Interior Department's issuing of leases at depths far greater than the 200-meter isobath constituted de facto extension of the U.S. continental shelf based on the exploitability clause of the Geneva Convention on the Continental Shelf. Although under the Convention resource jurisdiction would not affect other uses of the area, the military still feared that such limited resource sovereignty would gradually expand, through the phenomenon of "creeping jurisdiction," to full territorial sovereignty. This, the military feared, would ultimately close off U.S. military access to coastal areas around the world. To avert this outcome, Defense proposed limiting the size of special purpose or resource zones in the oceans.

With regard to seabed minerals, the Defense Department sought international agreement on a continental shelf extending no farther than the 200-meter isobath. To sell such a scheme to other governments, the Defense Department proposed the establishment of a generous and powerful seabed mineral regime in the area beyond the narrow continental shelf. In an unsuccessful effort to convince the skeptical petroleum industry of the merits of such a boundary, the Defense Department pointed out that 94 percent of the world's continental margins were off foreign shores. To gain access to these, it was far better for the petroleum industry to deal with an impartial international seabed authority than to deal bilaterally with unpredictable national governments that might resort to harassment, profit squeezing, or outright expropriation. The technological superiority of the U.S. petroleum industry and the dominant role that the U.S. government would play in an international seabed authority would assure favorable treatment for U.S. companies.

Inherent in the Defense position was a readiness to risk the petroleum industry's resource interests in return for internationally agreed-upon rights of transit. The industry predictably opposed such a tradeoff and fought it vigorously through the Interior Department. The industry's ready access to information and to policymakers within the government contributed to its effective and early input into the policy process.

The hard minerals and marine science interests were less fortunate. Throughout 1969 and 1970 neither hard minerals nor science was adequately represented in the closely held policy deliberations within the government. The primary concern of the hard minerals industry has been the nature of the regime rather than the location of the continental shelf boundary. Of interest to the industry is the manganese nodule. Because nodules of commercial value are rarely found on the continental margin, setting the continental shelf boundary at any point up to the outer edge of the margin will have no significant effect on the miner of nodules.

For tactical purposes, the hard minerals industry was willing to support a narrow but expanding boundary, *if* such a boundary could be used to buy a satisfactory seabed regime entailing minimal financial exactions and a weak international authority to register claims and grant exclusive licenses to exploit. Although the industry was willing to trade the petroleum industry's interest in the boundary for such a regime, it soon found the Defense Department to be a dangerous ally. To induce other nations to agree to a narrow continental shelf, Defense was urging the establishment of a generous and powerful seabed regime to administer the exploration and exploitation of seabed resources and to allocate substantial revenues from these activities to an international development fund. The hard minerals interest was unsuccessful in resisting the Defense Department position. Because of its position on the boundary, the hard minerals interest had lost the support of the petroleum industry, and within the Interior Department petroleum took priority over hard minerals interests.

The interests of marine science were somewhat different. The scientist has sought to include explicit guarantees for legitimate scientific research, as distinguished from commercial and military investigations. Such guarantees necessarily imply the absence of a similar freedom for military uses and have been strongly resisted by the military. The National Science Foundation has failed to override this military opposition.

An additional interest with limited influence on ocean policy until the past year is that of the Department of State. The State Department's guiding objective is to advance U.S. ocean interests in international negotiations while maintaining ordered and harmonious relations with other nations on the broad range of ocean issues. To achieve policy control, State has made strenuous efforts to resolve domestic disagreements over ocean issues. Since the seabed issue was first introduced in the United Nations in 1967, the State Department has encountered a series of obstacles and has been placed in the unenviable position of having to stall in the face of growing international pressures.

The first difficulty was that of resolving internal bureaucratic contention over control of ocean policy. This was definitively resolved in 1970 when the legal adviser, John Stevenson, became the head of a consolidated Interagency Law of the Sea Task Force.

A second difficulty in formulating a unified seabed policy was the growing dispute between the departments of Interior and Defense. In a successful effort to forestall the imposition of a boundary policy by the State Department, the Department of Defense requested an Under Secretaries Committee review of the seabed boundary question. In response to this request, the White House issued a National Security Study Memorandum (NSSM) in July 1969 proposing that, in the absence of interagency agreement, the Under Secretaries Committee meet to consider the position that the United States should take in the United Nations regarding the location of the continental shelf boundary.

Between the July 1969 NSSM and the January 1970 meeting of the Under Secretaries Committee, the State Department intensified its efforts to reach a compromise acceptable to both sides. To accommodate the interests of Defense and Interior, State proposed an intermediate zone between the

200-meter isobath and the edge of the continental margin. In this zone, the coastal nation would enjoy control over the exploitation of seabed resources. While responsible for enforcing standards against pollution and navigation hazards, the coastal nation could not exclude other nations from conducting scientific research or military activities on the continental margin beyond the 200-meter isobath. The State Department compromise further stipulated that a small royalty of 2 percent, based on the value of resources exploited in the zone, would be paid to an international community fund.

The compromise received a mixed reception. While Interior did not object to it strenuously, the Defense Department rejected it flatly. Defense argued that an intermediate zone would be temporary at best and that giving the coastal state exclusive jurisdiction over resource exploitation on the continental margin would jeopardize the freedom of other nations to use that area for other purposes. Explicit guarantees of access for military or scientific purposes, Defense argued, would simply not be acceptable to coastal nations. Only combining a narrow continental shelf with a satisfactory international regime would halt proliferation of unilateral national claims.

Seabeds: Power to the NSC

With this final failure to reach agreement, the Under Secretaries Committee meeting was scheduled for January 29, 1970, and the major contenders assiduously recruited allies within the bureaucracy. Interior consolidated the backing of the Commerce Department and won the added support of the Bureau of the Budget and John Ehrlichman's White House staff. The Defense Department found backing within the Justice Department and the National Security Council. And, behind its intermediate zone proposal, the State Department lined up the Transportation Department and the National Science Foundation.

Given the obvious power of the major antagonists—the petroleum industry and the military—allies seemed scarcely necessary to ensure that the Under Secretaries Committee would not render a judgment adverse to either interest. In any case, under the NSC options system the Committee did not have the power to impose a decision. Chaired by the then Under Secretary of State Elliott Richardson, the Committee's mandate was limited to submitting a report to the president's special assistant, Henry Kissinger, for review and consideration by the president. The result of the meeting, therefore, was a foregone conclusion. The only decision taken was to send the policy dispute further up the NSC ladder with Under Secretary Richardson's recommendation accompanied by position papers from the dissenting agencies.

In the month and a half immediately after the Under Secretaries Committee meeting, the Defense Department and its supporters mounted a vigorous campaign against the State Department position. In response to these objections and in his capacity as chairman of the Under Secretaries Committee, Richardson proposed a fourth policy position on the continental shelf boundary and the seabed regime. The new position was an obvious compromise between the State position on an intermediate zone and the Defense position in favor of a narrow continental shelf. Richardson proposed that the concept of the intermediate zone be retained but that the zone be expressly incorporated into the international regime. Within the intermediate zone, the coastal state would have the exclusive right to grant concessions and to collect substantial royalties which would be allocated to international economic development. Richardson's proposal differed from the original State position on the outer limit of the national continental shelf boundary and the size of royalties to be allocated to the international community. It promptly superseded the earlier State proposal as the new official State Department position.

The reactions of both Defense and Interior to the revised State Department position were revealing. The Defense Department continued to prefer its own concept of preferential bidding rights for coastal nations, but it deemed the new proposal acceptable as a "fall-back" position since it explicitly stipulated that national sovereignty would end at the 200-meter isobath. The Interior Department was far less sanguine about Mr. Richardson's proposal. Interior's main objection was to the provisions that would give the international community discretionary authority in the intermediate zone and would only allow the coastal state to act as "trustee." Such authority would mean that the international community, of which developing nations constitute a majority, would have the power to decide upon and to impose production controls, to fix high royalty payments, to impose other onerous restrictions upon the coastal state, or to exclude the coastal state altogether from its trusteeship zone. Finally, the Interior Department expressed concern that the Richardson proposal, unlike its predecessor in the State Department, called for large royalties to be paid to an international fund. The Interior Department urged, therefore, a return to the abandoned State position on the shelf boundary and a seabed regime.

With the formulation of the Richardson proposal and the retention of the original State Department proposal at the insistence of Interior, there were four policy options to be considered by the White House. Although these were sent to the president in March, no decision was made until the end of May. The continental shelf/seabed regime issue had to compete with seemingly more urgent matters for the time and attention of busy presidential advisers. A more fundamental source of delay, however, was the difficulty White House officials had mastering the complex technical and legal issues of the seabed question. Mr. Kissinger was particularly reluctant to involve himself in a subject with which he had little experience. Hence the problem was shoved aside.

This state of affairs might have persisted indefinitely had not other parts of the White House intervened in the agency dispute. Because the continental shelf/seabed regime problem spans domestic as well as foreign policy considerations, the Interior Department solicited the support of John Ehrlichman, the president's adviser for domestic affairs. Unlike Mr. Kissinger, Mr. Ehrlichman was quite prepared to take a position on this question after an initial briefing by Interior Department officials. Mr. Ehrlichman was concerned that an executive branch policy in support of a narrow continental shelf would expose the president to the politically damaging charge of "giving away" the nation's mineral estate. Therefore, Ehrlichman opted for either the Interior Department or the original State Department position. NSC officials received Mr. Ehrlichman's intervention in a foreign policy matter with less than complete enthusiasm. They were concerned that American strategic interests would be gravely endangered by the wide continental shelf policies of the Interior and original State positions. Thus, the lines were firmly drawn between the president's foreign and domestic affairs advisers, and the issue was once again stalled.

External events, however, combined to force strenuous efforts within the White House to negotiate a mutually acceptable options paper for the president. While the United Nations Seabed Committee was pressing ahead with its deliberations, a growing number of countries were laying claim to extensive offshore jurisdiction—Brazil to a 200-mile territorial sea and Canada to a 100-mile pollution safety zone. News of the interagency dispute was leaking to Congress and the press. The Senate Interior and Insular Affairs Committee was threatening to hold hearings exposing the interagency dispute, and to issue a report on its own in the absence of a prompt presidential decision.

The challenge, therefore, was to prepare an options memorandum for the president that was acceptable to both Ehrlichman and Kissinger. Of paramount concern to Ehrlichman in the first drafts by the NSC was the omission of the original State Department position as one of the options to go to the president. This position, in Ehrlichman's view, offered the best compromise between domestic and foreign policy considerations. The Defense Department position did not ensure national control over the valuable petroleum resources of the U.S. continental margin. The Interior Department position, on the other hand, ignored the problem of creeping jurisdiction. And, in a contest between the Richardson and the first State Department positions, Ehrlichman preferred the latter since it recognized the inherent legal rights of states to the resources of their continental margins.

The Ehrlichman views were taken into account in the final version of the option paper sent to the president over Kissinger's signature at the end of April. The NSC staff, however, was responsible for structuring the memorandum, giving it an obvious advantage in determining the president's decision. After setting out the four agency positions and their rationales, and after explaining Ehrlichman's support for the original State position, Kissinger recommended that the president choose either the Defense or the Richardson option. The Richardson position thereby became the obvious middle position and was adopted by the president.

After months of delay while the issue made its way to the White House, the president's decision was taken after only brief consideration and on the basis of a carefully constructed set of options. Once President Nixon selected the Richardson option, the "NSC system" again took over. In cooperation with the State Department, the victorious agency, the NSC staff drafted a National Security Decision Memorandum conveying the President's decision to the heads of all interested federal agencies. The NSDM outlined the principles that were to govern a prospective treaty to be submitted to the UN Seabed Committee. It also specified that the State Department would be responsible for preparing the treaty, the U.S. negotiating position, and the necessary legislative measures, in coordination with Defense and Interior.

The stipulation that the State Department coordinate its efforts to negotiate a seabed treaty with both Interior and Defense merely confirmed the fact that the NSC system reserved all critical foreign policy issues for White House decision. From the time of the June 1969 National Security Study Memorandum, the State Department had been effectively precluded from making an independent decision on the seabed regime without the agreement of all affected agencies. The January 1970 meeting of the Under Secretaries Committee was simply one further step in the progress of the decision to the White House. Elliot Richardson, chairman of the committee, did not have the authority under the NSC system to impose a decision. His recommendations simply went to the president as one of several options advanced by the dissenting agencies. The options as they reached the president were carefully structured and articulated by Kissinger and his staff, with the intervention in this instance of Ehrlichman. At the top of the pyramid was the president, advised by Kissinger to adopt the Richardson or the Defense option. The success of the Richardson position lay as much in its presentation as in its intrinsic merit or persuasiveness. No doubt Kissinger's and Nixon's personal rapport with Richardson was an important factor in their choice.

While the NSC options system reserved the key or disputed ocean policy decisions for the White House, the implementation of those decisions was left to lower-level bureaucrats. A key role thus remained for the technicians who had mastered the complex legal, geological, strategic, and economic ocean issues.

Seabeds: The President's Policy

The "president's seabed policy" was announced by John Stevenson, the legal adviser, and Ronald Ziegler at a White House press conference on May 23. It called for the renuncia-

tion of national claims to seabed resources beyond the depth
of 200 meters and for the establishment, beyond this point,
of an international regime to govern the exploitation of seabed resources. Two types of machinery would be created to
authorize resource exploitation in this international seabed
area. To the edge of the continental margin, an area called
the "trusteeship zone," the coastal state would administer
exploitation as a trustee for the international community. In
return, the "coastal state would receive a share of the international revenues from the zone in which it acts as trustee."
Beyond the continental margin, international machinery
would authorize and regulate exploitation and would collect
"substantial mineral royalties" to be used for economic assistance to developing countries.

When the UN Seabed Committee met on August 3, 1970 the
United States presented its "United Nations Draft Convention
on the International Seabed Area." Five officials from the departments of State, Defense, and Interior had drafted the 78
articles and five appendices of the Convention. This lengthy
and complex document, rather than the president's May 23
statement, quickly became the focus of domestic opposition
to a narrow offshore resource zone. Even before its presentation to the Seabed Committee, the Congress and the Interior
Department had strenuously opposed many of its provisions
and had succeeded in securing some modifications. Then,
with its tabling at the Geneva meeting, the domestic
contention over the extent of the continental shelf merged
with United Nations debate over the breadth of an economic
resource zone.

Territorial Seas, Straits, and Fisheries

The U.S. seabed proposal was designed to encourage other
nations to adopt a narrow continental shelf policy. Defense
Department officials also hoped that the seabed proposal
would have a positive effect on separate negotiations then
underway regarding the territorial seas, international straits,
and fisheries. These issues had been grouped since 1967 and
1968, when they were first discussed with the Soviets and
then the U.S. allies. Policymakers handling this tripartite
package of issues were distant from agency officials managing seabed policy.

Among the three issues, those of a strategic importance—
the straits and territorial seas—were accorded primacy.

Fisheries was incorporated within the policy package as a tradeoff for concessions on straits and territorial seas and because the fishing industry did not object. The U.S. was prepared to recognize a twelve-mile territorial sea only if freedom of transit through and over international straits were guaranteed by international agreement. If the breadth of the territorial sea were universally extended to twelve miles, 116 international straits would be covered by territorial waters. In these straits, high seas corridors would cease to exist and transit would be subjected to the legal regime of innocent passage. To avoid the application of coastal state discretion to U.S. vessels, it was necessary to guarantee the right of freedom of transit.

Among fishing nations, the United States ranks sixth, and it fishes off its own coasts as well as off those of other nations. According to the U.S. proposal, a coastal fishing nation could reserve a portion of the catch off its shores for its own fishermen, the amount to be determined by the extent of its investment in or economic dependence on offshore fisheries. At the insistence of the Department of Defense, this proposal deliberately omitted the concept of a fishing zone that might evolve into an area of expanded coastal state jurisdiction.

U.S. proposals regarding preferential fishing rights were primarily determined by nonfishing interest groups that were responsive to foreign policy considerations—to the need to balance Soviet and Japanese distant water fishing interests with the coastal interest of developing countries and to the need to persuade the latter to accept a twelve-mile territorial sea and freedom of transit through straits.

Reasons for the early lack of policy input by the U.S. fishing industry were twofold. First, the fishing industry, unlike the petroleum industry, simply did not know that discussions were underway within and between governments and that the Department of Defense was determining the fisheries position in exchange for concessions on straits and the territorial sea. Second, internal differences existed within the industry. With the public announcement of U.S. policy on straits, territorial seas, and fisheries of February 18, 1970, the industry was first apprised of governmental discussions. Although the reference to preferential rights was quite sketchy, it was sufficient to alarm the distant water segments of the U.S. fishing industry. Their reaction to the preferential rights approach was analogous to that of the Soviet Union and Japan. The U.S. coastal fishermen, on the other hand, shared the interests of the developing coastal countries in reserving offshore resources for themselves. Neither segment of the industry, however, appreciated being excluded from the policy deliberations. Despite their differences, they agreed that if they were to have a say in determining U.S. fisheries policy, they would have to act in concert.

The first indication of the tenuous resolution of industry differences was visible in the adoption of the "species approach" presented by the U.S. government to the UN Seabed Committee on August 3, 1971. Here, the concept of preferential rights for the coastal state was applied only to stocks that were adjacent to the coast or that spawned in fresh water. Highly migratory oceanic stocks were excluded, thereby protecting the U.S. tuna fleets fishing off the west coast of Latin America. In its approach to the problem, the U.S. fisheries proposal of 1971 resembled the 1970 U.S. seabed proposal.

While U.S. positions on fisheries and seabed minerals evolved during domestic and international negotiations, the U.S. position on straits and territorial seas has not. The military remains adamant that the right of a vessel to freely transit an international strait cannot be left to the discretion of a coastal state. The only modification of this position has been a U.S. willingness to accept internationally agreed upon safety standards and to allow the coastal state to designate corridors suitable for transit through straits.

The linking of the issues of straits, territorial seas, and fisheries in the U.S. statement of August 3, 1971 reflected the official U.S. policy of keeping continental shelf and seabed issues separate from other law of the sea questions. The government thereby hoped to preserve its packages of trade-offs—a narrow continental shelf for a generous seabed regime and freedom of transit through and over international straits in exchange for a twelve-mile territorial sea with preferential coastal state fishing rights in the area beyond.

In the course of 1971 and 1972, this division of issues, and the tradeoffs thereby implied, gradually broke down because of a combination of pressures. First, domestic interests were becoming more active in the formulation of ocean policy. As the involvement of these interest groups increased, the priority formerly accorded U.S. strategic considerations over resource interests declined. Second, and at cross purposes with domestic pressures, foreign nations were pressing for a single international conference to handle all law of the sea issues. Developing countries were hopeful that by combining and trading on all law of the sea questions, they would gain greater concessions from the maritime nations.

U.S. bureaucratic machinery for ocean issues was consolidated in early 1970. Separate staffs for continental shelf and seabed issues on one hand and straits, territorial seas, and fisheries on the other were merged into single offices in the departments of State, Defense, and Interior. John Stevenson's task force was set up at State, with representatives of all affected federal agencies, including State, Defense, Interior, Commerce, Justice, Transportation, the National Security Council, the CIA, the Office of Management and Budget, and the U.S. Mission to the United Nations.

In response to strong industry pressure, an Advisory Committee on the Law of the Sea was formed in early 1972 with members representing all the U.S. domestic special interests. The official purpose of the Advisory Committee is to advise John Stevenson in his dual capacity as chairman of the task force and as head of the U.S. delegation to the UN Seabed Committee. The domestic interests have even succeeded in gaining representation on the U.S. delegation as observers.

The increased participation of other ocean interests has reduced the ability of Defense Department officials to further strategic interests by determining policy in other areas. Whereas the military previously intervened in seabed as well as fisheries policy, it now concentrates on policy inputs relating strictly to military mobility—that is, to straits and territorial sea boundaries affecting navigation. This may reflect the reassertion of military over civilian control within DOD. Law of the sea policy has been taken away from the legal office and officially turned over to International Security Affairs (ISA). But, in fact, the policy is handled primarily by the Joint Chiefs of Staff with limited ISA input.

As for the petroleum industry, after a strong blast at the 1970 U.S. Draft Treaty on the Seabed, it has lapsed into virtual silence on ocean policy. In part this silence has been made possible because the trend toward increasing zones of off-

shore jurisdiction makes industry efforts in this direction unnecessary. A more important consideration in altering petroleum industry behavior, however, has been the rapidly changing international and domestic environment in which petroleum policy is formulated. The successful negotiating tactic
of producing nations operating as a bloc has undermined
earlier industry confidence that it is safer and more profitable
to deal bilaterally with foreign governments than with an international regime. An international regime, dominated by
producing nations, might conceivably be preferable.

The newly discovered "energy crisis" also complicates the
ocean policy picture for the petroleum industry. In the future
the United States will be importing vast quantities of petroleum from the continental margins of other producing nations. Because estimated reserves of the U.S. continental
margins do not begin to meet projected U.S. demand for
energy, the industry argument for laying claim to the entire
margin to avoid dependence on foreign supplies of petroleum
is clearly weakened. Moreover, as U.S. imports grow, problems of ocean transport of petroleum will grow. Extensions
of coastal state jurisdiction for pollution or resource purposes will threaten the petroleum shipper as they now
threaten military mobility.

From Oil Lobbyist to Oil Diplomat

As the ocean interests of the petroleum industry have become more diverse, a single policy has been increasingly difficult to elaborate. Whereas the domestic sectors of the major petroleum companies formerly controlled ocean policy in
cooperation with the Interior Department and its National Petroleum Council, international segments of the industry, with
close relations to the Department of State, are playing an increasing role. The involvement of new segments of the industry is visible in changes in personnel—the disappearance of
the colorful, outspoken oil man lobbying conspicuously
through the Interior Department and the appearance of the
quiet oil diplomat working skillfully and quietly with the Department of State.

The hard minerals interest, formerly neglected by the Interior
Department, is now taking up the major portion of the depart-
ment's efforts on law of the sea policy. Shocked by the U.S.
Draft Treaty on the Seabed, the industry responded by vigor-

ous congressional lobbying and the introduction of legislation (S.2801) that would establish a congenial seabed regime. The American Mining Congress and high-level officials from major hard minerals industries are playing a growing role in the formulation of policy for a seabed regime by forcing a greater executive branch responsiveness to their demands. Industry representatives are also active in international negotiations—defending proposed legislation from attacks by developing nations while urging that other developed nations pass similar legislation. The resources and attention of the Interior Department, formerly devoted to petroleum, are now largely devoted to the needs of hard minerals interests.

The fishing industry is also faring better than it did a year ago, and it, too, has resorted to Congress to gain the attention of executive branch policymakers. The fishing industry is the only interest group with two seats on the U.S. delegation to the UN Seabed Committee, reflecting the divergent interests within the industry. The industry has managed to maintain the difficult alliance between distant water and coastal and anadromous interests by means of frequent, albeit heated meetings and exchanges, and it has played a direct role in the formulation of the official U.S. species approach.

The new participation of interest group representatives has reduced U.S. flexibility in international law of the sea negotiations and made it increasingly difficult to establish a scale of priorities among U.S. ocean interests. It has led to a new degree of parity between all the interests, most visibly between U.S. strategic and resource interests. The August 1972 statements to the UN Seabed Committee reflect this new parity most clearly. While there has been no change in U.S. policy toward straits or territorial seas, new emphasis is being placed on American interests in ocean resources. Only a year after the introduction of the first version of the species approach stressing U.S. support for international and regional regulation of coastal fishing, the United States indicated that it is prepared to accept coastal state management of coastal and anadromous fisheries.

The United States is also becoming increasingly conservative in its approach to a seabed regime. Most significantly, it no longer contemplates limiting national jurisdiction to the 200-meter isobath. In response to strong domestic and international pressures in favor of a broad continental shelf or some form of economic resource zone, the United States has moved toward accepting a limited intermediate zone of jurisdiction. Although the U.S. government has not submitted any articles officially superseding its August 1970 position on the continental shelf and seabed regime, recent U.S. policy statements reveal this changed attitude. In an area extending to the outer edge of the continental margin or to some agreed distance from the shore, the United States now says it would accept coastal state regulation of the exploitation of mineral resources, subject to international standards and compulsory settlement of disputes. Other uses of the area are not to be restricted, and pollution controls are to be internationally determined. Revenues from seabed resources would be shared with the international community, and foreign investment would be protected from expropriation.

The International Perspective

While domestic industry pressures limit U.S. policy flexibility and make fewer tradeoffs possible, international efforts to combine disparate law of the sea issues in a single conference are designed to increase the tradeoffs made by maritime nations. International pressure led to the December 1970 decision to convene a single Law of the Sea Conference on a broad range of ocean issues. As of the March and August 1972 meetings of the UN Seabed Committee, the number of agenda items had been expanded even further to twenty-five items.* How these diverse agenda items will be handled by the UN Seabed Committee, much less negotiated, is as yet unclear.

The trend toward a split between developing coastal nations and developed maritime nations was most pronounced in 1971. Led by the Latin American nations, twenty-five countries had by then extended claims to, or evidenced a willingness to accept, offshore zones of 200 miles. Since Latin America is surrounded by extensive and economically attractive ocean areas and overwhelmed by expansive American power to its north, the 200-mile claim reflects its economic

*Some of the new items include landlocked countries, rights and interests of states with broad shelves, rights and interests of shelf-locked states and states with narrow shelves or short coastlines, regional arrangements, high seas, archipelagoes, enclosed and semi-enclosed seas, artificial islands and installations, the development and transfer of technology, dispute settlement, zones of peace and security, archaeological and historical treasures on the ocean floor, and peaceful uses of ocean space.

and strategic interests as well as strong nationalist senti-
ments. Such claims, however, do not necessarily serve the
interests of developing nations in other areas of the world. In
Africa and Asia very few nations had identified what their
ocean interests are. Developing country support for the Latin
American position in 1971 was primarily a reaction against
the great powers.

Only in 1972 have developing nations begun to arrive at national ocean policies on the basis of particular geographic
and resource situations rather than in reaction to developed
nations. Support for a 200-mile territorial sea is waning. A
group of developing nations have forced inclusion on the
agenda of items on the rights and interests of shelf-locked
states, states with narrow shelves or short coastlines, and
landlocked states, indicating increasing efforts to distinguish different national interests in the oceans. As it
becomes apparent that the ocean interests of all developing
nations are not alike, the coalitions will become more complex. The landlocked or shelf-locked nations may discover an
interest in restricting the extent of coastal state jusrisdiction.
Nations bordering semi-enclosed seas or nations with
limited resources off their coasts may find that extensive offshore claims benefit others more than themselves. The fact
that the United States stands to gain the most territorially
under a regime of 200-mile territorial seas can scarcely be
comforting to developing nations.

The first break within the coalition of developing states occurred in 1972 with the development of the "patrimonial sea"
concept at African and Caribbean regional conferences. This
concept involves an extensive economic zone of limited
coastal state rights that would not restrict the maritime
activities of other nations. As the U.S. position has evolved
away from restricting coastal state jurisdiction in offshore
areas, it has moved more in the direction of something
approximating the "patrimonial sea" concept. But it is still
premature to expect a compromise in 1973 along the lines of
an economic resource zone.

The process whereby the developing nations are differenti-
ating their particular interests in the oceans has only just begun. The United States has progressively lost its negotiating
flexibility as the participation of U.S. domestic interests in
the policy process has increased. Although 1973 will no

doubt see an organizational session of a general Law of the
Sea Conference, the Conference itself will probably take
place at the earliest in 1974. At present, prospects are bleak
for a successful conference, one that would result in internationally accepted Law of the Sea Conventions. If the conference fails, the democratization of U.S. foreign policy toward the oceans will, by freezing the U.S. negotiating position, have contributed substantially to that failure.

CONTRIBUTORS

M. A. ADELMAN is professor of economics at M.I.T. His essay is based on a lecture at the Tokyo Institute of Energy Economics. He is the author of *World Petroleum Market.*

C. FRED BERGSTEN is a senior fellow at the Brookings Institution and was assistant of international economic affairs on the senior staff of the National Security Council from 1969 through May 1971. He is the author of *Approaches to Greater Flexibility of Exchange Rates.*

HAROLD VAN BUREN CLEVELAND, the author of *The Atlantic Idea and Its European Rivals*, is vice president for international economics at the First National City Bank, New York. He was formerly director of Atlantic Policy Studies at the Council on Foreign Relations.

RICHARD N. COOPER is provost and Frank Altschul Professor of International Economics at Yale University. He has served in government as a senior staff economist with President Kennedy's Council of Economic Advisers, as deputy assistant secretary of state for international monetary affairs (1965-66), and as a consultant to the National Security Council (1969-70). He has written *The Economics of Interdependence* and numerous articles and essays on international economics.

JOHN DIEBOLD is chairman of the Diebold Group, Inc., an international firm of management consultants. Part of this article was prepared for the Second Atlantic Conference of the Chicago Council on Foreign Relations.

ANN L. HOLLICK is assistant professor at The Johns Hopkins School of Advanced International Studies. She is also executive director of the university's Ocean Policy Project.

LAWRENCE B. KRAUSE served on the staff of the Council of Economic Advisers, 1967-69, and is now a senior fellow at the Brookings Institution. Mr. Krause is the author of *European Economic Integration and the United States* and *Sequel to Bretton Woods: A Proposal to Reform the World Monetary System.*

WALTER J. LEVY is an oil adviser to industry and government. His essay, based on a paper he presented in 1973 to the Europe-America Conference in Amsterdam, will be part of *The New Atlantic Challenge.*

EVAN LUARD teaches international relations at Oxford and has recently completed a book on the control of the seabed. Additional books by Mr. Luard include *The International Regulation of Civil Wars: Ten Distinguished Authorities Examine the Role of International Organizations in the Regulation of Civil War* and *International Regulation of Frontier Disputes*.

HARALD B. MALMGREN, formerly a senior fellow at the Overseas Development Council (Washington, D.C.), is now deputy special representative for trade at the Office of the Special Trade Representative for Trade Negotiations in Washington, D.C. He is the author of *International Economic Peacekeeping in Phase II.*

THEODORE H. MORAN was formerly assistant professor of political science at Vanderbilt University. He is now research associate at the Brookings Institution, where he is working on the Multinational Corporations and U.S. Foreign Policy Project. His book *Economic Nationalism and the Politics of "Dependents": The Case of Copper in Chile, 1945-72* will soon be published.

YASUO TAKEYAMA is board chairman and editor-in-chief of the Tokyo daily *Nihon Keizai Shimbun* (Japan Economic Journal), which has a circulation of 2.4 million. He is also an economic adviser to the Japanese government.